Developing Online Content: The Principles of Writing and Editing for the Web

Irene Hammerich

Claire Harrison

Wiley Computer Publishing

John Wiley & Sons, Inc.

NEW YORK · CHICHESTER · WEINHEIM · BRISBANE · SINGAPORE · TORONTO

Publisher: Robert Ipsen

Editor: Cary Sullivan

Developmental Editor: Christina Berry

Managing Editor: Penny Linskey

Associate New Media Editor: Brian Snapp

Text Design & Composition: Pronto Design Inc.

This book is printed on acid-free paper. ∞

Published by John Wiley & Sons, Inc.

Published simultaneously in Canada.

This publication is designed to provide accurate and authoritative information in regard to the subject matter covered. It is sold with the understanding that the publisher is not engaged in professional services. If professional advice or other expert assistance is required, the services of a competent professional person should be sought.

Library of Congress Cataloging-in-Publication Data:

ISBN: 0-471-14611-0

Printed in the United States of America.

10 9 8 7 6 5 4 3 2 1

CONTENTS

Claire **Harrison**, president of CANDO Career Solutions, Inc., is an award-winning writer and editor with 25 years' experience working for government and corporate clients. She writes on social, cultural, and health issues, and she is also a specialist in developing career information products. In addition to writing and editing, Claire's print experience includes consulting with clients on production, particularly in the areas of design and illustration. Her Web works ranges from writing and editing Web documents to building sites from scratch, and assisting clients in the concept development, information architecture, and navigation design of public and Intranet sites.

Claire's expertise also extends into the areas of creative writing, journalism, and teaching. She has published novels and poetry, written travel articles and book reviews, and is an instructor of writing and a frequent writing conference speaker. She is currently completing her M.A. in Applied Language Studies and is a member of the Society for Technical Communication, the Canadian Society for the Study of Rhetoric, and the Canadian Association for Teachers of Technical Writing.

Claire was born in Brooklyn, New York and grew up in Cold Spring Harbor, New York. She now makes her home in Ottawa, Ontario.

Irene **Hammerich** is the founder, CEO, and Senior Partner of Inner Action Inc., a company that specializes in Web and CD-ROM development, digital-media creation, and training. An experienced manager, she assists government, corporations, educational institutions, and other organizations in developing strategies for Web site development and long-term management plans. For her achievements, Irene was a 1999 nominee for Pioneer category for the Canadian Women in New

Media Award. Irene is also a Founding Partner in Focus48, a company devoted solely to Web application software development.

Irene has extensive teaching experience. She is now a Professor for the Full-Time Post-Graduate Interactive Multimedia Program and the Fast Track Multimedia Web Specialist Program at Algonquin College in Ottawa—two programs for which she is also Acting Program Coordinator and Project Manager. As well, she actively contributes to the new media community as an educator by speaking at conferences, workshops, and seminars.

Irene was born in Toronto, Ontario, had a short break along the ocean of Nova Scotia, and now makes her home on the Mississippi Lake outside of Ottawa, Ontario.

ACKNOWLEDGMENTS

First, to Karen and John whose support and encouragement kept us going. Secondly, to Jackie, Laura, Jim, and Tracy whose work behind the scenes made the difference. And thirdly, to others in our families and on staff who put up with us. Many thanks.

W e wrote this book to help professional writers/editors deepen their understanding of the Web as a new communications medium, and to assist them by providing practical advice and solutions to the challenges they'll encounter in their work. It is also our hope that this book will demonstrate the value of writers/editors to others involved in the Web development process. We believe that, with professional communicators working to improve standards in Web text, the nature of the Web will change from a design-first medium to a word-and-design medium where the two modes are equal in significance and work together to deliver information clearly and effectively to the Web's millions of users.

Irene Hammerich

Claire Harrison

CHAPTER 1

A Funny Thing Happened on the Way to the Web

What's Inside:

- **Informational sites—new opportunities for professional writers/editors**
- **A brief history of the Web from a writing/editing perspective**
- **The Web site development process**
- **Roles of the writer/editor on a Web production team**
- **Analyzing sample job ads**
- **Overview of Web writing/editing tasks and skills**

In 1998, we met with a Web/CD-ROM developer concerning his company's work on a project that we were managing. The material was riddled with text omissions and errors of spelling and punctuation. When we pressed him for better quality control, he shrugged and said to us: "Nobody reads text anymore." We tell this story not only to illustrate the interesting issues that can arise on a Web production team but, more importantly, to demonstrate a general mind-set with regard to the Internet that is now—happily for those of us who care about words—undergoing change.

What the developer didn't know then was that his view of the Web as a medium primarily for design, graphics, animation, and video was not going to last. The online world, as it turns out, is *not* post-reading. In fact, current research shows that text is the first and foremost concern of users when they visit a Web site. Usability researcher Jakob Neilsen (2000:100) notes: "Usability studies indicate a fierce content focus on the part of users. When they get to a new page, they look immediately in the main content area of the page and scan it for headlines and other indications of what the page is about." In our experience, corporations, governments, and other organizations are increasingly turning to professional writers/editors to help them develop readable, coherent, accurate, and grammatical online text.

The Informational Site: Uncharted Territory

In the past, available Web-related work for professional writers/editors was primarily in online news and e-zines. As a result, there are already many books, articles, and courses devoted to

Let's Speak the Same Language

Terminology in the Web world is chaotic. People use the same term for different things, or different terms for the same thing. Here are some definitions to ensure that we're all speaking the same language.

Content: Written material on a Web site. When written text is enhanced by graphics and video and audio materials, these elements become part of the content.

Writing/Editing: Writing/editing text on a Web site. Please note that the terms *Web writing* and *Web editing* (and also *authoring* and *scriptwriting*) are also sometimes used to refer to programming in the Internet world.

Client: Person(s) responsible for the creation/maintenance of a Web site. The term encompasses many job titles such as project manager, knowledge manager, Webmaster, and information technology (IT) manager. If you're an in-house writer/editor, this person may be your boss!

Content Specialist/Subject Matter Expert: Person(s) who "own" the content through their specific knowledge of the topic.

Visuals: All forms of design and graphics such as color, backgrounds, and navigation icons as well as the media mix of illustrations, photographs, and animation.

Audio/video components: Elements of the site, created in a studio or on location, that are inserted as clips in the Web site.

Navigation: The routes that users take through a Web site to move from Web page to Web page.

work in that field. This book is designed to fill an important gap by providing useful theoretical and practical information about writing/editing for another, very significant part of the Web world—that of governments, corporations, educational institutions, non-profit organizations, and professional associations. These organizations require a variety of Web sites such as:

- *Public Internet sites*—accessible to any person seeking information.

- *Intranet sites*—in-house Web sites that can't be accessed by outsiders and are designed to provide employees with organizational information.

- *Extranet sites*—which OneSoft Corporation (1999:55) defines as the "bridge between the public Internet and the private corporation intranet. The extranet connects multiple and diverse organizations on-line behind virtual firewalls, where those who share in trusted circles can network in order to achieve commerce-oriented objectives."

- *Business-to-business (B2B) sites*—while accessible to any Web surfer, their purpose is strictly to inform other businesses about their products/services.

- *Business-to-consumer (B2C) sites*—while accessible to any Web surfer, their purpose is strictly to market products/services to interested customers.

For the purpose of this book, we'll call these *informational* sites as opposed to those that are news-oriented, those that supply training and require knowledge of curriculum design, and those that provide entertainment such as games and music.

This Book Is for You if...

Everyone working on informational sites—clients, designers, writers, editors, content managers, and programmers, for example—is learning on the job. Katherine McCoy, Senior Lecturer at the Institute of Design, Illinois Institute of Technology (1999:8), succinctly describes the problem from the design perspective: "Most of the pioneering graphic designers who specialize in new media today have had to acquire this knowledge informally, largely through trial and error, in the context of professional design practice." As a writer/editor, you are, or will be, in

> Web writers/editors have to learn on the job.

the same boat. Your client and other members of your Web development team will not be helpful because writing/editing is not their area of specialty. You will not know, until you're in the thick of it, what skills you can transfer to the Web from print, and what skills you may have to develop to help a Web production team achieve a high standard of excellence in content development. And, most significantly, you may learn good rules of thumb for online writing/editing, but these rules won't help you understand why the Web is a new writing and reading medium and they don't provide principles that can guide your writing/editing decisions.

Therefore, this book is for you if you're a **practicing professional writer/editor** who's interested in, or already in the process of, developing content for the Web. Your background may be in general organizational/corporate communications, technical writing, public relations, advertising, journalism, fiction, speechwriting, screenwriting, or playwriting.

This book is also for other experts on Web development teams who are interested in understanding the principles behind good content development and how a professional writer/editor can contribute. People who will find this book useful are:

- **Knowledge managers** and **business analysts** who provide strategies for the digital delivery of an organization's data and information.

- **Project/production managers** who oversee Web production teams including writers/editors.

- **Content specialists** and **subject matter specialists** who must adapt their knowledge and/or existing information to the Web.

- **Content contributors/publishers** who add information to large corporate/government sites through products such as Lotus Notes and other technologies.

- **Information architects, information designers**, and **content strategists** who organize content for the purposes of structure and navigation.

- **Web site designers** who must deal with the interactions of text and visuals on the Web page.

- **Content managers** and **content librarians** who must maintain and update content on existing sites.

- **Marketing specialists** who need to ensure that content meets the marketing goals of their organizations.

- **Professors**, **instructors**, and **teachers** who provide courses, seminars, and workshops in professional writing, workplace/collaborative writing, and/or writing for new media.

What You'll Learn

This book presents a discussion of the Web as a new communications medium, based not only on our personal experiences in developing Web content, but also on the work of researchers in applied linguistics who study writing and reading, analysts who study the effect of Web development on human cognition, and usability experts who test the interactions between users and Web sites. In addition, we'll tell the stories and report on the insights of professional writers/editors and other specialists who work in Web development.

Online Writing/Editing Challenges

Throughout the book, we'll address the many challenges that Web writers/editors face in developing content for this new medium such as:

- Why do users read so quickly online and what does this mean for content development?

- What is the best way to structure information that is logical and accessible to users?

- How should online text be written, formatted, and presented to make it consistent, coherent, and easily readable?

- How do visuals create meaning on the Web page and interact with text?

- What are the benefits of nonlinear reading and how can writers/editors use strategic linking to help users gain knowledge?

- What are the fundamentals of developing Web content that exist regardless of ongoing advances in technology? At the same time, how can technology be used to enhance Web content?

- What issues are involved in writing/editing for a global audience?

- What should be considered to make a site accessible to persons with visual, motor, and other disabilities?

- What are the best practices for maintaining content after a site has been launched?

Career Advice

This book is also designed to help professional writers/editors in their career development. You already have excellent writing/editing skills, know how to organize and synthesize information, and are accustomed to creating audience-based text in other media. What you're looking for now is a guide to best practices for Web writing/editing that allows you to approach content development with confidence and increases your marketability in this new field. Therefore, we'll also examine the business of being a Web content developer. In this book, we'll answer questions such as:

- How do I get into the field of Web content development?

- What value do I bring to the process of Web development and how can I explain this to clients?

- If I'm a freelance writer/editor, what should I know about estimating, contracting, and scheduling?

- What skills will I need to be an effective member of a Web development team?

- How can I ensure that my professional standards with regard to text and its presentation will be incorporated into a final Web product?

Resources to Further Your Knowledge

At the end of every chapter, we'll also provide a list of print and online resources relating to that chapter's content. Given the vast amount of information already published about Web development, we've chosen quality over quantity and have included those resources that we find most reliable and useful. As well, we've tried to provide a range of resources that will appeal to people with a variety of interests and tastes, from those who want to "tread lightly" to those who wish to delve into the theory and research.

Examples, Exercises, and Links on Our Web Site

The companion Web site at www.wiley.com/compbooks/hammerich provides additional information for your use. On it, you'll find:

- Examples of Web pages that demonstrate various aspects of design such as how color can affect content delivery.
- Exercises for those who wish to practice strategies described in the book.
- Downloadable checklists and other teaching tools.
- Links to the Web resources provided at the end of each chapter.

Getting from There to Here

A funny thing has happened on the way to the Web. Content became "king" not once, but twice. And, in between, developers got caught up in the excitement of the look-and-feel and interactive potential of Web sites, and lost sight of the most important people of all—the users.

Back in Them Olden Days

The Internet began in 1969 as a way for universities and the U.S. military to exchange information about science and technology, using rudimentary hypertext software that enabled readers to connect one document to another or one bit of information to another. But the early Internet had major problems. As Tim Berners-Lee (2000:18), the creator of the World Wide Web, describes it: "The Internet was up and running by the 1970s, but transferring information was too much of a hassle for a non-computer expert. One would run one program to connect to another computer, and then in conversation (in a different language) with the other computer, run a different program to access the information. Even when data had been transferred back to one's own computer, decoding it might be impossible."

> Text was the medium of the early Internet.

By the early 1990s, Berners-Lee and his associates had solved the major technological problems that finally allowed the Web to be a single global information network as we know it today. But early Web sites were essentially print documents "dumped" online. Although developers in multimedia CD-ROM technology were eager to migrate to the Internet and incorporate audio, video, and animation onto the Web, the technology was too cumbersome and computers too slow to allow users to make efficient use of multiple media effects. Written content, then, was the medium of the early Web. People used it to get textual information, even if presentation and readability was less than optimal.[1]

Fast Forward to Today

Rapid advances in technology with regard to visuals and audio/video components, downloading speeds, and information management involving databases opened the doors to innovations in design and interactivity. Excitement built around the possibilities of the visual impact of Web sites, rather than how such innovations could enhance written content. Business, governments, and other organizations turned to designers, not writers/editors, to create their Web sites. Many design houses, in turn, evolved into Web production firms and added technology specialists to program sites and develop complex functionality such as search engines and databases. These events, combined with an overall cultural trend towards more use of visuals in print documents,[2] were fueled by a belief that design and technology bells-and-whistles were the key factors in attracting users to a site and creating *stickiness*—the ability to keep them there.[3]

The result was that text was generally ignored. Many Web site owners continued to dump existing print materials on their sites while others created content without much concern for readability. Sloppiness with regard to spelling, grammar, and punctuation prevailed. The perception was that text was "dead," no one read anymore, and a picture was always worth a thousand words anyway. However, to paraphrase Mark Twain: "The report of the death of Web text was an exaggeration." Studies began to show that user behavior was at distinct odds with the conventional wisdom. Two studies were particularly influential:

> Research shows today's users focus on text.

- John Morkes and Jakob Neilsen (1997), usability researchers, discovered that much of the writing on the Web—which was wordy, often promotional in tone, and presented in lengthy paragraphs—was not suitable for Web reading and discouraged readers from staying on sites.

- The Stanford-Poynter Eyetrack Study 2000 provided users with head-gear that tracked their eye movements as they surfed news Web sites. This research found that users looked at text before moving their attention to graphics.

Users, it turns out, look at text first and graphics second—and they want clear, concise content. Explosive growth in the number of Web sites, all of which compete for user time and attention, means that no site can afford to turn off readers with badly conceived and written content. It's no surprise that text is resurfacing as a major focus of Web developers.

New Roles for Writers/Editors

As a professional writer/editor working in other media, it's likely that you play a minor role, if any, in the production of your words in their final form. For example, speechwriters don't deliver their words; playwrights and scriptwriters don't customarily produce their theatrical works; journalists, novelists, and corporate communicators are usually not involved in the design and print of their publications. Generally, the writer's/editor's role is finished when production takes over, with the exception of copyeditors who work with page proofs and scriptwriters/playwrights who may work on-site for revisions.

There are two main reasons why this is the case. First, speeches, plays, films, newspapers, reports, newsletters, and so on have long-established conventions (for both writing and production) based on a solid understanding of usability. Those working in traditional media can learn by reading or referring back to examples which set enduring levels for excellence. Great speeches and plays are printed in anthologies; classic novels remain in print; Oscar-winning films and Emmy-winning television shows are stored on tape; and governments and major corporations archive their publications. The second reason is that technological change has occurred at a relatively slow rate in traditional media as compared to the Internet, giving everyone the time to experiment, evaluate results, and decide whether or not the new technology adds value to their processes and products. These media are also supported by an infrastructure of critical reviewing and prizes that provide writers/editors and producers with constant feedback on success and failure.

Communications Milestones

- Oratory and theatrical performance have been around as long as humankind.
- The Gutenberg printing press was invented in 1436.
- Mass circulation of print materials occurred after the development of steam-powered presses in the 1800s.
- Film production and radio broadcasting have had a century's worth of development.
- Television production began after World War II.
- The first computer was hooked to the Internet in 1969.
- The World Wide Web started in 1993.
- The Google search engine was founded in 1998.

The Web Is a New Frontier

In contrast, the Web today is like the Wild West, a geographical frontier of the past where there was so little law and order that people made the rules up as they went along. The Web is, metaphorically, a new communications frontier with few existing guidelines. According to usability researcher Jared Spool (as quoted by Head:1999): "The only definable trends on the Web are change, experimentation, and uncertainty…[and] a standard for good Web writing is far from being established, let alone practiced." And with digital technologies changing so quickly and bandwidths expanding so rapidly, what can be included on sites is undergoing dramatic change. For example, five years ago, audio- and video-clips took too much time to download; today, they are increasingly part of site content. Constant and dramatic change means that what was experimental yesterday is a convention today, and likely to be passé tomorrow.

> Web conventions happen almost overnight.

Analysis of the Web as a communications media is also a new area of research, drawing in investigators from areas such as psychology and cognitive science, physiology and ergonomics, software engineering and computer science, art and design, and composition and reading. Researchers began to publish articles and books about usability and user impact in the early 1980s and the academic discipline of human-computer interaction (HCI) appeared in the late 1980s. As in any research field, it can take years for theory to evolve and good practice to result. Also, as HCI specialist Christine Faulkner (1998:1) notes: "HCI is a discipline concerned with the optimization of these two complex systems: computers are highly complex machines and human users are highly complex organisms." Combine these complexities with the constant evolution of computer technology and human pleasure in the new and different, and you have a field of study where the parameters are changing constantly, making it difficult to establish enduring theories that will lead to solid principles for practice.

And, finally, there is virtually no public historical record with regard to the Web. Sites disappear, leaving nothing behind for exemplars, either good or bad. Although the International Academy of Digital Arts and Sciences has Webby Awards to celebrate excellence on the Web, these awards are obscure in comparison with the Oscars and Pulitzer prizes. The result is that almost everyone who works in Web development makes judgments based on his or her own experience as a user. Only a few know about researchers who analyze Web sites for usability with regard to readability, visuals, and navigation, and even fewer are aware of the work being done by semioticians who have started to explore how different modes of communication interact and make meaning when combined in a document.[4]

As we conducted the research for this book, we were struck by how much the Web has been affected by fads rather than rationality. Buzzwords pop up and disappear. Good ideas arise, get discarded when a new bell-and-whistle appears, and then are resurrected when users remain unhappy with content, design, or navigation. For example, in the late 1980s, researchers in technical communications were already concerned about the effect of design on text. Roger Grice (1989:41) wrote: "Use of color may aid in initial learning by making the information more distinctive or memorable. But use, actually misuse, of color can be a distraction, and the color may get in the way of use and understanding…If color is used with no apparent reason, users may spend time and energy trying to figure out meanings for the colors, wasting their time and possibly misinterpreting the information in their attempt to derive a reason for the uses of color." Cautious analysis like this, however, disappeared beneath the deluge of experimental online designs, animation, and so on.

> Web development has been affected by fads.

But what goes around in Web research, seems to come around. Now, usability experts are suggesting that the overuse of color, graphics, and animation is getting in the way of users' ability to read and understand content. When it comes to Web development, the online world is constantly reinventing the wheel. And, when problems arise, developers often go back to traditional media for answers, guidelines, and rules. The truth is that, although the Web *is* a new medium, it can also be viewed as a new delivery tool for the same type of content that exists in other media such as text in print, audio on radio, and audio/video on film and television. Therefore, one of the aims of this book is to demystify the Web and dig beneath the hype, fads, and buzzwords to get at the essential, enduring principles of good information structure and online writing.

Making a Difference: Your Contribution

Writers/editors are the new kids on the Web block. This means you'll bring new knowledge, a fresh perspective, and a different vocabulary to the medium. You're likely to find yourself involved in every aspect of site development because a Web site, unlike a book or film, is an ongoing process, not a finished product. New technologies mean design, navigation, and database changes. New organizational needs and goals require content change. And users often won't come back unless a site demonstrates that it has *freshness*, that is, it continuously reinvents itself. As the person most knowledgeable about content in this ever-changing environment, you're likely to take on production roles that you never experienced as a writer/editor in other media. For example:

> Writers/editors bring a new "eye" to the Web.

- If you're writing on a topic that you know well, you may also function as a content specialist, helping to develop or revamp the concept of the site and what information it should include.

- If you're helping to build a site from scratch, you may work with, or actually be, the information architect or content strategist, organizing topics into hierarchical levels and determining navigation.

- If you're still working on the site after it has been launched, you'll be a content manager or content librarian working to upgrade content, add new information, and continually build and check linkages.

And, no matter at what stage you enter the development process, you may also find yourself acting as:

- A project manager, if your organizational skills are strong and recognized by the client to the point that he/she passes many management tasks over to you.

- An Internet site assessor who visits other Web sites to analyze similar sites for content, technology, and design and their effect on user appeal, usability, and readability.

- A design consultant, helping the client/project manager/designer make judgments on color, fonts, and visuals from the perspective of enhancing text.

- A statistics evaluator who assesses user information regarding time spent and pages visited to determine how the site can be improved or revised.

- A focus-test advisor, providing scenario-setting questions for users to see if they can easily find information.

- A usability tester yourself, testing the site to ensure that the content and navigation work well together.

- Your own copyeditor and proofreader, as many clients don't hire specialists to perform these functions.

You and the Process

Given the possible roles you could play, you may be wondering when you'll actually be writing/editing. Figure 1.1 provides an overview of the process of Web development, although you should note that this process can vary based on the size and scope of the project. Essentially, however, developing a Web site should be a straightforward process with the writer's/editor's tasks fitting into a logical sequence.

Each step in a site's development brings together those team members with the required specialties to move the process forward. The team may be small with each individual working on many tasks, or large with specialists in different areas. In the steps outlined below, you may be working with other team members to accomplish your tasks. Please note that the timelines for many of these tasks overlap.

Consulting on the Product Concept

If you're part of the initial stage of the development process, you'll take part in brainstorming sessions and possibly focus-

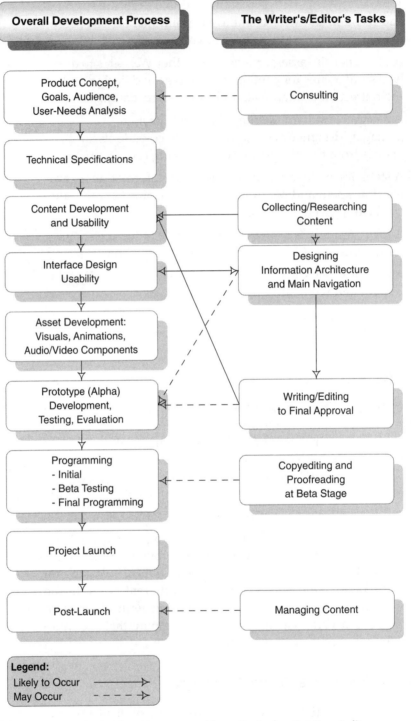

Figure 1.1 Web site development and how the tasks of writers/editors fit within the process.

Creating Main Navigational Links

On most projects, I'm not only the writer, I'm also playing a key role in the site's navigational structure. My goal is that, within seconds, a person can tell whether to stay and read, or move on to another page. To make it easy to find information quickly, I usually recommend a three-column approach, with the main menu on the left and the sub-menus on the right. The left column stays basically the same, so you can always find your way around the site. The right column might have sub-categories of the main topic, related topics, or helpful links. Up top goes the most important information. Wherever possible, I try to keep the site's section names short and informative. If these names are too clever, they may become confusing.

Teresa O'Connor, Independent Consultant
www.2a-T.com

testing—the time when site owners and other team members take an idea and begin to give it substance. At this point, concepts about the goals of the site and the target audience are established, while considerations with regard to potential content and the site's look-and-feel begin to emerge.

Collecting/Researching Content

Your task is to firm up content which consists of:

- Gathering information, if you're going to be developing all the content from scratch
- Working with content specialists, which means you'll need to obtain the content and/or set up a schedule for its delivery
- Collecting already existing materials, either in print or on an already existing Web site, that require updating

Designing Information Architecture and Main Navigation

As you're doing the preliminary work on the content, you'll also develop, or assist the information architect in developing, the preliminary information structure and navigation pathways. In addition, you'll work with the Web site designer to determine what visuals and audio/video components are appropriate. Your task, at this point, is to identify elements of the content that need specific graphical treatments. For example, one of our Intranet projects included fact boxes, quotes, and tips as well as regular text. The designer had to determine how best to present these different elements in a consistent style throughout the site. With this information, the designer can begin to create the design—from the overall look to the smallest element.

Writing/Editing to Final Approval

In this step, you'll either create new content, update existing content, and/or edit text submitted by one or more subject matter specialists. However, even if most of the site is based on content delivered by others, chances are you'll have to create new text for areas of the site such as "FAQ's," "Help," and "About Us." Web writing/editing means developing content Web page by Web page. This doesn't mean you compose on the Web site itself. Putting the words online is the programmer's task. Rather, you develop content in a word-processing program for delivery to the programmer. (For more information on the nuts-and-bolts of online writing/editing, see Chapter 7, "Writing/Editing *for* the Web Page; Writing/Editing *to* the Web Screen.")

If you're a freelance writer/editor, your work may end with content approval, but if the client wishes and the budget allows it, you may be asked to take part in testing and evaluating the prototype—the stage when some of the elements of the site are put together for the first time. Whether freelance or in-house, your role will be to look at the text within the context of the navigation and design. How do the words look on the screen? Are they easily readable? Are there problems with fonts, margins, link titles, and so on?

Copyediting and Proofreading at Beta Stage

You may participate in this step if the client has the desire and/or budgetary flexibility to put the text through copyediting and proofreading during the Beta testing of the site. We suggest that you work from a print-out of the site, no matter how many pages are involved. If you don't, you may miss a page. It's also extremely difficult to copyedit and proof onscreen because that would require making notes for the programmer as opposed to providing marked-up copy which is much easier to follow. At the same time, you must keep track of text that won't appear in the print-out such as mouse roll-overs and pop-up windows. You'll have to check this type of text onscreen.

Managing Content

It's a common fallacy that, once the site has been launched, everyone can walk away from it. Every site requires a maintenance plan that may involve members of the original team. For example, the client must evaluate results through feedback from users

When the Process Isn't Followed

My organization built two applications for our job matching site—one for internal users and another for work search candidates who visit the site. The internal application included several weeks of scrutiny, analysis, and focus-testing. On the other hand, the external application had, maybe, three days of discussion with zero input from my marketing group. When we got the product, it was a mess. The language was organizational jargon that would befuddle users, and it was filled with broken sentences and bad grammar. I'm passionate about having text perfect online, which meant I spent hours and hours editing the 400 pop-up messages alone. What we learned from this experience was that people like me should be involved in the process from the get-go.

Andrea Ritter, Content Editor/Provider

and usage statistics, address any technical issues that may arise, and ensure that content remains current. As the writer/editor, you may continue to work on such tasks as adding new material, updating original material, archiving content, and creating new links. (For more information on content management, see Chapter 9, "Keep CALM: Content and Logical Management.")

The extent of your involvement with the Web team depends on whether you're on staff or freelance. If you work in-house, you're likely to be highly involved; if you work off-site, the organizational budget will determine how much time the client will be able to use your services. However close or distant you may be from other members of the team, a key point to remember is that site development involves many other people. Some may be full-time employees; others may be outsourced contractors. Some team members will be very visible to you; others will be tucked in the background. Chances are, you'll be working most closely with the client and/or project manager, the designer, and content specialist(s) if your main role is writing/editing.

How Much Technology Do You Need to Know?

The technologies that underlie Web development are changing so rapidly that even the technology experts are in a constant state of catch-up. Design specialist Randy Weeks (1999:16), writing in a book for Web designers, asks: "Do you know every difference between every version of every browser with regard to every Java, Java-script, ActiveX, animated GIF, table layout, frame design, download method, XML, SGML, PC vs. Mac display/load/transfer consideration? Neither do the experts. They may know them today, but this afternoon they'll have to brush up. Next week, they'll have to be talking about changes, and next month they'll be loading patches, adjusting code and writing new, better and crash-free ways of doing almost everything."

If the technology experts can barely keep up, how can you be expected to understand this continually changing environment? If you're like most writers/editors, you want to work with content, not technology. Some of you may even consider yourselves techno-phobes. On the other hand, you may have a curiosity about technology and, if you work in Web production, willingly get more involved with the technical aspects of development. Whatever your leanings, you'll find that Web writing/editing requires a basic understanding of technology with regard to its *potential* to deliver content.

Although technologies have changed considerably since Alex Soo-jung-Kim Pang (1998) was involved in developing an electronic equivalent of the *Encyclopedia Britannica*, his story of the tussle between content and technology is both fascinating and typical.

> The experience involved in creating [a] set of timelines created for the 1998 Britannica CD…The basic screen interface consists of a column with years, flanked by two large columns for text; on the outside are two small columns for pictures. Navigational buttons and pull-down menus surround this main body. This design allows readers to load into each text column a different subject, such as science and literature, or architecture and women's history, and thus to compare them. The timeline was created in Shockwave. Since the program is four megabytes, this is something of a technical *tour de force* as Shockwave was designed for creating small animations and programs. All the data—pictures, writing, everything—are in a special Shockwave-only format.
>
> As the project unfolded, we discovered a variety of things that required us to make changes in the design, text, or programming. The need to keep loading times short—a Shockwave animation reloads every time you go to it, rather than being cached—forced us to keep the pictures relatively small, and put a 250-entry limit on each subject. The original design called for a timeline that displayed ranges of dates, as many printed timelines do. However, the sorting engine that figured out which entries belonged where, and wove together entries from two different subjects, couldn't handle such complexity. This in turn required revising the timeline text. Entries on things as broad as the development of Gothic art or the start of the Renaissance had to be rewritten to refer to specific years or events. Since each timeline entry occupied a

To Program or Not to Program

At the moment, some Web writers/editors are getting involved in actual HTML programming as a result of job requirements, the need for additional skills in order to find work, or simply from a desire to be involved in that aspect of production. We consider programming tasks as part of the technical component of site development rather than content development. If you wish to develop skills in this area, you'll find numerous books on this topic in your local library and bookstore. The HTML Writers Guild (www.hwg.org) also provides comprehensive information and online resources.

fixed amount of space, no entry could be longer than a certain number of characters. Any change to the design—such as resizing the space, or changing the point size of the type, or switching to a new font—would affect that limit, and force yet more changes in the text. However, readability had to be balanced against content: the easiest-to-read entries would have been so short as to be almost meaningless.

You'll also need to know how your writing/editing decisions affect the work of the team's designers and programmers. For example, if you add internal links, you'll alter the information architecture and increase the work of the programmer. In turn, you'll need to understand what technologies are available and cost-effective for your client and will meet user needs. For instance, would animation or video instead of written text be a better content solution for a particular section of your site? If so, does the project budget allow for the costs of animation or a video shoot? How will animation or video affect the download-ing of the site? Answers to questions like these will influence how you can organize and deliver information.

> You need to understand how technologies affect content delivery.

Throughout this book, and particularly in Chapter 8, "Content + Technology: A Surprising Alliance," we'll provide information about technical issues of Web development to help you understand:

New Opportunities for Writers/Editors

The more experience you have in new media, the easier it is to adapt to writing or editing for it. You have to surf the Web and soak in different styles. You need to look at the kind of sites you want to write or edit for. If it's corporate, then visit business sites. Pick out the ones you like and analyze them. There are a lot of doors opening in areas such as corporate Intranets and e-learning, and content is exceedingly important. Equally important for the growth of informational sites is the fact that governments which were funding the infrastruc-ture for the Web—the wires and pipes—are now starting to look at what's going down the pipes.

Kim Daynard, Communications and Content Consultant
Shrewd Expression
www.shrewdexpression.com

- The technical vocabulary used by members of Web teams.

- How different technologies affect Web development and usability.

- The pros and cons of different technologies.

- Which technologies have an impact on text presentation.

- Ways you can use technology to achieve your goals for content delivery.

Getting Work

Your ability to get work in informational site development will depend on many factors, including your writing/editing skills, your ability to search effectively for work, and the opportunities open to you. However, all the writers/editors we interviewed for this book spoke about the importance of knowing as much about the Web as possible—from the medium itself to the kinds of skills required to work within it.

The First Step: Surf, Surf, Surf

Have you ever analyzed your reaction to different Web sites? Do you know what kind of sites hold your interest, and why? Your chances of writing/editing successfully for any medium—film, novels, theater, how-to publications—increase exponentially when you spend a lot of time studying that medium.

What Employers Want: The Job Ads

One strong indication that content is becoming king in Web development is the increasing number of job ads posted online and listed in newspapers for Web writers/editors. Such ads hardly existed in the late 1990s when Web project managers didn't consider writers/editors essential to developing Web content. Exploring job ads in depth, including reading between the lines, will help you better understand what employers are looking for when hiring Web writers/editors.

In the following section are three ads that employers posted during January, 2001 to The Writing Employment Center (www.poewar.com/jobs/index.html). We suggest you read these ads quickly just to get the gist and see what you think the

> ### *Web Writer/Creative Writer (not technical)*
>
> Responsible for developing themes and writing creative, user-oriented web content for broker, shareholder and public audiences within established Clients for the Client.com and global web sites. Review, revise, and update existing content. Compose letters, Emails, invitations, confirmations and other collaterals that support products and services delivered on the sites. Research competitive sites. Recommend template changes and improvements in processes and procedures.
>
> Job ad reproduced with permission of poewar.com.

job entails. After each ad, we discuss words/phrases in each ad to analyze the obvious, and not so obvious, clues to the skills required for Web writing/editing, and the many roles the writer and/or editor can be asked to play as part of the job.

Creative Writer (not technical): For many people in the writing field, the term *creative writer* means someone who writes fiction, poetry, plays, and so on. But in the business world, this term has different connotations. At first reading, *Creative Writer*, with the addition *not technical*, suggests two possibilities. The first is that the employer wishes to emphasize the fact the company does not want a writer who must also handle HTML programming and other technology-related tasks. A second possibility is that the employer has realized that content delivered by financial experts is too technical for the average user and wants a writer outside of the financial field who can bring fresh ideas to the subject matter as well as be able to express complex financial issues in a simple and clear manner.

Developing themes: Thematic development refers to the ability to highlight particular messages through the structure of a text. This suggests that the company has had difficulty organizing information in a way that helps it express its goals and needs.

Writing creative, user-oriented web content: The term *creative* is used here to describe a writer who can create readable prose for nonfinancial experts.

Global web sites: This information indicates that the writer will be developing content for two different audiences: users of the highly targeted Client.com site (which is probably being visited by an audience familiar with the company's financial products), and users of public sites. The writer may have to develop different content and write in different styles for these two separate audiences as well as have knowledge of *localization*—how to write so the content doesn't have a negative impact on people from other cultures. (For more information on localization, see Chapter 9, "Keep CALM: Content and Logical Management.")

Review, revise, and update: Because Web sites can be altered more frequently than print and at a lower cost, the writer will be expected to regularly update text, that is, acting as a content manager or content librarian. This task will also entail copyediting and proofreading.

Research competitive sites: Researching other sites will require the writer to analyze the following elements: content in terms of scope, style, tone, and delivery; how this content interacts with visuals and navigation; whether other sites have a competitive edge; and, if so, what extra value they bring to users.

Recommend template changes and improvements in processes and procedures: Because this sentence occurs right after *Research competitive sites,* it suggests that the two statements are connected and that the writer may be expected to make recommendations based on competitors' materials. However, the phrases, *template changes* and *processes and procedures,* also suggest that part of the online content involves delivery within designated formats, and/or there are forms that users must fill out on the sites. In either case, the writer must analyze template and form specifications, make judgments as to their usability, and alter the formats for greater ease of use.

Work closely with the Web Creative Manager: This phrase provides a clue to the organizational hierarchy built around the site's development. The Web Creative Manager is likely to be

Web Content Editor

As Web Content Editor, you'll work closely with the Web Creative Manager to drive online sales through effective, compelling content. In addition to providing top-level creative with regard to tone, messaging and information architecture, this challenging position plays a major role in maintaining the overall quality of site content. As Web Content Editor, you will plan, develop and organize content, and you will collaborate with content developers and visual designers during the creative process. This position will be proactive in identifying opportunities for enhancing site content and will play a supportive role in helping to develop the skills and capabilities of the content staff.

Job ad reproduced with permission of poewar.com.

the designer/technology expert who manages the site and has to deal with text coming from a number of content contributors who are not writers but specialists in their own field. Although it isn't clear from the ad what this company sells, reading between the lines suggests that these content specialists, who may be engineers or other technically oriented product developers, are either unable or unwilling to write material for the average user. In either case, it's likely the Web Creative Manager has been frustrated by the text and asked the company to hire a professional editor.

Drive online sales through effective, compelling content: The product developers have written the content, but the editor will have to massage, and likely re-write, text to give it punch and appeal. The emphasis on sales suggests that the writer must be able to write promotional materials.

Top-level creative with regard to tone, messaging and information architecture: The editor will have to develop a style to advertise the product(s) and promote the company's goals—concepts that are closely connected to developing *effective, compelling content*. The more interesting part of this phrase is *information architecture*. It suggests that the company may believe that the site needs to be revamped. This means the editor must also be capable of re-organizing the site's structure and navigation.

Collaborate with content developers and visual designers: The editor will be part of a team and have to develop an understanding of the needs, issues, and concerns of two separate clientele: the content specialists and the visual designers. This phrase also hints at past difficulties between these two groups. The editor may find him/herself in a mediating role.

Website Writer and Editor

Create, coordinate, write and edit multicultural tolerance stories for online delivery for organization website. Develop relationships with story contributors, sources and internal staff to ensure that current, relevant content is presented on the site; conduct regular reviews and audits of content to ensure innovation, interactivity, quality and relevance necessary for high volume visits; interview industry sources to obtain editorial material; adhere to prescribed deadlines; develop clear, concise and factually accurate copy; link information into appropriate magazine departments; maintain and apply advanced knowledge of new media concepts to relevant websites, capabilities, and projects.

Job ad reproduced with permission of poewar.com.

Enhancing site content: This phrase reiterates the issues of editing the content to be more appealing, but the employer may also be looking to the editor to make recommendations with regard to visuals and navigation.

Helping to develop the skills and capabilities of the content staff: The company wants better writing performance from its content specialists. The editor may have to act as a writing teacher/trainer—an interesting career dilemma because success in this aspect of the job may mean the editor could teach him/herself out of a job!

Create, coordinate, write and edit: This position is journalism-related, likely involving a periodic publication such as a monthly newsletter. The writer is expected to develop story ideas, gather information, write the stories, and act as his/her own editor. The journalistic aspect of this job is also demonstrated through phrases such as *interview industry sources* and *adhere to prescribed deadlines*. The type of stories required—about multicultural tolerance—suggests that the employer might be a non-profit organization.

Develop relationships: As an information-gatherer, the writer/editor will need to stay on top of the news and build good sources both internal and external to the organization. If the employer is a non-profit organization, as we speculate, this hints at a political aspect of the job, that is, enhancing relationships to build good will and possibly gain funding for the organization.

Conduct regular reviews and audits of content: The writer/editor will act as a content manager or content librarian. The term *audits* suggests that he/she will also be analyzing site-visit statistics to determine usage, and whether the content is still appropriate to the organization's current needs. Fact-checking may also be involved.

Clear, concise and factually accurate copy: Any writer/editor would be expected to provide clear and concise text. The phrase *factually accurate*, however, suggests that the writer/editor will have to apply rigorous journalistic standards to content by double-checking information and sources. Non-profit organizations are special interest groups and, as such, can be suspect with regard to credibility as they promote their agendas. Clearly, this employer wants to ensure a public image of integrity and reliability.

Apply advanced knowledge of new media concepts: The writer/editor is expected to be cognizant of, and understand, the most up-to-date technologies and design in Web development, and how they can be applied to this particular site.

Know the Tasks

As you can see from the analyses of these job ads, the work scope of a Web writer/editor is broad—well beyond that of professional writers/editors in other media. Table 1.1 outlines the range of tasks involved in Web writing/editing.

Table 1.1 An Overview of Web Writing/Editing Tasks

RESEARCH TASKS
Collect relevant print information from content specialists or library-style investigation
Gather other information through interviews with content specialists and other sources
Surf similar sites for ideas about information architecture, navigation, design, writing style, and so on

INFORMATION-ORGANIZING TASKS
Synthesize and organize information into logical groupings
Balance the client's/project manager's needs with those of the audience
Consider the various ways users might navigate through a site and ensure content will remain coherent
Structure information in logical ways at different levels of the site

WRITING AND REWRITING TASKS
Anticipate and write to users' needs and questions
Express complex ideas in accessible language
Write clear, concise text
Create short, explanatory headers and titles
Know when to make effective use of bulleted lists
Write text with "punch"

SUBSTANTIVE EDITING TASKS
Create a text style guide or adapt the house style guide for Web usage
Correct ambiguities at every level of text: section, paragraph, sentence, word

continues

Table 1.1 (Continued)

SUBSTANTIVE EDITING TASKS (continued)
Notice inconsistencies in facts, names, spelling, and other elements
Check all tables, charts, and figures for accuracy in text content and visuals
Reorganize written content for greater clarity
Improve flow and coherence of text
Edit paragraphs and sentences for greater clarity
COPYEDITING TASKS
Ensure that each level of head is consistent in presentation across the document
Check all titles against table of contents
Note inconsistencies in font styles, colors, and sizes
Ensure consistency in footnotes and bibliographies
Correct grammar and punctuation
Help the translation process (if there is one) by ensuring that *only* copyedited material goes to translator
PROOFREADING TASKS
Check text for details that occur because of production errors and omissions
Check text for any errors, omissions, or inconsistencies missed during the copyedit
Recognize when a text line breaks poorly and correct to enhance flow of meaning
Ensure that *all* corrections have been made properly
If text has been translated, compare the English and foreign-language versions for consistency in format
TEAMWORK TASKS
Listen well and understand the needs and concerns of others
Articulate your issues in a pleasant manner
Explain problems and solutions in a clear way
Focus on team goals
Adapt easily and quickly to change
Work under pressure
Work with a variety of personalities and temperaments
Acknowledge your mistakes
Keep a sense of humor

continues

Table 1.1 An Overview of Web Writing/Editing Tasks (Continued)

DESIGN TASKS
Visualize how text and graphics can work together
Evaluate font styles and color usage for greater readability
Recognize when design overpowers or enhances text
Recognize when a visual can be more effective than text
Suggest visuals to enhance or replace text

TECHNOLOGY TASKS
Understand technical terms and concepts at a basic level
Understand the capabilities and limitations of software products that involve programming
Know how information architecture affects navigation and vice versa
Understand how different technologies affect usability
Keep up to date with technological advances in new media

What's Next?

This chapter was designed to give you an overview of the state of Web writing/editing by combining theoretical and practical information with regard to developing Web content and working in the field. We believe that this combination of theory and practice is crucial for writers/editors who wish to excel at their craft. Experience has taught us that if writers/editors understand the theoretical underpinnings of Web content development, they will not simply follow rules of thumb, but have a better idea why the rules of thumb exist, when they should be applied, and when they will not suit a particular type of content. In other words, understanding the principles of Web content development will allow you to practice your craft more thoughtfully and, when you create innovative ways to deliver content, to have a better understanding of what will be appropriate to the medium. Therefore, the following chapters are designed to deepen your understanding of the context of Web content development and assist you by providing practical advice and solutions to the challenges you'll encounter in your work.

Resources for This Chapter

Books

Designing Web Usability: The Practice of Simplicity by Jakob Neilsen. To date, this book is the definitive work on usability. Chapter 3, "Content Design," provides good rules of thumb for writing online text. (New Riders Publishing: 2000)

The Non-Designer's Web Book by Robin Williams and John Tollett. A light read for individuals new to Web development. (Peachpit Press: 1998)

How to Write for the World of Work: Sixth Edition by Thomas E. Pearsall, Donald H. Cunningham, and Elizabeth O. Smith. A good resource for many different types of workplace text from proposals to instructions. (Harcourt College Publishers: 2000)

The Copyeditor's Handbook: A Guide for Book Publishing and Corporate Communications by Amy Einsohn. A guide for beginners and a refresher text for experienced copyeditors that includes exercises and answer keys. (University of California Press: 2000)

Weaving the Web: The Original Design and Ultimate Destiny of the World Wide Web by its Inventor by Tim Berners-Lee. A nontechnical history of the Web with thoughts about its future. (HarperCollins: 2000)

Web Sites

The Webby Awards (www.webbyawards.com). Links to sites chosen by the members of The International Academy of Digital Arts and Sciences as outstanding in their category.

Writer's Resource Center (www.poewar.com/index.html). Information for writers interested in all types of Web writing. Provides an Employment Center and Freelance Forum.

Poynter.org (talk.poynter.org/cgi-bin/lyris.pl?). Click on the second blue box to reach a Web page that provides discussion lists for online writers.

The Journal of Electronic Publishing (www.press.umich.edu/ jep/) and First Monday (www.firstmonday.dk/). Many articles in these scholarly journals describe case studies about content development and discuss issues of theory and practice.

Endnotes

1. There is an interesting print parallel that shows how difficult it is for one technology to completely overtake and transform another, and for developers to truly understand the new technology as a new medium for content expression. According to literacy researcher Kathleen Tyner (1998:19), early printers didn't try to make their books look any different than those that were handwritten. "Gutenberg's 42-line Bible is barely distinguishable from that of a master scribe. It took several generations before the look of the book changed from that of the manuscript and it was not until at least the mid-17th century that page numbers began to appear at the bottom of a printed page."

2. This trend is being explored by researchers in a variety of fields to determine causes and evaluate its impact. For example, document design specialist Karen Shriver (1997) provides an extensive overview of this change and ascribes it to developments in society and consumerism, advances in science and technology, changes in the way writing and graphic design are taught and practised, and professional developments in the field of writing, graphic design, and typography.

3. Deborah Shaw (2001), a researcher in information science, describes *stickiness* as "a term apparently first used to connote the user's difficulty in leaving a Web site in 1997 (Bentley, 1997). Stickiness refers to spiders' design of their webs with sticky filaments to capture insects which light on the web; in the business world, stickiness involves retaining users and driving them into the site (Bedoe-Stephens, 1999) or getting them 'to leave something of themselves behind' (Bo Peabody, quoted in Seybold, 2000)."

4. Discourse analysts Gunther Kress and Theo van Leeuwen (1996) were among the first linguists to realize that textual analysis must include the visual as well as verbal components in a multimodal document. Their framework for analysis provides one means of exploring how the mix of verbal and visual makes meaning for users. See Chapter 5, "Is Seeing Believing? The Art of Visual Rhetoric," for more information on this topic.

Audience, Audience, *Audience!*

We've noticed an interesting situation that arises, time and again, when we work with clients to develop informational Web sites. They're generally in absolute agreement with us that the site must be user-focused, but only rarely do they actually "walk the talk." These clients have content they want to put on the Web site, usually materials that have first been developed for print. When we suggest, tactfully, that the content isn't appropriately organized for Web sites or written for Web users, the clients nod, but the conversation almost always begins to veer towards jazzy graphics such as pop-ups and animation, and techno-props such as links, video- and audio-clips, and metatags for search engines. Surely, they reason, if all those good things are on the site, users will come and stay. Right?

Wrong. Users are exasperated with the delivery of online content, even users who are Web-savvy. During the course of our workshops and classes, we've collected a litany of complaints. Table 2.1 provides a summary of users' pet peeves.

We don't want to paint all clients with the same brush. Increasing numbers of clients do understand that writing content designed for the Web is as much a part of site development as design and navigation. This is why professional writers/editors

Table 2.1 Users' Pet Peeves

ABOUT	COMPLAINTS
Content	■ Too long
	■ Not relevant
	■ Lack of summaries
	■ Inconsistency in language—style and tone
	■ Punctuation and grammar errors
	■ Requires too much scrolling
	■ Includes banners and other advertising "junk"
Navigation	■ Inability to find content
	■ Too many clicks to get to content
	■ Too many links
	■ Poorly labeled links
	■ Buttons that look like links, but aren't
	■ Icons that are links, but don't look like it
	■ Dead-end pages
	■ Getting lost
Design	■ Too many fonts and colors
	■ Too much clutter
	■ Slow downloads because of too much graphic material
	■ Pop-up windows

are starting to get work in this medium. But, for every truly well-written, user-friendly site, there are hundreds of thousands of informational sites that fail the test. Why, we wondered, do we encounter resistance to content change? All the usability studies point to appropriately written text as crucial to a site's success, and our clients share, along with the general public, a dislike for poorly written Web text. Why, then, is it so difficult for clients to deal with language and so easy for them to deal with visuals and navigation?

We are all visual/action experts.

The answer lies in our biology. Our survival, as a species, depended on our ability to see and to act on what we saw, whether it came to hunting prey or protecting ourselves from predators. The result is that we all have a high level of expertise in these areas. In discussing vision, for example, cognitive scientist Donald Hoffman (1998) says that we are all creative geniuses:

> Your creative genius is so accomplished that it appears, to you and to others, as effortless. Yet it far outstrips the most valiant efforts of today's fastest supercomputers. To invoke it, you need only open your eyes…In a fraction of a second your visual intelligence can construct the strut and colors of a peacock, or the graceful run of a leopard, or the fireworks of an ocean sunset, or the nuances of light in a forest at dusk, or any of countless other scenes of such subtlety and complexity. In repertoire and speed you far surpass the greatest of painters…You are a visual virtuoso.

Our visual intelligence combined with our instincts regarding action affect the way we react to Web design and navigation. We know instinctively what we like visually and what we don't. Similarly, if a navigation path on a site doesn't suit us, we know it immediately.

However, reading and writing are not innate. These are learned skills that require years of education to achieve mastery and, even then, not everyone acquires them to the same level. If your clients have difficulty discussing text and prefer to talk about visuals and navigation, it's a good idea to remember that, at a very basic level, your clients are experts at pictures and actions. Your area of expertise—the written word—is generally out of their comfort zone.[1]

The Bubble Syndrome

> *Most human beings have an almost infinite capacity for taking things for granted.*
>
> **ALDOUS HUXLEY**

Clients are like figures inside the bubble toys that you shake to create a miniature snowfall. They're insiders participating in a particular workplace and living its assumptions and beliefs every day. It's very difficult for them to step outside the bubble and get an arm's length perspective. Furthermore, these assumptions and beliefs have a powerful impact on their language use.

In-House Language

Discourse analyst Norman Fairclough describes the bubble syndrome's impact on language as *naturalization*, where beliefs become so familiar to us that we accept them as merely common sense.[2] And, because beliefs are always housed and expressed in language, the terms and phrases around these beliefs become *naturalized*—familiar, comfortable, and accepted without question.

Even Intranet sites, those designed for employees of a particular company, can suffer from this problem. Large organizations have numerous divisions, national and global branches, and/or subsidiaries, each of which develops its own culture, attitudes, and jargon. When these divisions, branches, or subsidiaries decide to post their information on the company Intranet, they're often so attached to their own language and messages that they lose sight of the users, that is, their fellow employees.

Research on writing in the workplace has found that people who aren't trained as writers/editors but are content specialists such as engineers, economists, and scientists are doing more writing on the job than ever before. This kind of writing is usually collaborative with texts passed around, re-written or edited by colleagues, and approved or edited again by superiors—in other words, the texts go round and round inside the bubble.[4] Throughout this process, the content is refined and massaged with attempts to: 1) meld different authors' viewpoints, interpretations, and language into a coherent whole; and 2) create a document in a language that is reflective of, and acceptable to, the organization. Because the text has never left the bubble,

---

Our Everyday Metaphors are a Form of Naturalization

The term *key executives* is used so frequently in organizational settings that most of us forget that the word *key* is being employed here as a metaphor. A *key* is a tool for mechanical devices. When a CEO refers to executives as *keys*, he or she is displaying a mental model of the company as mechanistic, composed of wheels, cogs, and levers that must all run smoothly. Those key executives are the CEO's tools. From this perspective, *key* is less a complimentary term, designating important persons, than language used to reaffirm the organizational hierarchy with the CEO at the apex of power—the person who turns the *keys* and makes the machinery run.[3]

The Value of the Wordsmith

A Web site can often get major benefits from a freelance or contract writer—an outsider, in other words. The team has an overall strategy for their Web site, but the outsider may be the one who says, "Hang on. What is the purpose of this particular page? How does it fit in with your business strategy?" The contract writer may be the only one who challenges the client's assumptions and "corporatespeak"; who says, "I don't understand what that means," or, "If I were searching for a Web page like this, I would use the phrase _outdoor living—not exteriorization._"

A skilled Web writer also can deal with the content that all too often falls between the cracks. At present, techies and content managers are expected to do many jobs that really need a wordsmith. For example, who writes the links text? Who makes sure the text on the page is easy to scan? Who edits the boilerplate text of 404 error pages and those all-important forms? The answer is all too often— nobody, or somebody without any interest or expertise in language. Writers are needed to deal with the "badlands" between technical experts and business or marketing managers.

Rachel McAlpine, Web Writer and Training Consultant
Web Word Wizardry
www.webpagecontent.com

chances are that most of its language will be naturalized to that particular environment. Unless the organization is large enough to have staff writers/editors, this content often lacks clarity, is cumbersome and dense, and is likely to provide far more information than users want or need.

Meet the Online CIA

What happens when naturalized language appears on Web sites? Figure 2.1, an example of naturalized discourse, is text taken from the Web site of the U.S. Central Intelligence Agency (CIA). Knowing that a text has difficulties is only the first step; writers/editors must be able to pinpoint the precise problems and come up with specific solutions. We've provided the kinds

Retitle. This page doesn't actually explain "Who We Are."

Cut paragraph. Users aren't interested in the back story.

Get to the point. Cut most of paragraph.

Simplify and put in bullet format. Add bolded header.

Cut, simplify, and put in bullet format. Add bolded header.

Cut all text but program titles, put in bullet format, and add bolded header.

United States Intelligence Community

Who We Are and What We Do

Throughout history, the leaders of nations and armies have sought to be fore-warned of dangers and forearmed with information that reduces uncertainty and provides a critical edge for decisions. The effort to meet these fundamental needs of decisionmakers is what lies behind the practice of intelligence. That practice consists of collecting and interpreting information, overcoming in the process any barriers erected to keep secret the activities, capabilities, and plans of foreign pow-ers and organizations.

Today, intelligence is a vital element in every substantial international activity of the US government. Every day, the agencies and offices that make up the US Intelli-gence Community provide an important information advantage to those who man-age the nation's strategic interests--political, economic, and military. Intelligence organizations support a broad range of consumers, from the national level of the President, the Cabinet, and the Congress, to the tactical level of military forces deployed in the field.

For intelligence officers, this means maintaining an ability to warn policymakers and military leaders of impending crises, especially those that threaten the immediate interests of the nation or the well-being of US citizens. It also means giving govern-ment and military officials advance knowledge of long-term dangers, such as the threats posed by countries that covet weapons of mass destruction. It means help-ing to safeguard public security by countering threats from terrorists and drug traf-fickers. It means supporting economic security by uncovering foreign efforts at bribery and other schemes to tilt the playing field of international trade. And it means multiplying the effectiveness of US military forces deployed for operations.

A series of statutes and Executive Orders provides legal authority for the conduct of intelligence activities. Key documents include the National Security Act of 1947 (as amended), which provides the basic organization of the US's national security effort, and Executive Order 12333, which provides current guidelines for the con-duct of intelligence activities and the composition of the Intelligence Community. Together with other laws and orders, these two documents are meant to ensure that intelligence activities are conducted effectively and conform to the US Constitution and US laws. They also provide a statutory basis of accountability to the Congress.

The national intelligence effort is led by the Director of Central Intelligence (DCI), who oversees the Intelligence Community organizations described in more detail in the following pages. Resources for these organizations are tied together in the National Foreign Intelligence Program--the budget for these national activities, which support political, economic, and military decisionmakers, is developed by the DCI and presented to the Congress annually. Intelligence activities that are more narrowly focused and intended to support tactical military forces are funded separately in two programs within the Department of Defense. These programs--the Joint Military Intelligence Program and the Tactical Intelligence and Related Activities aggregation--fall under the aegis of the Deputy Secretary of Defense. In recent years, the line between national and tactical activities has become less dis-tinct and, in fact, national and tactical capabilities have been brought to bear on intelligence problems in complementary ways. The goal of intelligence, however, has remained constant--to support decisionmakers with the best possible informa-tion, no matter its source.

Figure 2.1 Text from the United States Intelligence Community Web site.
February 17, 2001. www.cia.gov/ic/functions.html

United States Intelligence Community

Overview of Activities

The Intelligence Community serves a broad range of clients from the President, Cabinet, and Congress to military forces deployed in the field.

> One brief, introductory sentence is sufficient.

Our activities include:

- Warning policymakers/military leaders of impending crises, especially those that threaten the immediate interests of the nation or the well-being of US citizens.

- Informing government/military officials about long-term dangers, such as threats posed by countries that wish to acquire weapons of mass destruction.

- Helping to safeguard public security by countering threats from terrorists and drug traffickers.

- Supporting economic security by uncovering foreign efforts at bribery and other activities designed to disrupt international trade.

- Enhancing the effectiveness of US military forces in areas of action.

> Provide consistent body format of bolded headers, simplified text, and bullets.

The legal authority for our activities is based on:

- The National Security Act of 1947 (as amended) which provides the basic organization of the US's national security effort.

- Executive Order 12333 which provides current guidelines for the conduct of intelligence activities and the composition of the Intelligence Community.

Our Funding is based on:

- The National Foreign Intelligence Program

- The Joint Military Intelligency Program

- Tactical Intelligence and Related Activities

> Links cut down text and provide interactivity.

Figure 2.2   Rewrite of the text in Figure 2.1 to make it user-friendly.

of editing notes in the margins that we'd jot down to ourselves as we thought about making this text user-friendly.

Now compare the text in Figure 2.1 with that in Figure 2.2, where we rewrote the text to make it more suitable for the Web.

In general, we cut text and simplified sentences to reduce the dense verbiage. As well, we:

- Eliminated clichés such as *tilt the playing field.*

- Created sub-heads to break up the text and bolded them for emphasis.

- Used bullets wherever possible for easier reading.

- Provided white space between bullets when the text was longer than one line.

- Created links for users who might be interested in gaining more information about particular items.

- Rewrote emotive language such as "countries that *covet* weapons of mass destruction" to "countries that *wish to acquire* weapons of mass destruction."

- Avoided use of *nominalizations*, that is, nouns derived from verbs, such as *reservation* which comes from the verb *to reserve*. Nominalizations, and particularly their over-use, make text weighty and hard to read because they are usually multi-syllabic, and create ambiguity because they eliminate time (verbs demonstrate time through tense) and agents, that is, who is doing what and to whom.

- Avoided passive voice in verbal processes such as "activities *are conducted* effectively." Like nominalizations, passive voice makes text ambiguous by concealing the agent performing the action.

Most importantly, we cut a great deal of naturalized discourse—the type of organizational jargon such as *aggregation, a critical edge for decisions*, and *an important information advantage* that is so familiar to the content developers it's likely they neither had any idea how strange it sounds to outside readers, nor how difficult it is to read on the Web.

William Horton, a leading authority on Web writing and new media design, says that when Web writers/editors develop content they must continuously think in terms of *seductive writing*: "You have to choreograph the reading experience so that users feel the content is personal, useful, and enticing." Horton says that every Web page is an information object that should provide users with many pathways to potential experiences. Web writers/editors should:

- Use words and phrases that relate to users' information needs.

- Organize the flow of information to convince users that the answers to their questions are never more than one or two clicks away.

- Create smooth transitions between paragraphs that point people forward.

- Keep users so curious that they'll keep searching and drilling down.

The problem with naturalized content is that it doesn't meet users' major goal, which Horton describes as "moving from question to answer with a minimum of pain." You might find it useful to print out the following piece of advice from Horton and put it somewhere in your workplace where it will be continuously visible:

"The key to a seductive Web site is immediate gratification."

The User Prism

Writing has traditionally been seen as a solitary pursuit. According to this tradition, when the writer is composing, he/she is acting as a conduit between the subconscious where the words exist and the paper (or computer screen) where the words appear. How this conduit actually operates is a mystery. Although some writing researchers continue to explore these fundamentals of composition, others have started to examine the development of text, not as a solitary pursuit, but as a form of social action between the writer and the reader.

> Writing/editing is a social action.

Writing and literacy researcher Deborah Brandt (1990:39) says: "To write words down is not to give them a detached life but to give them a public life—to make them shared." The text is not a one-way exchange from writer to reader, but an act of meaning-making to which each player—the writer and the reader—bring their knowledge. Brandt describes text as a place where writers and readers are dealing with a *situation-in-hand*. The writer plans the situation, structures the knowledge he/she brings to it, and presents it to the reader in the form of words.

Readers, coming upon this situation, develop plans for understanding it and, as they read the words, constantly monitor comprehension within the framework of their own background knowledge. The result is a powerful, interactive process. "Overall, the representations of the situation-in-hand that effective writers and readers create and maintain tend to be flexible, particular, and dynamic, growing in depth and breadth as an act of writing or reading unfolds."

You are likely to be well acquainted with the social process of developing content. But given the number of poorly written and organized Web sites, it's clear that this process is not well understood, if at all, by nonprofessional writers/editors. Rather than seeing the entire text as a situation of mutual and shared meanings, they focus on what they want to say from sentence to sentence. On the Web, this type of writing, combined with the use of naturalized discourse, results in:

- Irrelevant information.
- Unclear messages.
- Poorly structured information.
- Unsuitable style, tone, and terminology.
- Paragraphs and overall text that are too long.
- Text that is boring and/or hard to read.
- Uninformative headers and link titles.

Is Reading Print Different than Reading Web Text?

As a Web writer/editor, you need to know what users do when confronted with online text. Are their reading strategies completely different than when they read print materials? At present, Web usability researchers have given three labels to users' reading activities: *scanning*, *foraging*, and *consuming*. Although these sound as if users have different behaviors reading online, we suggest that, in fact, they are equivalent to four well-researched print reading activities: *skimming*, *scanning*, *intensive reading*, and *extensive reading* (see Table 2.2).

De-Naturalizing Content

> You must view content through users' eyes.

As a writer/editor, you're accustomed to writing with the audience first and foremost in your mind. You continuously filter everything you write through the prism of the reader's interests and work continuously to answer the following questions:

- What are the reader's needs and concerns?
- How can I ensure that this information is best presented to address these needs and concerns within the context of the product?

Table 2.2 Print and Web Reading Strategies

PRINT READING STRATEGIES	WEB READING STRATEGIES
Skimming: Readers quickly run their eyes over text to get the gist of it.	**Scanning:** When readers first run their eyes down a screen to see if the material is relevant to their needs, they're skimming the text as they would in a print document. Note that, at this point, it's unlikely that they'll scroll further if what they read doesn't interest them.
Scanning: Readers search for particular pieces of information that meet their needs.	**Scanning:** If the Web text meets their needs, readers will quickly focus on particular pieces of information and may scroll further. Highly visible text such as links and bolded/italicized words and phrases play an important role in this activity. You'll find more information about: ■ Links, in Chapter 3, "Organizing a Web Site: "Elementary, My Dear Watson" and Chapter 6, "Links, Logic, and the Layered Reader." ■ Bolded/italicized text in Chapter 4, "E-Rhetoric: A New Form of Persuasion."
Intensive reading: Readers read short texts to extract specific, detailed information.	**Foraging:** As with a print document, readers stop, having decided that the text is relevant, and read a short bit of content for more in-depth information.
Extensive reading: Readers read long texts usually for pleasure and global understanding.	**Consuming:** The vast majority of readers can't perform extensive reading online and prefer to print-and-read for a variety of reasons: ■ Studies show that 25 percent of users read slower online than from print text. ■ Many users develop eye fatigue when reading online text because of resolution. According to *Discover* (2000:94): "The visual resolution of a typical book—1,440,000 dots per square inch is up to 277 times sharper than that of an average computer screen." ■ Some users may have limited time to be online, because of cost or through use of public computers such as those in libraries and cyber-cafés.

Source: *Developing Reading Skills* by Françoise Grellet (1981/1995).

- How can I organize the material so that the reader will find it coherent, logical, and reliable?

- What type of language should I use so that the reader will understand this information?

- What is the appropriate style and tone to use for this particular audience and format?

- What writing devices—headers, leads, sidebars, tables, charts, and so on—can I use that will be informative and make reading easier and more comprehensible?

In short, you work at the process of de-naturalizing the content for the reader, and your primary objective is to entice the audience into reading your text. Your success depends on your sensitivity to language, particularly that of naturalized discourse such as "important information advantage" in the CIA's text, your ability to walk in the reader's shoes, and your dexterity at juggling the reader's needs with those of the client who's likely to be quite attached to his/her words. Research for this book (Harrison, 2001) shows how five freelance writers who work in different print-based media use certain mental strategies to de-naturalize text. As Table 2.3 demonstrates, each of these strategies leads them to take on different roles in their relationships with clients.

The Importance of a Vision

I've been in situations where the techies and designers have gotten together, figured out what they think is cool design and navigation, and then created a "content bucket." I'm supposed to fill in the few blank spaces with text. This is *brochureware*—completing 90 percent of the site and then just dumping some content in. What's missing is any strategy about users. A site has to build a good relationship with users, and you do that by meshing together what you have—the content, with what you want—the ultimate goal of the site, with what users want and expect. In other words, you have a vision, you execute that vision, and then you maintain it.

Hilary Marsh, Web Content Strategist
www.pen4hire.com

Table 2.3 How Writers De-Naturalize Text

THE ROLES	THE WRITERS' COMMENTS
The Repackager: The writers don't see themselves as authorial, but as people hired to find creative ways to deliver the client's material.	■ "It's not my stuff; it's not my voice." ■ "I develop, adapt, and edit their material." ■ "I package it the best way I can." ■ "I have no ego invested." ■ "Criticism doesn't bother me in a gut way, because it's not my material."
The Go-Between: The writers see themselves acting as intermediaries between the client and the target audience.	■ "I represent the consumer/reader." ■ "I have a real-world point of view." ■ "I take it from the audience's point of view, i.e., 'What is it that I'm going to remember from this?'"
The Facilitator/Collaborator: The writers feel that an important part of their work is to help clients better understand what they want to say, and why.	■ "I end up interviewing the client who has a hard time telling me the whole story because he/she assumes I know more than I do. And, they often keep talking around the subject and I keep pulling them back." ■ "It's a collaborative process. Sometimes I know more about the message than the client because I'm also writing for other clients and have a better understanding of the big picture than anyone else in the room. I help them tie things together." ■ "I'm a mirror for the client, saying back to them what they've told me in more audience-based ways. After the first draft, we negotiate language as collaborators, trying to balance their needs with audience needs."
The Pseudo-Insider: The writers take on the beliefs of their clients in order to write successfully, but keep these beliefs at an arm's length distance.	■ "I'm like an actor playing a role. I'm distant and yet involved." ■ "I try to find what it is that I agree with. You have to 'buy in'; make a private connection." ■ "I let part of my brain think the way they do. I represent them and have to express their messages." ■ "I put myself in another consciousness and see how the world looks to them." ■ "Part of your mind thinks their way, while another part remains the real you."

continues

Table 2.3   How Writers De-Naturalize Text (Continued)

THE ROLES	THE WRITERS' COMMENTS
The Challenger: The writers sometimes play the devil's advocate with the client to de-naturalize content.	■ "They'll say the propaganda, and I'll try to ask dumb questions such as 'What's your problem?' I try to be provocative in a goofy way. I want them to drop their guards and speak out." ■ "I act as a counter-force to the clients' acculturation which often works against clear communication." ■ "With more experience, I've learned how and when I can 'shake things up' so that I present my clients with a completely different way of viewing the issue."
The Risk-Taker: The writers believe that they can write text in de-naturalized ways that are "off-limits" to clients.	■ "It's not efficient for clients to take risks. They need to get approvals and don't want repercussions. So they use language that's already been approved and it tends to get replicated over and over and imported into new documents. We tug at the other end of the rope and offer them a contrasting way to say things." ■ "The clients are often timid and afraid and don't use real-life words. They write for the boss. I write for the audience." ■ "I'm given the benefit of the doubt for my lack of knowledge. That lets me say things in new ways."

Visualizing Users

Clearly, viewing the world through the user's prism is key to writing successful text whether in print or on the Web. How successful writers/editors actually do this at the cognitive level continues to be debated by researchers who study this issue. But the question that should concern all of us working in the field of Web writing/editing is just how accurately we represent users in our minds as we write or edit.

Document design specialist Karen Shriver (1997) describes three ways that print document developers determine audience:

Classification-driven audience analysis: Writers/editors and designers brainstorm and analyze target audience demographics. A strength of this method, says Shriver (1997:156-157), is that it compels "communicators to think about the needs and expectations of different groups." Its weakness is that it leads

to stereotyping, and communicators can "draw faulty infer-
ences about the audience's needs."

Intuition-driven audience analysis: Document writers/editors and
designers "imagine the audience and draw on their internal
representation of the audience as a guide to writing and
design." Because intuition is derived from "the gut," it can
clearly lead to inaccurate judgments. For example, Kirsch
(1990:226) interviewed five experienced print writers and found
that they "develop rich representations of audiences," but that
they became extremely attached to these representations, perhaps to the detriment of the audience. However, Shriver
(1997:159) notes that: "The strength of intuitive modes is that
they capture, in ways that others do not, the phenomenon that
skilled communicators are good at 'doing things with words
and pictures' that get the audience's attention and keep it."

Feedback-driven audience analysis: Document design teams
bring actual readers into the process of development in order
to gain the most accurate representation of the audience possible. Shriver (1997:162) says that the strength of this model is
that it allows writers and designers to witness how readers
"engage with documents in order to understand, access, and
use them for pragmatic purposes." A weakness of this model is
that it may provide vast amounts of data, particularly if many
users take part in the test group, and some of the data can be
irrelevant, idiosyncratic, or as Shriver puts it: "just plain
weird." Web users, for example, often have unrealistic expectations of a site. Also, bringing users into the Web development
process creates challenges in terms of cost and scheduling as
well as the possibility of major change. The result is that many
clients resist feedback-driven audience analysis.

In our experience, variants and combinations of these methods
are used in Web site development. We have both been in meetings
where clients and production team members brainstormed about
users, worked on Web sites where intuition drove content, and
had material focus-tested to see the results. What's important is
that, as a Web site's writer/editor, you remain aware of the pit-
falls of all three methods and seek the best route to meeting user
needs. The checklist in Figure 2.3 can help you cover the bases.

Thinking Global

One of the major issues regarding these approaches to visualizing users is that of global and/or multicultural audiences.

"Who's the Audience?" Checklist

☐ Who is the target audience(s)? How have we determined this?

☐ What are the needs, concerns, and goals of members of the target audience? How do we know this?

☐ Is the audience local, regional, national and/or global?

☐ How computer literate will your target audience be?

☐ Is the content delivered in a way that appeals to people with different learning styles such as preferences for content that is delivered visually or through audio?

☐ Are members of the target audience elderly and likely to require special types of text formatting and/or sizing of fonts and icons?

Will members of the audience have disabilities such as:

☐ Visual impairment or color blindness that could affect their ability to read text and see the content's graphic and video elements?

☐ Cognitive or visual disabilities that affect their ability to read text that moves or changes?

☐ Motor skills or mobility problems that might hinder their ability to use technologies that depend on devices such as keyboards and the mouse?

☐ Hearing impairment that could limit their ability to access the content's audio component?

Figure 2.3   A checklist for visualizing a Web site's audience.

No matter how a production team attempts to visualize users, team members are products of their own cultures and will be limited by their personal experiences within those cultures. This limitation affects how we create meanings for ourselves and others. Jay Lemke (1990:186) is a researcher in social semiotics[5]—a field of study which he describes as a "theory of how people make meaning. It asks how we make sense of and to one another and how we make sense of the world. It concerns itself with everything people do that is socially meaningful in a community: talking, writing, drawing pictures and diagrams, gesturing, dancing, dressing, sculpting, building—in effect everything." In other words, no word, object, or action exists as meaningful on its own. Rather, we give it meaning, and we do so through the "lens" of our own society, culture, and community.

International communications specialist Nancy Hoft (1995:266-267) cites color as an often-described example of a graphical element that can be interpreted differently by different nationalities or cultural groups within nationalities. However, she warns that responses to color are complex and affected by many factors including exposure to other cultures and the fact that colors are often used together. "For all these reasons, it is often dangerous to generalize about color and the reactions it is likely to induce." Given these caveats, she cites possible cultural interpretations of red.

- Thailand—most popular color
- China—prosperity, rebirth
- Malaysia—valor and might
- Ivory Coast—mourning (dark red)
- United Kingdom—first place
- France and the United Kingdom—masculinity
- United States—power, stop, danger
- India—procreation, life
- Many African countries—blasphemy or death

Creating Web sites for a global audience is clearly a tricky business. Technical communicator Kirk St. Amant (2000:12), in writing about global communications, notes: "While exchanges in this new online business environment generally involve the use of similar technologies and often use a common language (usually English), many cultural factors can affect communications. Even minor differences in expression can contribute tremendously to confusion and miscommunication."

> Writing for a global audience requires research.

Not every Web site is intended for a national or international audience, but many are. The cultural mosaic within countries and across the globe means that, as a Web writer/editor, you must add an additional social-semiotic layer to your questions regarding users, such as:

- Does our Web site communicate appropriately to our intended audiences?

- Will the words I've written/edited have a different meaning for people outside of North America?

- Will the visuals of the Web site such as the colors and graphical images be interpreted in ways that vary significantly from our team's interpretation?

- Are there alternatives, both textually and visually, that would be more culturally neutral?

People who work on Web production use the term, *localization*, to refer to the adaptation of a Web site to make it more acceptable to international users. (For more information on Web content and cultural issues, see Chapter 9, "Keep CALM: Content and Logical Management.")

Text in the Context of Design and Navigation

> Print writers/editors visualize the page.

If, in addition to writing/editing text, you've also been involved in the print production of your content, you've learned to write/edit with design requirements in mind. Print products often have page limitations and color restrictions because of cost. As you're creating, you're constantly visualizing how text will appear on the page of a tabloid, report, brochure, or newsletter. You may ask yourself questions such as:

- What material will the reader see on a particular page?

- How many words will fit comfortably on the page and still leave white space so the text can breathe?

- How can I condense the content to make it fit the required space?

- Will the information be more suited to one page or a double-paged spread?

- Are there visual methods—screened boxes, arrows, or icons—that will enhance readability?

- If the product will be in black-and-white, two-color, or four-color, how can the different colors be used to better enhance the content?

- When and how will an illustration or photograph add to, or replace, the text?

If you've worked with graphic designers, you'll also know that few of them read a complete text because of time and budget constraints. Therefore, when you sit down with the first design, you'll discover that the graphics may have enhanced the readability of your text in some ways and detracted from it in others. You, along with the client, will make suggestions to improve the presentation of the text. The graphic designer will then go back to the drawing board and return with a revised design. This process will continue until everyone is happy, or time and budget issues force all concerned into trade-offs and compromises.

Is Designing for the Web Different than Designing for Print?

As Table 2.4 demonstrates, the tasks of Web designers are much broader than those of print graphic designers. The process of Web design involves more than graphics, including the use of multiple media, the programming of Web materials, and the development of other Web elements such as databases, chat rooms, discussion groups, and so on. For this reason, most Web design houses employ or sub-contract technology specialists.

Technology and Presentation

The role of the writer/editor in Web development is broader than that of a writer/editor for print materials. You need to understand the technology of the Web in much deeper detail than you need to understand print technology, because your content decisions—from the organization of information to what goes on the Web page—will affect the design, navigation, programming, and costs of the site. Although the questions you ask yourself will, in some respects, be similar to those you asked as you developed print products, you will have to broaden the questions to consider technology-related issues. Figure 2.4 provides a checklist of questions you should ask when developing content.

> Web writers/editors visualize the site, page, and screen.

A Question of Accessibility

As we discussed earlier in this chapter, making a site user-friendly may involve issues of accessibility for those who are disabled. The World Wide Web Consortium (W3C:1999)—an

Table 2.4 A Comparison of Print and Web Design Tasks

	PRINT DESIGNER	WEB DESIGNER
Visual Tasks	■ Uses overall content structure to design document in required format such as textbook, magazine, novel, and so on. ■ Creates design templates for document pages, dealing with such issues as pagination, margins, color use, and final paper quality. ■ Creates front-page or cover design. ■ Uses color to highlight text and visuals. ■ Develops design elements for different text features such as headers, bullets, and callouts. ■ Works with illustrators and photographers to create a successful merge of visual elements, text, and the overall design. ■ Inputs text and prepares layouts. ■ Fine-tunes final design with text in accordance with client wishes.	■ Uses information architecture to help design the user interface. For more information, see Chapter 3, "Organizing a Web Site: 'Elementary, My Dear Watson.'" ■ Creates design style guide that determines the look-and-feel of a site's Web pages as well as features such as headers, bullets, and navigational information. ■ Creates "Splash" and/or "Home" page designs. ■ Employs color to highlight text and visuals, using the Web-safe color palette so that text and visuals can cross multiple platforms and monitors. ■ Works with programmers, illustrators, photographers, and video and audio specialists to create a successful merge of visual elements, text, and the overall design. ■ Inputs text into design. ■ Fine-tunes final design with text in accordance with client wishes.
Technology Tasks	■ Uses appropriate design software to prepare print-ready copy. ■ Understands potential and limitations of different print technologies and print presses.	■ Uses appropriate design/programmer software to prepare Web site. ■ Understands the potential and limitations of different Web browsers such as Internet Explorer and Netscape Navigator.

Table 2.4 (Continued)

	PRINT DESIGNER	WEB DESIGNER
Technology Tasks (Continued)		■ Understands the potential and limitations of different servers.
		■ Understands the potential and limitations of user technologies such as the speed of computer processors, monitor resolutions, and modem bandwidth accessibility.
Production Tasks	■ Not involved in final print production.	■ Builds databases, internal site search engines, chat rooms, discussion groups, and other Web elements, if required.
		■ May transfer Web site onto client's server or deliver the Web site on CD-ROM.

international organization of more than 500 corporations, institutions, and government departments—has established guidelines under the Web Accessibility Initiative (WAI) to assist developers in building sites to accommodate the needs of many different kinds of users. For example, with regard to content, they suggest:

> Content developers should make content understandable and navigable. This includes not only making the language clear and simple, but also providing understandable mechanisms for navigating within and between pages. Providing navigation tools and orientation information in pages will maximize accessibility and usability. Not all users can make use of visual clues such as image maps, proportional scroll bars, side-by-side frames, or graphics that guide sighted users of graphical desktop browsers. Users also lose contextual information when they can only view a portion of a page, either because they are accessing the page one word at a time (speech synthesis or Braille display), or one section at a time (small display, or a magnified display). Without orientation information, users may not be able to understand very large tables, lists, menus, etc.

A Text and Technology Checklist

☐ How will content appear on monitors with different resolutions?

☐ Does the text comfortably share the "real estate" of the screen with navigational information?

☐ Is the use of visuals on the site enhancing or detracting from the content?

☐ Does the information architecture organize material in a way that is logical and coherent? Does it help users develop a mental map of the site?

☐ Are the navigational visuals and text clear and obvious to users?

☐ Will the information be more suited to one Web page or spread out among two or more pages? And, if I determine that the content does require additional pages, how will this affect the information architecture, navigation, and programming?

☐ Are there visual strategies—tables, charts, illustrations, animation, audio- or visual-clips—that will enhance usability?

☐ How will the addition of these elements affect the time it will take users to download the site onto their computers?

☐ What plug-ins/players may be required for additional elements?

☐ Should the site provide a print-friendly version of the content for users?

☐ Should the site deliver some content using a different mechanism than the standard Web page? (For more information on alternative formats, see Chapter 8: "Content + Technology: A Surprising Alliance.")

Figure 2.4 Technology-related questions with regard to text.

As this guideline indicates, users' ability to access text is highly dependent on technology and presentation. If you are working on a site where the client wants to ensure more accessibility, then you and your production team will have to develop content, design, and navigation strategies to meet user needs. (For more information on accessibility, see Chapter 9, "Keep CALM: Content and Logical Management.")

Typos and Other Gremlins

As the site's writer/editor, you will also play a role that is relatively new to Web content development—the copyediting and proofreading of text. In the print world, a typographical mistake or punctuation error essentially "lives" forever, visibly trapped in the published text. Although copyediting and proofing standards in print are not as high as they used to be, nevertheless many print clients are willing to spend money to hire copyeditors and proofreaders to ensure a quality presentation.

On the Web, the situation is different. To paraphrase a line from the film, *Love Story*: "A Web mistake means never having to say you're sorry." Why? Because a Web site is not a final product, but an ongoing process. Web text errors can be changed easily and rapidly. However, making Web text changes still involves staff resources, such as having someone on the team who has the time and skill to spot mistakes, and assigning a programmer to fix body-text errors or a designer to correct text within a graphic.

> Many clients take a low-budget approach to final Web text.

Although most clients understand that ungrammatical, misspelled text irritates users to the point of "turning them off" a site, we find that they don't want to apply the same rigorous copyediting and proofreading processes to online text that are applied to print. Clients must deal with so many scheduling, budgeting, and approval issues involved with Web site production that a few missing commas seem rather trivial, especially as they can always be added at a later date. Also, the costs of site development can be extremely high and, not surprisingly, clients resist additional costs for items that don't seem terribly significant. In fact, we've even worked for a client, admittedly on a tight budget, who refused to have his staff check over content at all. The result is that copyediting/proofreading tasks and costs are rarely factored into project schedules and estimates; consequently, many texts lack a high-quality presentation.

We hope that, as a writer/editor working on Web site production, you'll help change this low-end approach to text presentation. You'll probably point out errors that your client and other team members haven't noticed. Your concerns with how text appears online are likely to be new to them and should make them more sensitive to text presentation. And, most importantly, your high standards should, albeit slowly, raise their levels of awareness about the function of high-quality text presentation in attracting and keeping users on a site.

Why Do Users Read (So Fast)?

*It is a very sad thing that nowadays
there is so little useless information.*

OSCAR WILDE

Online readers are in a big hurry. Research shows that they hop, skip, and jump over text; avoid fluff such as promotional writing, logos, and mission statements; are impatient and goal-driven; and so ruthless that they will leave a site within seconds if it doesn't meet their needs. The interesting question is: Why do they act this way? "That's self-evident, isn't it?" you might be thinking. Users read because they want information, and they read quickly because modern life is busy and hectic, and none of us has a minute to spare. But we believe that these answers aren't sufficient to understand user behavior and that, as information providers, we need to know why users are willing to:

- Read Web sites, despite readability, design, and navigation problems.

- Keep clicking to find further information, although they are sometimes disappointed.

- Use search engines although they often feel like they're on a wild goose chase.

- Persevere although they frequently get lost and frustrated.

> The function of knowledge drives user behaviors.

Although users often do find the information they need, they clearly do so at great expense in terms of their time and effort. Why? What is it about their need and this information that keeps them at it so relentlessly? We believe the answer lies in the function of knowledge in modern Western societies, and this function has a direct impact on Web content development.

To understand the functions of knowledge today, you need to consider two simultaneous evolutions: 1) the technology of knowledge, that is, *how* it has been dispersed; and 2) the reason for the knowledge, that is, *what* knowledge has been dispersed, and *why*. These evolutions are complex and interconnected. Literacy researcher Kathleen Tyner (1998:16) notes: "A full understanding of contemporary literacy is impossible without a complementary understanding of 20th-century wars, postcolonialism, postindustrialism, human rights movements, social institutions, and hypercapitalism that have intervened to change the way that literacy is used in the 20th century." We can't even begin to explore these subjects in any depth in this book, but we believe that an overview will help you better understand user behavior.

With regard to *how* knowledge has been dispersed, there have been three major technological innovations:

- The alphabet, which allowed people to express knowledge in more efficient ways than through earlier forms of writing such as pictograms.

- The printing press, which provided the means for easy duplication of knowledge and its distribution en masse.

- The computer, which provides people, for the first time, with two significant capabilities: easy access to the knowledge at the global level, and the opportunity to contribute to that knowledge as they please.

Precomputer Knowledge Seekers

Imagine yourself back a couple of millennia. You live in a small community (in modern terms) that has powerful sources of local and spiritual information—priests, shamans, scholars, elders. You may or may not be literate and, if there are books, they are hand-scribed and few in number. The information that you gain is primarily through oral means such as stories, sermons, lectures, and gossip. If you are fortunate enough to be in a socioeconomic class of this community that enables you to attend a school, your job will be to memorize what is already known.

Writing researcher Richard Lanham (1976:2) describes the education, from a teacher's perspective, of a young Greek, circa 500 B.C.

> Start your student young. Teach him a minute concentration on the word, how to write it, speak it, remember it. Stress memory in a massive almost brutalizing way, develop it far in advance of conceptual understanding. Let words come first as objects and sounds long before they can, for a child, take on full meaning. They are looked at before they can be looked through. From the beginning, stress behavior as performance, reading aloud, speaking with gesture, a full range of histrionic adornment. Require no original thought. Demand instead an agile marshaling of the proverbial wisdom on any issue.

In other words, nothing more was expected of a rhetorically trained Greek than to voice old wisdoms in clever, playful ways.

Of course, every era in human history has had its critical, creative thinkers—Aristotle, Copernicus, Columbus, Newton, to name a few—but behind these individuals were millions of ordinary people who were not expected to generate new ideas. Literacy researcher Myron Tuman (1992:39) describes reading education in the United States during the pre-industrial age as primarily oral recitation where "students were required to recite aloud passages memorable for their rhetorical, ethical, or patriotic fervor." In short, nothing much had changed since the ancient Greeks.

> Precomputer readers sought deeper understanding of a truth.

The industrial revolution changed human society in a multitude of ways—from workplace tasks to the evolution of modern nations. In doing so, it also had an effect on the purpose of gaining knowledge. According to Tuman (1992:39), the average person was no longer expected just to master the traditions of his/her parents, which in many cases no longer applied to Western ways of life, but was taught, through writing and reading, "to create and comprehend ever-deeper understandings of the world." Reading, in schools, became a silent activity, and students were tested on their ability to read short prose passages and answer comprehension questions.[6] The ultimate goal of this type of education was "to increase the likelihood of producing the one truly powerful interpretation that will deepen our collective understanding." In other words, the function of knowledge from the industrial age to that of computers was, as a writer, to create a new "truth" or, as a reader, to study this new "truth" in depth. This is the way most of us today were taught to learn and think.

Living in the Information Age

> Information Age readers seek many opinions.

Now, we have reached the computer age, a time when the knowledge of the global community is online—a vast bedlam of multicultural voices, beliefs, and writings. In fact, thinkers whose ideas have not, or wouldn't be, picked up by traditional media have found "voice" on the Web because it's a social space where everyone can become a publisher. As Tyner (1998:22) notes: "…as the egalitarian ability for anyone to create—as well as receive—information increases, questions of information veracity and interpretation intensify. Traditional gatekeepers of

The Disappearance of the "First Speaker"

Although the French philosopher, Michel de Certeau, published his seminal work, *The Practice of Everyday Life*, in 1984 before the advent of the Web, his discussion of the history of writing and reading is relevant to today's online user behavior. de Certeau believed that, when God, the "First Speaker," was our society's only authoritative source of intellectual "truth," reading and writing was essentially directed toward the deciphering of his words as found in the Bible. In fact, these words were so powerful, that people used them to guide all aspects of their lives—from sexual practices to determining legality. When society's certainty in these works weakened, along with the institutions that supported them, people essentially lost the "language" that they could understand and trust. As a result, de Certeau explains, the disappearance of the "First Speaker" created a craving for substitute speakers—other voices providing other "languages."

information—media professionals, clergy, librarians, teachers, parents—are increasingly ineffectual in their ability to provide interpretive frameworks for information." We can no longer seek any one "truth" in depth because there are so many possible and equal "truths." We seek information, but for every piece of information that we find, a second, third, and fourth opinion can be discovered with a click of our mouse.

Philosopher James Slevin (2000:16), in his book *Internet and Society*, explores how this lack of "truths" creates anxieties for us:

> Feelings of security and uncertainty can be particularly acute during what [sociologist] Giddens calls "fateful moments". These are occasions when individuals 'are called on to take decisions that are particularly consequential for their ambitions, or more generally their future lives' (quote: Giddens, 1991:112). Making a decision, for example, to invest time in a period of study can be particularly complicated, often involving a wide range of "experts" and "authorities" advising a wide range of different trajectories of action. There are no taken-for-granted solutions and the individual has to develop skills in order to gather together and process this information, weighing up the likely risks and uncertainties related to different outcomes. Modern every-day life is rife with such moments.

We're also bombarded with overwhelming amounts of information. Dow Jones Reuters Business Interactive Limited (2000) notes that: "Every day, approximately 20m [million] words of technical information are recorded. A reader capable of reading 1,000 words per minute would require six weeks reading eight hours every day to get through one day's output. At the end of that period he would have fallen five and a half years behind in his reading." The result is what information architect Richard Saul Wurman (1989:317) terms "information anxiety": "I believe it is a myth that the more choices you have, the more appropriate actions you can take and the more freedom you enjoy. Rather, more choices seem to produce more anxiety."

Too many voices, too much information, too many choices—the result is a population of nervous and apprehensive surfers, racing through Web sites, picking up information from here, there, and everywhere.

The Needs of Mouse-Riders

The real future for online content is in what people will bother to sit and stare at on a screen, and I don't believe it's entertainment. I see two streams. One is commercial—sites that deliver prices, bargains, and catalogs where users will endure Flash and other bells-and-whistles. The other stream is for the vast millions of people who want content they can't find anywhere but the Internet. For them, mouse-riding will be worth large chunks of time to meet three compelling needs:

- The need to be informed such as on, say, consumer issues, investigative reports, balance sheets, government releases, and so on;

- The need to be educated about stuff that won't justify reading a book or entail a search through a mountain of old magazines; and

- The need to be reassured about issues such as health, loneliness, inadequacies, and anxieties.

D.V. Sridharan, Web Site Owner
www.goodnewsindia.com

As users surf, each bit of information, either remembered or printed out for safekeeping, becomes part of their own personally created content. As Tuman (1992:42) says: "There is no pre-existing text, with its own special vision of the world, that we as readers are required to grasp; instead, the text comes into existence through our own manipulations and decisions as we sit at the terminal." Lanham (1993:104-105), looking into the future of education, provides this scenario of how students will be able to create their own texts. Compare it to his description of the education of the young Greek, circa 500 B.C.

> Imagine a student brought up on computers interacting with the volatile text I've described in earlier chapters. She is used to moving it around, playing games with it, illustrating and animating it. Now let her…sift a dubious classic like, say, "Love's Labor's Lost." Imagine her charting the rhetorical figures, displaying them in a special type, diagramming and cataloguing them, and then making hypertext animations of how they work. She'll use another program now on the market to make her own production, plotting out action, sight lines, costumes, etc. And then a voice program to suggest how certain lines should be read…Or make it into a film. Or simply mess around with it in the irreverent way undergraduates always have, mustaching the Mona Lisa just for the hell of it.

In the Information Age, then, knowledge no longer comes to us by tradition or through the reading of a valued thinker or artist. Rather, we build it ourselves through our own ingenuity and technical dexterity. To do this, we constantly need upgraded software, faster processor speeds, and more time surfing. It's no wonder, then, that we race through Web sites, relentlessly seeking that one bit of information we need to add to the pile we've already accumulated, and try to make sense of it all. In a world drowning in information and peopled by experts from many fields, we repeatedly plunge into that vast, confusing sea of data, facts, and opinions. Today, the function of knowledge is no longer to gain depth in feeling, insight, and revelation in order to understand a truth, but to continually gather already existing knowledge in the hopes of weaving our own truth(s).

To Sum It Up

Keeping the attention of drive-thru users will be the greatest challenge you face in developing Web content. You must constantly

> The drive-thru user will be a continual challenge.

view the world through their prism and convince your clients and other members of your production team to do so as well. You must also write/edit with a continual focus on the site's visuals and navigational elements because the Web, far more than print, is a highly stimulating, multiple-media environment. In addition, you may be required to do so for an international audience or those with disabilities that affect accessibility.

In the chapters to come, we will explore ways in which you can address user needs by:

- Organizing information well.
- Developing your rhetorical writing skills.
- Becoming a strategic thinker with regard to visuals.
- Exploring the ways linking can help readers build knowledge.
- Knowing and exploiting the differences between the Web page and the Web screen.
- Learning about technology solutions to problems of online persuasion.

Resources for This Chapter

Books

InformationAnxiety2 by Richard Saul Wurman. Thoughts about how people approach and use information in a world overflowing with data. (Que: 2001)

Language and Power by Norman Fairclough. Designed for nonspecialists, this book about discourse analysis provides an excellent discussion of naturalized language. (Longman: 1989)

Web Sites

Useit.com (www.useit.com). The Web site of usability expert Jakob Neilsen. Covers and updates many issues with regard to making sites more audience-friendly.

Web Accessibility Initiative (www.w3.org/WAI). Guidelines, checklists, and tips for making sites more accessible to users with special needs.

Learning Styles Resource Page (www.oswego.edu/~shindler/ lstyle.htm). Although designed primarily for teachers, this site is rich in information and links.

The Society for the History of Authorship, Reading and Publishing (www.indiana.edu/~sharp). Links to a huge variety of resources about reading.

Semiotics for Beginners (www.aber.ac.uk/media/Documents/ S4B/semiotic.html). An overview of the field of social semiotics with excellent links to top thinkers in this field. Good for people who wish to delve deeper into theory.

Endnotes

1. There are many books about how people see, perceive, and understand the visual world. An interesting place to start is Rudolf Arnheim's 1969 book, *Visual Thinking.* Arnheim, who was a pioneer in the psychology of art, was one of the first researchers to prove that visual perception is a cognitive act that is not different from other forms of mental reasoning. Ann Marie Barry's 1996 book, *Visual Intelligence,* provides a modern perspective on this viewpoint, with an update on recent neurological and scientific knowledge about vision, and explores the emotional impact of visuals. For more information on online visuals, see Chapter 5, "Is Seeing Believing? The Art of Visual Rhetoric."

2. Norman Fairclough (1989, 1992, 1995a, 1995b) is a Professor of Language in Social Life at Lancaster University in the United Kingdom. He has written extensively and thoughtfully on the connections among language, power, society, and the media. His Web site is at www.ling.lancs.ac.uk/staff/norman/norman.htm.

3. Lakoff and Johnson's 1980 book, *Metaphors We Live By,* is an enlightening discussion of metaphors that we use, without considering them metaphors, in our everyday life, and how they help us develop concepts about life.

4. With so many professionals writing at work, universities are trying to determine how best to prepare students for workplace writing tasks. The result has been research since the early 1980s on workplace writing, and interesting observations on the composing process, and the role of different genres of text in academia and the workplace. Samples of this research in this area

are Dias, Freedman, Medway and Paré (1999), Spilka (1993), Bazerman and Paradis (1991), and Odell and Goswami (1985).

5. Social semiotics is a fascinating field for writers who wish to explore how words make meaning within different social contexts. Researchers in this area are interested in three different ways that language creates meaning: 1) through the words we use to discuss our experiences, known as the ideational function; 2) through the words we use to express our feelings, known as the interpersonal function; and 3) through the words we use to create language as understandable, known as the textual function. Excellent texts on this topic include Hodge and Kress (1988), Lemke (1990), and Halliday (1994).

6. Although it may seem that the oral tradition has completely disappeared, there are still venues for storytelling. Some radio stations such as National Public Radio (NPR) and the Canadian Broadcasting Corporation (CBC) still include storytelling, and a number of storytellers perform in schools, libraries, and so on. Storytelling might have a resurgence on the Web as audio technologies become more sophisticated. As well, storytelling may be a way for the visually impaired to gain greater pleasure from online experiences.

Organizing a Web Site: "Elementary, My Dear Watson"

What's Inside:

- Basics of site architecture, navigation, and the graphical user interface
- How to choose content for different types of sites
- Mind-mapping as an organizing strategy
- Linking and appropriate clicks to content
- Site maps

The major problems facing the development of products that are safer, less prone to error, and easier to use and understand are not technological: they are social and organizational.

DONALD A. NORMAN (1998)

Whether you're experienced in writing/editing a speech, a press release, an annual report, a film script, or a feature story, you possess two very significant skills when it comes to organizing information on a Web site:

1. **You know how to structure information so that the flow of content is logical and coherent.**

2. **You've learned to write/edit with the reader constantly in mind.**

These skills, when combined, are extremely important, because many of your team members will not have them, or will not have honed them to the same degree that you have. Although everyone knows how to organize information in ways that make sense to themselves, most people have trouble stepping beyond the personal to create alternative organizing schemes that may be more accessible to others. As usability specialist Adam Smith (2001) notes:

> At a very basic level we have a strong tendency to see ourselves as being archetypal and our current situation as being "normal." Most of us are not conditioned socially, nor primed cognitively, to spend a lot of time thinking about people who aren't like us or situations that are not familiar—and for obvious reasons. But as a result we fail to appreciate the differences, small and large, that exist between us.

In this chapter, you'll learn about different aspects of organizing and presenting information on a Web site. As information in today's world and users' needs for it are growing at a rapid rate, Web sites are becoming larger, more complex, and increasingly dependent on databases and internal search engines. However, as information designer Robert Horn (1999:16) points out:

> Simply storing large amounts of information on computers and retrieving it does not solve our information needs. In fact, gigantic storehouses of information overload us with too much information and burden us with navigational problems that... sometimes make us feel that we are "lost in cyberspace." What we need is not more information but the ability to present the right information to the right people at the right time, in the most effective and efficient form.

Organizing a Web site in this environment presents a major challenge for the development team. The important thing to remember is that, if you participate in the early stage of a site's development, your skills at organizing information can help you make a valuable contribution to the process.

Organizational Basics

> There's no single solution to organizing information.

Web navigation specialist Jennifer Fleming (1998:45) notes that organizing information is about demonstrating the relationships among items in such a way that they're easy to find. However, this isn't always easy because "the problem with knowledge is that it's not made up of simple linear relationships. It's a messy interrelated thing." Take the fictional detective Sherlock Holmes, for example. Say you had to organize the following bits of information about his life:

Cape and hat

Apartment

Dr. Watson

Professor Moriarty

Mrs. Hudson

Violin playing

Deduction methods

Published monographs

Pipe

What ways could you create relationships among these items/people? According to information architect Richard Saul Wurman (2001:40-41), "While information may be infinite, the ways of structuring it are not." He says that there are five ways to organize information:

1. **Alphabet:** "This method lends itself to organizing extraordinarily large bodies of information, such as words in a dictionary or names in a telephone directory."

2. **Time:** "Time works best as an organizing principle for events that happen over fixed durations."

3. **Category:** "Category pertains to the organization of goods...different models, different types, even different questions to be answered, such as in a brochure that is divided into questions about a company."

4. **Location:** "Location is the natural form to choose when you are trying to examine and compare information that comes from diverse sources or locales."

5. **Hierarchy:** "This mode organizes items by magnitude from small to large, least expensive to most expensive, by order of importance, etc."

Using Wurman's list, you could most logically organize Sherlock Holmes' items/people in three of the five ways: alphabetically; chronologically according to when they first appeared in Holmes' life story; and by category, that is:

- Numerically—how often each item/person appears in the published stories or films.

- By description—Watson's comments about each item/person.

- In his own words—how Holmes refers to these items/persons.

- Comparatively—for example, did Hercule Poirot or Nero Wolfe smoke a pipe or play an instrument?

- Referentially—where these items/persons have been referred to in scholarly journals or articles about mystery stories.

Each different method of organization that you use will create a different meaning for users of a Web site. As information and interface designer Nathan Shedroff (1999:270) states:

> Information is also not the end of the continuum of understanding. Just as data can be transformed into meaningful information, so information can be transformed into knowledge and then, further, into wisdom. Knowledge is a phenomenon we can build for others, just as we can build information for others from data. This is done through interaction design and the creation of experiences…

In addition to different methods of organizing information for users, Web sites deliver information to them through three different technology routes.

1. **Without databases:** Sites without databases, generally, have a small number of pages and are coded using HTML or Web Editor.

2. **Database-supported:** Sites supported by databases are usually mid- to large-size and provide users with content coded with HTML or Web Editor plus search engines to access additional material.

3. **Database-generated:** Sites with database-generated pages usually have a great deal of data, and the information is only dynamically compiled into pages when users request it through search engines or use mechanisms such as customized portals/gateways where they can determine what, when, and how they will view the information.

NOTE
When creating sites with databases, information architects organize data into groupings. We find it useful to think of these groupings as *storage buckets.* For example, when a user types a keyword into a search engine, it may dip into one or more *buckets* to bring up the requested information.

Architecture ➔ Navigation ➔ The Gooey GUI)

Web sites allow users to access information through different underlying technologies. However, no matter how information arrives on the users' screen, all sites are composed of three major elements that contribute to the user's ability to access content easily—the information architecture (IA), navigation design, and graphical user interface (GUI).

Information Architecture (IA)

IA is the organizing of information into logically related groupings so users can navigate effectively through the content and find the information they seek.

> IA is structuring a site to best meet user needs.

The Days of IA Guesswork are Over

In the early days of the Internet, we made educated guesses when it came to information architecture. We can't afford to do that anymore. Information systems are so complicated today—they vary greatly in their content, business strategy, and user needs—that we can't rely upon educated guesses about design. Instead, we need multi-disciplinary teams that weave together their respective skills, expertise, tools, and techniques into a unified methodology. Anyone who deals with information as important and valuable stuff in and of itself—ethnographers, linguists, data-modeling specialists, marketing people, cognitive scientists, technical communicators, usability researchers, and many others—could be at the table.

And content is an area that still is quite misunderstood. Too many companies focus on technology—what their content management package should be, for example—rather than what their content is and how users will use it. One explanation is that they confuse the unstructured text that is clogging up their sites with data, that is, something that's easier to model and search. Because data is relatively easy to deal with, they assume that text is too, and don't invest the extra effort that text deserves.

Louis Rosenfeld, Consultant
www.louisrosenfeld.com

Peter Morville, Executive Director
Argus Center for Information Architecture
www.argus-acia.com

As part of this process, the development team will create a hierarchy among the groupings. If you compare this process to that of a building and decorating a house, it means deciding on how many floors the house will have and where certain items will go in it. What groupings would fit in the basement? Which would be more suitable on the first floor, the second, and so forth?

Developing good IA is crucial for any Web site. Steve Toub of The Argus Center for Information Architecture (2000:2,3) notes that flawed architectures can have significant effects on usability.

- Lower revenue on e-commerce sites due to failed searches: "One consulting firm observed that 56% of search engine queries on e-commerce sites ended in failure and claimed that this translates into a loss of billions of dollars."

- Lower revenue on e-commerce sites when users can't find what they want: "One market analyst report states that when looking for products, 62% of online shoppers had given up at least once."

- Lost employee productivity due to poorly designed Intranets: "One oil company's head of information services reported that 35% of an employee's time is wasted looking for information…"

Who creates the IA for a Web site? This question is more complex than most people realize, because IA has two different aspects—content, and the technology that supports content. "Knowledge manager," "information architect," "information designer," and "content strategist" are job titles that generally refer to people who think about IA from the standpoint of content: How should information be organized and how should this organization be revealed to users? On the other hand, database architects, networking architects, and data modelers are people who think about structure from a technology perspective: What technologies can be used and what technological structures built that will allow users to access the information they need?

The titles are confusing and, in fact, people's roles in IA may overlap depending upon their technological know-how. Because this field is in such flux, keep in mind that job titles are ambiguous and people have different ideas about their roles. Take, for example, "information designer." Writing researcher Michael Albers (2000:161) points out that: "It's ironic that one of the complex problems information designers face is defining information design. Any article or book you find on information design contains a definition. Unfortunately, these definitions rarely match." For some people, information design is just another term for Web design, that is, creating the GUI. For others, it's the creation of content within design, using knowledge of cognitive issues such as learning styles, the effects of presentation, issues of cultural impact, and so forth, to make a site most effective for users. Others go even further. Document design and usability specialist Janice Redish (2000:163) says: "My definition of *document design* or *information design* has always been, first and foremost, the 'whole.' Information design is what we do to develop a document (or communication) that works for its users." According to this definition, information design is the overall process of development including planning, organizing, designing, drafting, testing, gathering feedback, and keeping content up to date.

Navigation Design

Navigation design is the connection between IA and the design of the graphical user interface (GUI). During this stage of a site's development, the production team determines the pathways, from the simple to the intricate, that will allow users to move easily among the groupings of information. As your team builds these groupings, some of the navigation will become immediately obvious.

Navigation provides site travel possibilities.

To return to the house metaphor, some of these pathways will be like staircases, leading users to drill up or down through the site. Others will be like corridors that lead users to information that exists on the same level. These staircases and corridors are represented by links.

- **Main navigation links** provide pathways to and from the main site sections. Such links must be clearly visible and have short, informative titles. If you and your team are having trouble determining a title for a site section, you may have to reconsider your architecture. Poor titles often reveal poor structure, such as content that is too varied to fit within one information group.

- **Shortcut links** allow users to access important information without drilling down through the site. Typical shortcut links are "What's New, " "Press Releases," and "Disclaimers." These links provide significant information for users that they might not notice if such information wasn't given special linkages.

- **Converging links** bring users from different locations to the same point. You may find that a content page contains information that pertains to two or more site sections. It's not necessary to make a decision to only link the content page to section A, rather than B or C. Rather, you can have pathways in A, B, and C that link to the same Web page.

- **Hypertext links** create additional connections both down and across a site's sections and add layers of information to those that already exist through the main architectural structure. (For information about hypertext links, see Chapter 6, "Links, Logic, and the Layered Reader.")

- **Redundant links** are links that are duplicated on one Web page, that is, they show up in more than one location on the page. At one point in Web history, redundant links were considered taboo. However, as new sites are developing, these links are appearing for specific items. These include links to articles, to people, or to other sections of the site. A typical example is that of the OSHA site (Figure 3.18) where the links in the navigation left bar are duplicated in the page's text.

The Graphical User Interface (GUI), or The Gooey

The graphical user interface (GUI) is what the user sees on his or her screen from the "Home" page and throughout the site. It acts as a shield, representing the architecture and navigation of the site and providing access to the site's information without actually revealing the organization of information behind it. As Shedroff (as quoted in Wurman, 2001:28) notes:

> Information comes from the form data takes as we arrange and present it in different ways. One of the most confusing points for many people is that the presentation and organization of data are entirely different. The organization of data itself changes the meaning of it, or at least its interpretation…The presentation of the very same organization of data can vary drastically, from verbal (or textual) to visual, to auditory, or to something else entirely.

Designing a good GUI is like building a house where visitors can't get lost and can easily identify the purpose of each level, room, corridor, and staircase. The GUI, therefore, has three major functions:

1. Help users develop a mental map of the structure of the site.
2. Provide a good overall look-and-feel to the site.
3. Assist users in reaching the information they want.

Elements of a well-designed GUI include:

- **Visual metaphors** that users can understand immediately. For example, the trash can image is a real-world metaphor for dumping unwanted files.

- **Internal consistency in the look-and-feel** of different site sections, as appropriate for users. For example, on a children's site, the "Parent" section is likely to have a different on-screen appearance. However, a government site that alters design throughout will cause user confusion.

> Consistency is key to a good GUI.

- **Consistency in the use of icons** throughout the site. For example, the "Help" button—which is labeled with text—shouldn't turn into a visual of a question mark on another Web page. To avoid confusion, consistency also includes following conventions that users find on other Web sites such as underlined links.

- **Lack of clutter** so that users can find the content and links that they need. Technical communication specialist David Farkas and information designer Jean Farkas (2000:343) also suggest that the design should ensure that: "…the most important links appear high enough on the page to be visible without scrolling," and "when pages must scroll, provide visual cues to encourage users to scroll down to links that are below the scroll line." (For more information on scrolling, see Chapter 7, "Writing/Editing for the Web Page; Writing/Editing to the Web Screen.")

Getting Started

You've been asked, as an in-house writer/editor, to join a Web development team for your company. Or, maybe you're a freelance writer/editor, and a new client wants to meet you and see what you can contribute. You want to be knowledgeable, but perhaps you don't have experience in building/recreating a

Web site, or you've never worked for the organization before. What information can you bring to the table that would be immediately useful and, if you're a freelancer, help you get you the work you want?

As we noted earlier, organizing information is difficult for many people. Your ability to speak knowledgeably about IA in general, and that of the client's site in particular, is likely to demonstrate that you have the required expertise. It's also important to remember that a first meeting is an opportunity to discuss many other issues regarding the site such as its production, content, team members, and schedules. (For a checklist of important questions to ask at the first meeting with a client, see Chapter 10, "The Business of Web Writing/Editing.")

Find the Right IA Model

All organizations are essentially unique, but they fall within generic categories such as government, business, professional associations, and so on. And the generic categories of organizations have information that falls within typical content groupings that are relevant to users. Each content grouping has the potential of becoming one of a Web site's major sections (also known as *key content areas, channels,* or *themes/streams*). Table 3.1 provides seven models for informational Web sites by organizational type.

These IA models present possibilities for site sections that are logical and practical for users. However, many organizations forget or ignore such user-friendly structures. Usability experts Jakob Neilsen and Kara Coyne (2001), noting that major corporations spend millions of dollars on public relations (PR), tested the Web sites of such organizations to see if they contained even basic PR information:

> In our study, 20 journalists attempted to use the press areas of 10 corporate websites to gather information for story assignments. Among other tasks, the journalists tried to find basic information about each company's financials, management, and commitment to social responsibility, along with a PR telephone number.

> On average, journalists found the answer to each of these simple questions only **60% of the time**. If these sites were being graded in a U.S. school, the average grade would be no higher than a D.

In our experience, the more you know about an organization and its competitors on the Web, the more focused, directed, and efficient you'll be in discussing the client's or team's needs.

Table 3.1   IA Models of Informational Web Sites

TYPE OF ORGANIZATION	WEB SITE SECTIONS
Governments	■ Policies
	■ Laws/Regulations
	■ Reports
	■ Announcements
	■ Directories
	■ Programs/Services
	■ Legal/Privacy/Security Statements
	■ Tourist Information (usually on the sites of state/provincial and municipal governments)
Large Corporations	■ About Us
	■ Product/Service Information
	■ Product/Service Support
	■ Dealer/Resellers
	■ Investor Information
	■ Press Releases
	■ Education/Tutorials
	■ Testimonials
	■ Career Opportunities
	■ Worldwide Locations
Small- to Medium-Sized Businesses	■ About Us
	■ Product/Service Information
	■ Product/Service Support
	■ Contact Us
Not-For-Profit Organizations	■ Mission/Vision/Values
	■ Board of Directors
	■ By-laws
	■ Membership
	■ Fundraising
	■ Sponsorship
	■ Useful Links
	■ Research Meeting Areas*
Professional Associations	■ General Information
	■ Membership Information/Benefits

continues

Table 3.1 IA Models of Informational Web Sites (Continued)

TYPE OF ORGANIZATION	WEB SITE SECTIONS
Professional Associations (continued)	■ Chapters
	■ Annual Conference
	■ Publications/Newsletters
	■ Education/Training
	■ Certification
	■ Professional Opportunities
	■ Members Only
	■ Resources/Links
E-commerce	■ Products/Services
	■ Marketing Information/Special Offers
	■ Policies: Privacy, Security, Personal Protection
	■ Product Support/Customer Service
	■ Corporate Information
	■ Newsletters
	■ Help Desk
	■ Inventory Information
	■ Online Surveys
	■ Registration Form
	■ Shopping Cart
	■ Account Information
Intranet	■ Product Information
	■ Company Organization/Executives
	■ Company Policies
	■ Recognition/Awards
	■ Newsletters
	■ Industry Information
	■ Job Postings
	■ Marketing and Sales
	■ Technical Documentation
	■ Employee Benefits/Support Programs
	■ Work Team Meeting Areas*
	■ Educational Opportunities
	■ Libraries
	■ Company Directories

* Online meeting areas are cyber-workplaces where users can work on projects, share information, and contribute to the knowledge base.

We've also found that clients often have no idea where to start with their sites and will welcome your input when they realize that your ideas and opinions are well informed, thoughtful, and insightful. Use the checklist provided in Figure 3.1 to pull together your ideas for a Web site's architecture before meeting a client and/or the production team for the first time.

Choose Navigation Priorities

Imagine that you've clicked on a Google search hit and landed on the page of a Web site. Perhaps you glance at the content, and then try to find out where you are on the site. Or, perhaps you look at the main site sections to see if the site has potentially good information. What happens if you can't find what you want? You begin to wonder about the credibility of the site, and chances are, you leave in a hurry. Usability researcher Steve Krug (2000:62) uses the term *persistent navigation* to describe the navigation elements that should or could appear on every page of a site: "Done right, persistent navigation should say—preferably in a calm, comforting voice: 'The navigation is over here. Some parts will change a little depending on where you are, but

---

An Information Architecture Model Checklist

☐   Match the organization to its model.

☐   Surf the Web to find other organizations of the same generic type to see what variations exist.

☐   Surf the Web to check other organizations within the same industry because variations on the models can often be industry-specific. For example, sports teams usually fall within Small- to Medium-Sized Businesses, but their sites, designed for fans, are likely to vary greatly from that of a hardware company. A museum is generally a government-run operation, but its target audience will be visitors and its site structure will differ from, say, the site of a federal agency.

☐   Consider what you already know about the organization, its goals, and potential audience, and how its information would fit into the model's typical site sections, or vary from it.

☐   Prepare a rudimentary information architecture plan for the site.

Figure 3.1   Prepare good IA ideas for a first meeting.

it will always be here, and it will always work the same way.'"
Krug's five elements of persistent navigation are:

- The organization's ID or logo.
- A way home.
- A way to search.
- The Web site sections.
- Utilities that provide assistance such as "Help."

In our research of informational Web sites, we've identified a variety of navigation elements, other than those linking users to site sections, that you should consider when building a Web site. We find that many of these elements are often forgotten during a site's development, and may only be caught at the end of the process when the site undergoes review. In Table 3.2, we've prioritized these navigation elements to help you and your client decide on the fundamentals for your site.

You may find that, during the Web development process, there are elements that you don't need or that the priority rankings of these elements may change. Either way, your role as a participant in building a Web site is to make sure that the client is aware of potential navigation and content elements.

The Case of the Chaotic Content

You've reached the stage where you understand the client's needs and those of the target audience. You may have a model in mind that would suit the client's content. However, that content is still in a raw form. It may be:

- Grouped into categories, but these categories aren't appropriate to the Web site
- Not grouped in any way, and the client expects you to create the organizational structure
- A mixture of the above

In addition, the content may be coming to you from a bewildering array of sources. You may get print publications from the public affairs department, reports from content specialists, print-outs from the organization's Intranet, competitive materi-

Table 3.2   Priority of Navigation Elements

PRIORITY	NAVIGATION ELEMENTS
Obligatory Although the organization's ID or logo must appear on every Web page, we don't consider it a navigation element. In many cases, the ID or logo doesn't act as a link.	■ Home/Main Menu ■ Site Map/Table of Contents/Index ■ Contact Us ■ Shopping Cart or equivalent (for an e-commerce site requiring financial transactions)
High Priority Although we include "Help" here, site builders shouldn't use "Help" as a crutch when they can't figure out how to make the site more accessible to users.	■ Search (for large sites) ■ Language Selection (for sites aimed at different language audiences) ■ Plug-In/Player Links (when required to use the site) ■ Help (for sites where users may require assistance to achieve their goals)
Medium Priority	■ What's New ■ Useful Links ■ Search (for small sites)
Low Priority	■ Chat/Discussion Groups ■ FAQ's ■ Glossary ■ User Surveys
Nice to Consider	■ Print Buttons (print-friendly items)

als from other organizations, and supporting resources. In short, the content that you must organize is likely to be in a chaotic condition.

We've found, through hands-on Web development and teaching experience, that one of the best ways to make sense of content is to use a technique called mind-mapping, which was created by learning expert Tony Buzan when he was trying to figure out the best way for students to take notes. As Buzan (1999) explains:

> A Mind Map is a powerful graphic technique which provides a universal key to unlock the potential of the brain. It harnesses the full range of cortical skills – word, image, number, logic, rhythm, colour and spatial awareness – in a single, uniquely powerful manner. In so doing, it gives you the freedom to roam the infinite expanses of your brain. The Mind Map can be applied to every aspect of life where improved learning and clearer thinking will enhance human performance.

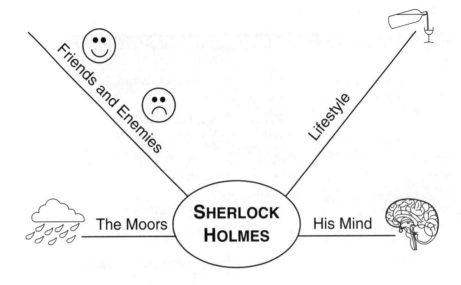

Figure 3.2   First branching in a Sherlock Holmes Mind Map.

Mind-Mapping: IA Revealed

Mind-mapping is a technique that allows you to build a graphical display of information in an informal way that encourages creativity and innovation. Based on a trees-and-branches approach, mind-mapping allows you to choose a central theme, word, or concept, and then create information pathways from the center, starting with large branches that show major content groupings and ending with smaller branches that reveal ever-finer details. In terms of a Web site, mind-mapping can bring you from the major site sections, through subsections, to individual page information quickly and easily.

Figures 3.2 through 3.4 show the evolution of a simplified mind map around the character of Sherlock Holmes.

- **Figure 3.2:** We've given the central theme four major branches of information—The Moors, Friends and Enemies, Lifestyle and His Mind.

- **Figure 3.3:** We've added a secondary level of branches to the major pathways. As well, we included three tertiary branches under Cases.

■ **Figure 3.4:** We've added dotted lines to show lateral connections among the branches. Remember, information is messy!

Mind-mapping can be a powerful tool for organizing information into a logical pattern, and is based on *associative thinking*. (For more information, see Chapter 6, "Links, Logic, and the Layered Reader.") Jason Sawaya, one of our Web design students, used mind-mapping during university to help him organize information for exams and now uses it to develop his Web projects. According to Jason, "Mind-mapping is about opening your mind to anything. You use words that trigger subideas that, in turn, lead to other words. The important thing to remember is that mind-mapping is very subjective because it's based on your background knowledge, experiences, memories, and personality."

Mind-mapping can be used for a wide variety of tasks—from organizing To-Do lists to writing books. Writer Anne Bartlett

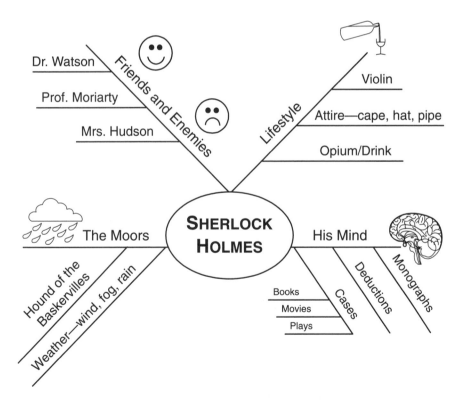

Figure 3.3   Secondary and tertiary branching in the Sherlock Holmes Mind Map.

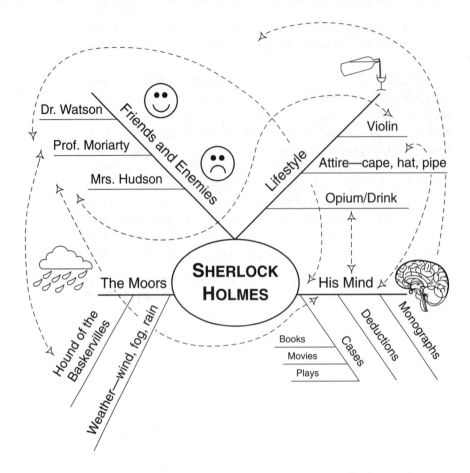

Figure 3.4 Lateral connections among the branches in the Sherlock Holmes Mind Map.

(2000) describes how she used mind-mapping to organize her chapters for a joint biography of a married couple and not lose track of where her information came from.

> The sources were diverse—several books, a pile of unindexed newspaper cuttings, brief snippets of information noted down in phone calls and library visits, taped interviews, medical reports, photos, and copies of various government papers.

> Following Buzan's procedure, I wrote the name of my subjects in the middle of the page. Then I made two branches, one for George and one for Maude. From there I draw more branches, each branch representing a section of each of their lives…

> I wanted my map to be more than a planning tool. I needed it to be a kind of index, so I referenced each branch to the source of infor-

mation, e.g., page numbers, interview numbers, photographs. It took me two days to map all the information.

When I had finished, all the main topics and their subtopics (and sub-sub-sub-topics) were laid out before me. I could see the gaps in the information, and what was the most important information to my subjects, as these areas were dense with source material.

With that overview, the structure of the book became immediately clear, I had regained control of the material and I knew where to find what I needed for each chapter.

Mind-mapping, then, is a paradoxical process. On one hand, you're creating organization out of informational chaos. On the other hand, you achieve this by using a chaos of ideas to generate the process. The goal is to let creativity loose and not limit ideas by making judgments about them or forcing them into any type of hierarchy. Table 3.3 provides tips to brainstorming Web site architecture with a client and other team members.

When you and/or your client brainstorm a mind map, you'll find that natural information groupings begin to appear in hierarchical levels. These groupings will be intimately connected to the organization's needs and the site's goals, and will have labels that are specific to the type of content. In our experience, clients may not realize the potential size of their site until they go through the mind-mapping exercise and see the information structure emerge. This doesn't mean, however, that all the contents of a mind map will end up on the Web site itself. The ultimate content depends on budget and time constraints.

The Site Structure: Solving the Mystery

The next step is to re-draw the trees-and-branches diagram into a site structure that will show the levels of hierarchy, that is, the vertical linkages. As Figure 3.5 demonstrates, when the Sherlock Holmes Mind Map is transformed into a site structure, the large branches became the first level of the information hierarchy, that is, the main Web site sections, while the narrower branches have been transformed into second- and third-level information.

Site structures fall within three types of models: tree, linear, or a mixture of tree and linear. For example, Figure 3.5 reflects a hierarchical structure of information known as a tree model. Each model discussed below has its own advantages and limitations.

Table 3.3 Tips to Group Mind-Mapping

ASPECT OF MIND-MAPPING	TIPS
Process	■ Use large paper/blackboard/whiteboard.
	■ Start with a center circle or box representing your key theme. If you're starting from scratch, the topic might be "Our Web Site." If you already know a site section, it could be "Our Products."
	■ Let everyone on the team call out ideas. Put *every* idea into the mind map, regardless of how trivial some may seem.
	■ Use keywords or phrases. The shorter the phrase, the better. One-word titles are best.
	■ Look for more linkages among branches (associations) as the map begins to fill.
	■ Allow for divergent thinking before convergent thinking can begin. Let the lines on the map ramble—relationships will begin to be obvious as this happens.
Aids	■ Use color for visual impact—giving each main branch and all its attaching branches and twigs its own color.
	■ Use images and symbols whenever possible. Have members suggest graphics.
	■ If a branch has a source, such as a print publication or content expert, note the source next to the branch's title.

Tree Models

A tree model starts with a central topic and then organizes subtopics down through multiple branches. Figure 3.6 shows a traditional tree model in which there are no lateral information links, that is, each subtopic stands alone and isn't connected to others. For example, in a Web site with this structure, you would always have to return to the "Home" page or click on the title of another subtopic (depending on the site design) to access another part of the hierarchy.

Narrow trees: Web sites with a narrow tree model provide limited menu items selections, usually less than six, so that users need to drill down to deep content. (See Figure 3.7.) Although information in this type of model may broaden out at a deeper level, the

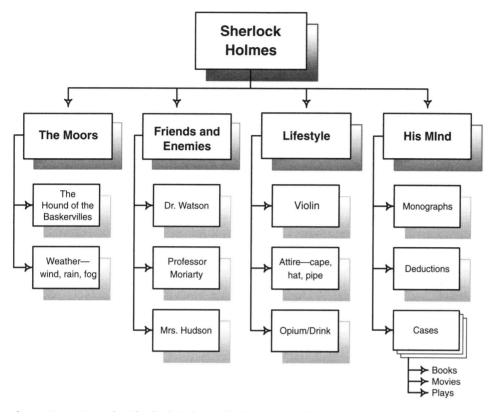

Figure 3.5 From the Sherlock Holmes Mind Map to a site structure.

site offers only a limited number of entry points. This type of site is useful when an organization has distinctly different audiences. For example, an e-commerce site may have a public area as well as a secure area for fee-paying customers.

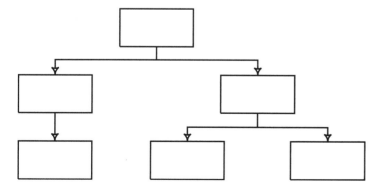

Figure 3.6 A traditional tree model.

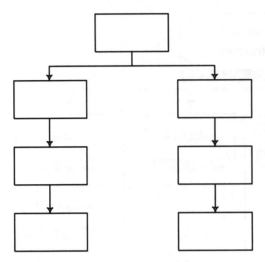

Figure 3.7   A narrow tree model.

Wide or Broad Trees: Sites with this model have many content areas, usually six or more, that users can click into from the main level. As Figure 3.8 illustrates, some of these content areas may have deep structures while others can be shallow. A Web site with this structure is useful when: the audience includes many different types of users; there's a great deal of content that is difficult to group into only a few areas; and/or huge volumes of content are generated by different underlying databases.

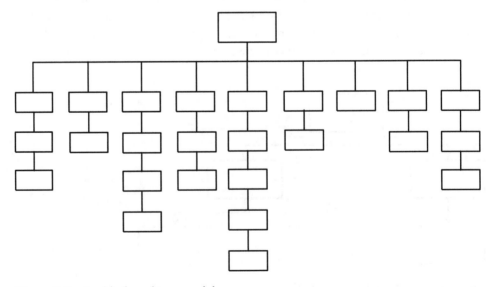

Figure 3.8   A wide/broad tree model.

Figure 3.9 A book-style linear model.

Linear Models

In the tree models we described above, there were no lateral connections between content. Linear models reflect equality among related chunks content as opposed to a hierarchical structure.

Book-style: Figure 3.9 shows a simple linear pattern that resembles the structure of a book. Users can move backwards and forwards through the pages, using buttons with labels such as "Previous" and "Next." Parts of children's sites that involve story-telling often have book-style structures where parents can click forwards and backwards through the narrative.

Book-style with alternative choices: Figure 3.10 shows a simple linear structure where users occasionally have a choice between two paths as they navigate through the structure. This structure is useful for an educational site that provides alternative learning routes or an e-commerce site that is selling two models of a single product—for example, a computer with two different types of monitors.

VCR-style: Figure 3.11 illustrates a type of simple linear style where users can leap ahead or backwards along a linear path, a pattern of use that is similar to the fast forward or rewind functions on a VCR or cassette tape machine. This type of site is used for educational sites as it allows users to move freely within a tutorial, that is, to link back to the beginning of the tutorial for review, or jump to the end so that they can complete a test or an evaluation process.

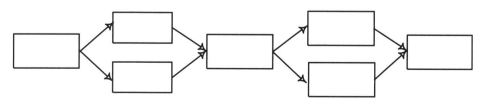

Figure 3.10 A book-style model with alternative choices.

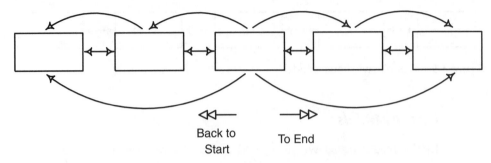

Figure 3.11   A VCR-style model with fast-forward and rewind.

Linear with Offshoots: As Figure 3.12 demonstrates, linear models can also have independent chunks of information that act as off-shoots from the main pathway. The offshoot is useful for an informational site with some very specific information not related to other content on the site. The risk with this model is that the user may end up in a dead-end location.

Mixture Models

In general, no site falls entirely within a tree or linear model. Rather, they're mixtures of tree and linear models, allowing developers to organize content in a way that provides users with the flexibility to jump from Web page to Web page, site section to site section, and even leave a site. We find that

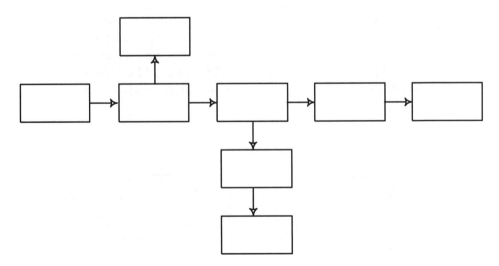

Figure 3.12   A linear model with an offshoot.

clients sometimes have difficulties with mixture models. They may find the surface organization to be illogical and worry that users will not get information in the appropriate order. These models can also be confusing for users if they're not organized well and the appropriate navigational "signals" are missing. If you're part of the IA team, you must work with the client to ensure that the content in each section retains its logic whether a user starts at the beginning, enters in the middle, or begins at the end.

A composite/hybrid model: As Figure 3.13 demonstrates, this model allows the user to travel through the site by using a variety of information paths. An information path can be based on topics, themes, business functions, and so on. A problem with this model is that users can find themselves in dead ends or back in locations already visited.

A web model: This model (see Figure 3.14) looks like a spider's web with long paths and lateral links. Users require continual navigation "signals" to position themselves accurately on the site using this model.

A grid model: As Figure 3.15 shows, this model allows users to travel horizontally, vertically, and laterally. This type of access to content may confuse users if they move from their point of entry into the depths of a site very quickly and try to find their way back.

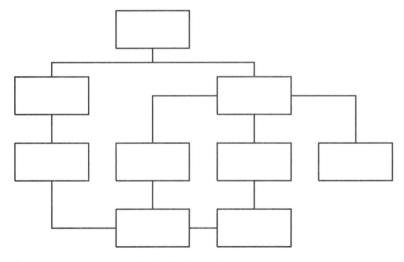

Figure 3.13 A composite/hybrid model.

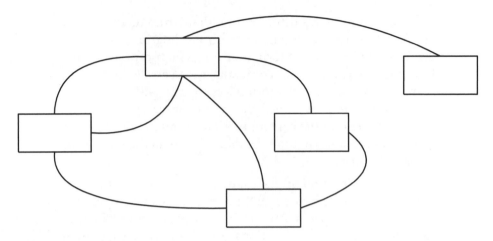

Figure 3.14 A web model.

A Tale of Two Web Sites

What happens when IA on a site doesn't work well? Two Web sites—CanLearn Interactive (www.canlearn.ca/English/eng.cfm) and the U.S. Occupational Safety & Health Administration (www.osha.gov)—demonstrate narrow tree models that are too confining for the content. Each site is loaded with information, but the developers couldn't figure out how to design the GUI in a way that wouldn't overwhelm users. They chose to put large chunks of related content under fewer headers rather than increase the number of headers to reflect the quantity of material. The challenge that each site's developers faced was: How can we let users know about everything the site has to offer?

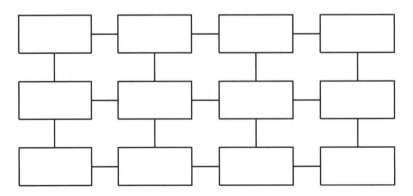

Figure 3.15 A grid model.

CanLearn Interactive is a site about educational and training opportunities. It is filled with useful information such as learning planners and databases of educational institutions and occupational information. As Figure 3.16 demonstrates, the developers of the site chose a minimalist approach, treating the site as if it were a guidance counselor and the user was a visitor to the guidance counselor's office.

The result is that the first two major content sections have completely ambiguous titles: "Getting Started" and the "Road Ahead." For example, we thought that "Getting Started" would include self-assessment quizzes and an overview of different kinds of educational institutions. However, as Figure 3.17 shows, "Getting Started" presents users with such links as "Site Map," "FAQ," "Glossary," and instructions on site use—links you would expect to see in navigation areas.

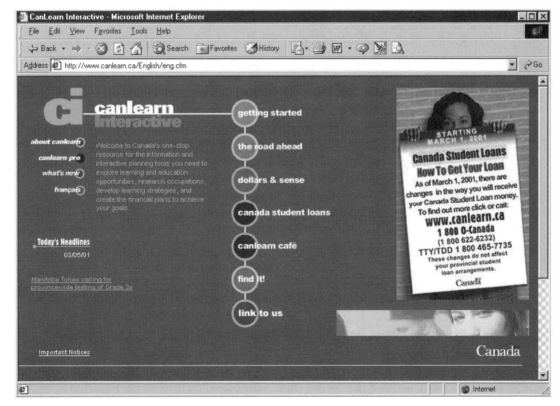

Figure 3.16 The CanLearn Interactive "Home" page.
(April 25, 2001: www.canlearn.ca/English/eng.cfm)

Human Resources Development Canada: Reproduced with the permission of the Minister of Public Works and Government Services Canada, 2001.

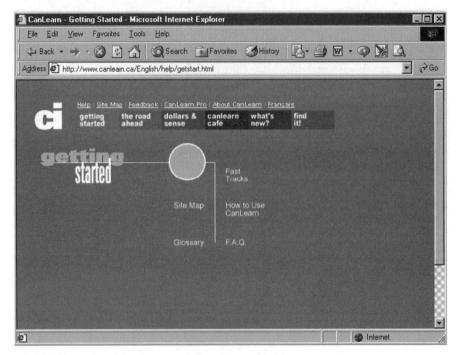

Figure 3.17 The CanLearn Interactive "Getting Started" page.
(April 25, 2001: www.canlearn.ca/English/eng.cfm)

Human Resources Development Canada: Reproduced with the permission of the Minister of Public Works and Government Services Canada, 2001.

The OSHA developers also provide a narrow-tree solution to the problem of having a great deal of content, but used a different approach to reveal the scope of the content. Note that the OSHA "Home" page (see Figure 3.18) has a left-hand navigation bar with seven main site sections which are repeated in the text. These redundant links also have other links. The result is that users are confronted with so much content and so many links that they're at a loss where to look first—a problem compounded by the black-and-red color scheme. In this case, a broader tree structure would have been more appropriate, or the developers could have used pull-down menus to reduce the clutter. However, when analyzing the structure of a site like this one, it's important to remember that the developers may have been limited in their choices because of accessibility concerns and technology issues. For example, the developers may have decided not to use pull-down menus—technology that supports a narrow-tree solution—because some users might not have the technology to view such menus.

Figure 3.18 The OSHA "Home" page.

July 4, 2001 (www.osha.gov)

Navigation Patterns

Like most aspects of usability, navigation is invisible when it's working, but when there's a problem, users can get completely stuck.

USER INTERFACE ENGINEERING (2000)

Trends and technology affect navigation patterns.

Navigation patterns begin to emerge at the IA's early development stages. You'll begin to see possibilities for both vertical and horizontal ways that information can flow. The Web designer supports these patterns in the GUI which provides navigation information. Conventions in GUI design, like many aspects of Web development, have come and gone with great rapidity. In the early days of the Web, location of the navigation information, usually at the bottom of the screen, compelled users to make cumbersome mouse and cursor movements. The current trend in GUI design includes the following basic elements:

- The top navigation bar for links to corporate information, search engines, and site maps.

- The left-hand navigation bar for main content site sections.

- Bottom-of-the-page links for utility items such as policy links, privacy links, and copyright statements.

- The right-hand navigation bar for add-ons such as advertising, sponsors, surveys, opinion polls, or advertising links to similar products through affiliate programs. Generally, this bar doesn't carry main content navigation, because some users might not be able to view it on their monitors. In the future, technological advances such as Web pages that automatically adjust to different monitors may allow developers to use this bar for different purposes.

NOTE An affiliate program allows site owners to link to another site where users can purchase products/services. If they do so, the owner of the original site receives a commission.

<u>**help**</u>

Figure 3.19   A word plus the underline serves as a link.

Navigation Links

Earlier in the chapter, we discussed links according to their function. Visually, a link can either be a word or words, a graphical icon, or an icon with words (see Figures 3.19, 3.20, and 3.21).

Farkas and Farkas (2000:344) note: "Potentially, icon links offer some significant advantages over text links. A familiar icon can be processed more quickly and easily than a text link. Many icons communicate across language barriers. Finally, icons can be made visually interesting and attractive, and can be incorporated into a Web site's overall visual design." If you have any doubt, however, about an icon's ability to communicate to users, suggest that the designer use either a different icon or include text with the icon.

Whatever type of links your team creates on a Web site, here are some rules of thumb that your team should follow:

- Text links should be visible and noticeable—underlining is the current convention, although the color of the link now varies.
- Graphical links should be visible and noticeable—putting the icon on a button aids visibility.
- Link text titles should be informative and brief—users need to quickly understand where the links will take them.
- Unusual links should provide special instructions—for example, "Click on the picture to view the video," or "Click on the picture to hear the interview."

Figure 3.20   A graphical icon serves as a link.

Figure 3.21   A graphical icon plus text serves as a link.

How Many Clicks to Content?

In the early days of the Web, developers were click-happy, and users often had to drill down through many layers to get to content. For example, we rebuilt a site, originally created in 1996, with some content that was 14 clicks deep! Not surprisingly, as users became annoyed and frustrated by this practice, a rule of thumb emerged—no more than three clicks to content. To be fair to early site developers, advancing technologies such as pull-down/fly-out menus on navigation bars have helped today's developers reduce required clicks to content. (For more information on how technology can enhance content delivery, see Chapter 8, "Content + Technology: A Surprising Alliance.")

When we start a site-rebuild, one of our first tasks is to do a test count of the number of clicks to content. If the problem is bad—far too many clicks before reaching a page other than a menu page—then the content has to be redesigned, and a very conscious effort made to flatten the navigation structure. In our experience, the three-click rule is an ideal to keep in your mind, but it may not work in practice. In the redesign of the site described above, the team made every effort to live by the rule. However, certain sections of the site were too complex and had content that required six clicks from the "Home" page. In these sections, we made a deliberate attempt to ensure that deeper-level pages were not just menu pages, because we wanted users to feel that they were getting practical information at every level. Therefore, many fourth- and fifth-level pages had meaningful information as well as links to deeper content.

Site Maps

The development of the information architecture and navigation design can eventually lead to a site map which is a graphical representation of the content of the site, or a site index or table of contents which presents a text version. Site maps are a relatively new addition to the Web. Information design specialists Paul Kahn and Krzysztof Lenk (2001:72) describe this evolution:

> When we designed our first web site for a commercial client in 1994 there were only 300 .com sites registered and most web sites were a few hundred pages at most. By the summer of 1995 it was evident to many web designers and developers that simply following links or searching for words was not enough to support navigation on most web sites. There were hundreds of thousands of web sites and many contained tens of thousands of pages. By early 1996 site maps began to appear as a regular feature of many sites.

To return to our house metaphor, a site map can be thought of as the equivalent of the floor plans for a house. Such plans are easier to draw when the building is small, but the task grows more difficult if the building is larger. Would it be possible to represent Buckingham Palace or the Pentagon on one single page? The same problem applies to graphical site maps. Although creating maps for small sites is relatively easy, developing maps for large sites—particularly those with thousands of pages, data organized into large databases, and/or content coming in different modes such as text, video, sound, and so on—is extremely difficult. Information visualization specialists Brian Johnson and Ben Schneiderman (1999:152) point out that:

| Large sites are difficult to map. |

> A large quantity of the world's information is hierarchically structured: manuals, outlines, corporate organizations, family trees, directory structures, internet addressing, library programs…and the list goes on. Most people come to understand the content and organization of these structures easily if they are small, but have great difficulty if the structures are large.

Researchers in the area of information visualization (IV) continue to research the best ways to present the information in large, complex sites. However, in general, these sites use maps that show only major information groupings rather than full-site depth.

Web Detection

The more you know about Web navigation, the more valuable you'll be to the client and the production team. Table 3.4 provides you with tips to building knowledge in this important area of Web development.

Table 3.4   Tips to Learning about Navigation

ASPECT OF NAVIGATION	LEARNING TIPS
Navigation Design	Pick a site and first draw a chart of its high-level menu items.
	Take one site section and follow a flow of information stream down to its deepest page. By repeating this exercise for a variety of sites, you'll be able to see how navigation is linked to the IA.
	Keep an eye out for dead-end spots where users find themselves with nowhere to go except by using the "Back button," and loops of content where users can get caught and can only exit the loop by leaving the site.
Links	Determine how well main navigation links are titled and whether they accurately reflect the content of the main site sections.
	To spot redundant links, look for similar link titles on navigation bars and in the body of the text. Trace them to their respective pages. If the pages are identical, you've found a redundant link.
Site Maps	Look at as many site maps as you can. For each one, ask:
	■ Does the site map help me understand the content of the site?
	■ Does the site map help me understand the breadth and depth of the site?
	■ If the site map is graphical, does the type of graphic work well? Could there be a different way of visualizing the site that would be preferable?
	■ If I click on an item, does it take me to the actual page? If not, where does it send me? Will this type of linking frustrate users?
Search Engines/ Databases	Check whether sites have search engines instead of site maps. Is the search engine more useful for the site? Do you think a site map would also help users?
	To determine the complexity of a database, click on a link to bring up a Web page. Now using a keyword from the Web page title or contents, use the search engine. Do you get the same page? (For more information on databases, see Chapter 8, "Content + Technology: A Surprising Alliance.")

To Sum It Up

Earlier in the chapter, we demonstrated how a mind map about Sherlock Holmes could lead to a site structure that revealed the IA of a Web site. However, that process is only the starting point for developing a Web site. To demonstrate how the site structure shown in Figure 3.5 leads to the navigation design and GUI, we've created the "Home" page for a fictitious Web site: "The World of Sherlock Holmes" (see Figure 3.22 on page 98). Note how the four main branches of the site structure have become the main content site sections on the left-hand navigation bar. Users can run their cursor over these buttons to view second-level content through the use of fly-out menus. (To see this, visit our companion Web site at www.wiley.com/compbooks/hammerich.)

Because this fictitious site is run by a fictitious non-profit organization, The Association for the Study of Sherlock Holmes, we've also included some of the links often found on non-profit sites. (See Table 3.1.) However, it's important to remember that Figure 3.22 represents only one GUI possibility for "The World of Sherlock Holmes." For example, another GUI could have shown all of the navigation routes at the first and second levels, or conversely, hidden the navigation structure through the use of visual metaphors (no text) for the site. For example, instead of words, the link "His Mind" could have been a brain or silhouette of a head.

When the Web first began, sites were fairly simple and their organization was relatively easy. However, as sites grow larger and more complex, the task of organizing content is increasingly difficult. The creation of effective informational models and easy-to-use navigation is becoming more crucial to every site's survival. As the writer/editor of either a new or existing site, you must work with the client, designers, and programmers to ensure that the site's IA and navigation maintains the integrity of the information and its flow, and that the GUI has a look-and-feel that is appropriate to the architecture, information, and users' requirements.

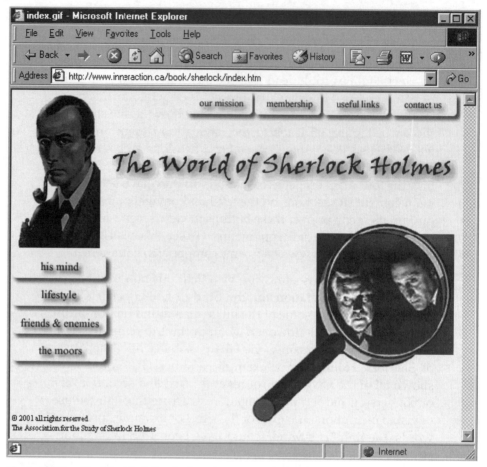

Figure 3.22 The World of Sherlock Holmes "Home" page.

Resources for This Chapter

Books

The Mind Map Book: How to Use Radiant Thinking to Maximise Your Brain's Untapped Potential by Tony Buzan with Barry Buzan. A full explanation of mind-mapping by its creator. Includes many illustrations. (Penguin Group/Dutton: 1993)

Information Architecture for the World Wide Web by Louis Rosenfeld and Peter Morville. A standard reference guide on building Web sites. (O'Reilly: 1998)

Don't Make Me Think: A Common Sense Approach to Web Usability by Steve Krug. Discusses the usability of the GUI and approaches to testing. (Macmillan: 2000)

Web Navigation: Designing the User Experience by Jennifer Fleming. Covers both information architecture and navigation design. (O'Reilly: 1998)

Web Style Guide: Basic Design Principles for Creating Web Sites by Patrick J. Lynch and Sarah Horton. A thoughtful review of the process of Web site development and the design of interfaces, sites, and pages. (Yale University: 1999)

The Essential Guide to User Interface Design: An Introduction to GUI Design Principles and Techniques by Wilbert O. Galitz. An excellent reference for GUI design. (John Wiley & Sons: 1997)

Mapping Web Sites by Paul Kahn and Krzysztof Lenk. An exploration of how mapping helps in the planning and design of Web sites. Includes innovative color illustrations that demonstrate the complexities of architecture and database sites. (RotoVision SA: 2001)

Web Design: The Complete Reference by Thomas A. Powell. An in-depth treatment of the theory, tools, and technologies for Web site planning, architecture, usability, navigation, and page layout. (Osborne/McGraw Hill: 2000)

Web Sites

Argus Center for Information Architecture (www.argus-acia. com). Provides recent and archived information on research, theory, and practice.

InfoDesign (www.bogieland.com/infodesign). Current articles about information design from a variety of specialists.

The Buzan Organization (www.mind-map.com). Mind-map creator Tony Buzan's site.

SiteNavigation.net (www.sitenavigation.net/snguide.html). Provides links to a variety of different sources and resources about site navigation.

OECD: Privacy Policy Generator (CS3-HQ.oecd.org/scripts/ pwv3/pwpart1.htm). The Organisation for Economic Co-operation and Development (OECD) provides a free service to organizations that want to develop online privacy policies and statements.

Could Your Site Use an FAQ? (cafe.trellix.com/features/details.asp?id=27). An article by Web writer Amy Gahran with useful tips on creating FAQ's.

Visual Logic (www.patricklynch.net). Articles, links, and book reviews by Patrick Lynch, the co-author of the *Yale Web Style Guide*.

AskTog: Human Interface Evangelism & Practical Design (www.asktog.com). A site that lays out principles for good GUI design and includes articles by Bruce "Tog" Tognazzini, a researcher in human-computer interaction.

User Interface Engineering (www.world.std.com/~uieweb/moreart.htm). Research articles from a company that specializes in GUI usability.

E-Rhetoric: A New Form of Persuasion

What's Inside:

- **Persuasive text in the Information Age**
- **Capturing the attention of the "drive-thru" reader**
- **The characteristics of quality Web content**
- **Rhetorical strategies for Web titles, text headers, and conjunctions**
- **Tips to bolding and italicizing online text**

"Information," referred to as a commodity, is a myth.
Information always comes in packages...
and every such package has a point of view.
Even a database has a point of view.

TED NELSON (1999)

We were once at a meeting with a client who listened carefully to our ideas about the benefits of links for Web readers, that is, how users could develop knowledge through layers of nonlinear information. When we finished, it was quite clear that the client hadn't been persuaded in the least. "But how can we make sure," he asked, "that people will go through the information the way *we* want?" Of course, the answer was that we couldn't, but his comment reflected an emotion that many clients and writers/editors have about presenting material on the Web—a feeling of helplessness in the face of the user's control over content.

Users can enter a site at any point, leave before they finish reading a page, link to somewhere else on the site, leave the site altogether and, basically, ignore all our carefully laid plans for organizing information. Despite the fact that print media also has elements of this nonlinearity—readers hop around text through the use of indexes and tables of content, and skim and scan content to find what they need—we have, as print content developers, ignored this reality. We've believed that the structure of print—its visibility as a unit of use, such as a book, newspaper, manual, or brochure, and its page-by-page sequencing—means that, no matter how readers use the text, they must ultimately follow our thread of reasoning. Being in authorial control is, not surprisingly, a source of comfort, and we've enjoyed that comfort for a long time.

Death of the Author?

Early Internet theorists predicted chaos.

The Internet presents information stripped of sequencing and not encased in any visible unit of use. As literacy researcher Myron Tuman (1992:58-59) states: "First, the individual works lose their distinctive boundaries (their former clearly marked beginnings and endings) as part of a larger database, and second, the searching and eventual reading activity are themselves largely driven by the user or 'reader.' The author, when there is one (reference databases often being anonymous), has the task of providing the general context, not a single specific track, within which the reader moves." For many early theorists, the Internet appeared to mean the end of authorial control over content.

Hypertext Theories

Even before the Web existed, Internet researchers were concerned about how hypertext would alter the relationships among writer/editor, reader, and text. For example, early hypertext researcher Joseph Jaynes (1989:158) predicted cognitive chaos: "Readers *learn* by discerning and internalizing structure…When we learn, we do so in large part because we perceive—and come to expect—sequence. We scan a painting and absorb its meaning because we have a sense of what has passed and what is to come. When such expectations are violated—for instance, in the paintings of M.C. Escher—we experience a serious sense of disruption and dislocation."

Writing researcher Jay Bolter (1991:31, 233-234) believed that electronic writing would lead to cultural chaos: "It opposes standardization and unification as well as hierarchy. It offers as a paradigm the text that changes to suit the reader rather than expecting the reader to conform to its standards...As our written culture becomes a vast hypertext, the reader is free to choose one subnetwork or many, as he or she wishes. It is no longer convincing to say that one subject is more important than any other." These early researchers focused primarily on literary texts and a hypertext that allowed users to go anywhere within a document, and even enter their own text as commentary. It's no wonder that they envisioned a world where information would exist without order or stability.

Although more recent hypertext theorists agree that the Web is a new medium for writing and reading, they argue that the focus of these early researchers was too confining. As hypertext researcher A.S. Pang (1998) notes: "This work has proved quite useful in making sense of certain aspects of multimedia, but the problematic character of its analyses of authorship and reading reveal a number of weaknesses. It theorizes about an ideal rather than real technology, exaggerates the differences between print and electronic publishing, considers books to be the natural traditional form of 'text,' and focuses too narrowly on academic work and writing."

By focusing solely on literary works, early researchers ignored the value of many other kinds of documents. Hyptertext researcher Johndan Johnson-Eilola (1997:6) says: "...we must reject hierarchical structures that place creative writing (fiction or non-fiction) in high status and functional writing (instruction, databases) in low status...these things we think of as *tools*, a term that unfortunately downplays their deep implications for our ways of living in the world. These tools are actually texts..." The early researchers also ignored the realities of workplace writing, that is, the process of writing/editing that generates informational Web sites. Workplace documents generally involve multiple authors as people collaborate to develop content, and text moves up and down the approvals ladder with comments received at every rung. Multiple authorship, Pang (1998) asserts: "...break[s] apart the link between writing and creating that is at the very core of humanistic scholarship, which hypertext theorists have taken to be the print world's norm."

In other words, the prediction of the death of the author, as a creator, on the Internet was as much an exaggeration as the pronouncement that the interactivity and visual potential of the Web meant the death of text.

The Futurists

Some early futurists were also concerned, and some exhilarated, by the idea that computers and hypertext would mean the death-knell of the printed book—a forecast that has, as yet, not come to fruition. Other visionaries, who believe that the alphabet and print media taught us to think in a certain linear way, believe that non-linear digital delivery of textual content, mixed with a variety of media, may affect us profoundly. Literacy researchers Brent Robinson and Edward Versluis (1985:27) suggest: "It is a new medium with its own characteristics which will have important consequences for literate users—it may affect their facility in the reading process; it may alter their concepts of the nature of print material…; it may have other, possibly less obtrusive, effects upon the social, political and economic structure of a society which is dependent upon the free and efficient passage of information." Discourse analyst Gunther Kress (1998:72) is less tentative, stating that both language and visual modes produce messages, but that: "…the two modes produce quite distinctly different takes on the world," and through their interaction provide "…ways of organizing representations of the world [that] have the most fundamental consequences for an individual's or a culture's orientation in the world, so that this shift is bound to have equally fundamental repercussion in social, cultural and economic practices…"

> Web writing/editing requires a new type of creativity.

The scholars will continue to ponder, argue, and analyze, but what is most important for you, as a Web writer/editor, to realize is that the author is not dead, and that the Web is truly a new and different medium, requiring just as much creativity on your part as any informational product based on print. However, working in this new medium means that you'll have to re-adjust your thinking about many aspects of text, from its development to its presentation, and consider new methods, techniques, and strategies for presenting online information.

Rhetoric Returns!

rhet·o·ric Noun: 1a. The art or study of using language effectively and persuasively.

THE AMERICAN HERITAGE DICTIONARY

In Chapter 2, we described the education of a young Greek, circa 500 B.C., who learned to orate through memorization of what was already known. He would be renowned for rhetorical skill if he could speak persuasively on any topic. As writing researcher Richard Lanham (1976:4) notes in *Motives of Eloquence*: "Rhetorical man is trained not to discover reality but to manipulate it." The young Greek held no central values of what was right or wrong, what was appropriate or not, and what was worthy or not. Rather, he was a purely social being who knew all sides of the argument and was trained to take any side necessary. Aristotle described rhetoric as "the faculty of observing in any given case the available means of persuasion." The world, to rhetorical man, was essentially a *game* of language.

Rhetoric and the Challenger Explosion

In 1986, the space shuttle *Challenger* exploded after liftoff, killing all of its seven astronauts. Two O-rings had failed to seal, allowing fuel to leak. The day before the launch, engineers at Morton Thiokol who had developed the O-ring became concerned about the forecast of very chilly weather and the high risk of the O-rings not sealing at low temperatures. Within a few hours, they drew up 13 charts, faxed them to the National Aeronautics and Space Administration (NASA), and recommended that the mission be aborted. They expected that the facts would, essentially, speak for themselves.

In his analysis of these 13 charts, visualization researcher Edward Tufte (1997:45) notes that: "…there is a scandalous discrepancy between the intellectual tasks at hand and the images created to serve those tasks. As analytical graphics, the displays failed to reveal a risk that was in fact present." The result was that NASA officials were skeptical, the Thiokol managers decided that their engineers' evidence wasn't conclusive, and the company reversed its position. As Tufte (1997:40) says: "On the day before the launch of Challenger, the rocket engineers and managers needed a quick, smart *analysis* of evidence about the threat of cold to the O-rings, as well as an effective *presentation* of the evidence…" In other words, the lack of rhetoric at the written level and poor rhetoric at the graphic level were major contributors to the Challenger tragedy.

Western society, on the other hand, is far less playful. Although traditional rhetoric exists pervasively in our activities—just consider what politicians *say* versus what they *do*—we aren't comfortable with the notion that we could, or even should, switch moral gears at a moment's notice just for the sake of winning. In fact, we've become highly suspicious of anything that smacks of the kind of rhetoric that the *American Heritage Dictionary* (2000) defines as: "Language that is elaborate, pretentious, insincere, or intellectually vacuous." Given its bad reputation, you might be surprised to know that rhetoric is making a comeback, not in the Aristotelian sense, but in how we use language in a world where there are no verifiable truths—only ideas, concepts, opinions, and theories.

A New Definition

Writing researcher Lanham (1993:117-119), noting that words are the commodity of the Information Age, suggests that we need a better definition of rhetoric, that is, "the economics of human attention-structures":

> ...whenever we "persuade" someone, we do so by getting that person to "look at things from our point of view," share our attention-structure. It is in the nature of human life that attention should be in short supply, but in an information economy it becomes the crucial scarce commodity. Just as economics has been the study of how we allocate scarce resources in a goods economy, we now will use a variety of rhetoric as the "economics" of human attention-structure...a vital activity in our information society.

Today, the first goal of rhetoric is to gain attention.

Getting people's attention isn't, however, about the number of words you use, but how you use them. Technical communicator and design specialist William Horton (1997:42) demonstrates this by showing the number of words in "influential and not so influential documents."

- Lord's Prayer—56 words
- Gettysburg Address—266 words
- Ten Commandments—297 words
- Declaration of Independence—300 words
- Box of breakfast cereal—1,200 words
- U.S. Government order on pricing cabbage—26,911 words

In Chapter 2, we also described how writing is now understood to be a social action that takes place between the writer and the reader. This concept of writing is based on the rhetorical tradition, with its focus on persuasion through the choice of words, emphasis on the audience, and an understanding of the situation in which the words would be presented. Our Greek orator used a variety of strategies as he played the game of rhetoric. He planned his speech carefully, laying out the issues and building one convincing argument on another. His rhetorical strategies also included a careful crafting of his presentation. He would consider the modulation and pitch of his voice, when he would create telling pauses, his physical stance, his hand gestures, and the type of eye contact he would make with his audience. Each of these actions would be just as important as his words in persuading his audience that he was right.

In the print tradition, document developers are also rhetoricians. They must not only plan the text with the same care that the Greek orator prepared his speech, but they must also consider how that text is presented. Instead of stance, hand gestures, and eye contact—the rhetorical actions involved with speech—document designers use rhetorical strategies involved with the design of text such as headers (font types and sizes), colors (black-and-white or with color), and visuals (illustrations and photographs).

Lanham (1993:77) suggests that rhetoric on the Web is emerging as a combination of the oral tradition of the early Greek orator and written tradition of print. He says that, as readers: "We have to learn to alternate between these two kinds of syntax, verbal and visual…[with] sound and color rapidly becoming part of the mix…And if voice and musical sampling are added to the palette, we take yet another step back toward the full range of oral expressivity." In fact, this mix of traditions on the Web contributes to its realization as a new form of communications. Therefore, E-rhetoric not only means that you, as the writer/editor, must focus on text but that you must also include, as part of your repertoire of persuasive strategies, all the advantages of multiple media and interactivity.

But Whither Fact and Accuracy?

As rhetorician and document design expert Karen Shriver (1997:10) notes: "Document design is the act of bringing together prose, graphics (including illustration and photography), and typography for purposes of instruction, information, or persuasion. Good document design enables people to use the text in ways that serve their interests and needs." E-rhetoric is, to paraphrase Shriver, the act of bringing together text, photographs, illustration, typography, animation, navigation, links, and audio- and video-clips for the purposes of persuasion on the Web.

"Wait a moment," you may protest. "What about facts and accuracy? Do we sacrifice these important elements of information for rhetoric?" However, the fact and its close cousin, accuracy, are subjective and depend entirely on the sayer and the receiver of the statement. For example, the Morton Thiokol engineers were, they thought, creating indisputable facts with extreme accuracy. The NASA officials thought otherwise.

> Facts and accuracy are subjective.

In Chapter 2, we briefly mentioned social semiotics, a field of study that examines how statements make meaning. Social semioticians believe that a statement, whether fact or opinion, has a meaning only within its context of situation, and this meaning can change when the situation changes. Even science, usually considered the bastion of fact and accuracy, is social and, therefore, subjective. Sociologist Bruno Latour (1987:29, 33) demonstrates how scientific writing creates meaning and uses rhetoric through the use of citations.

> By themselves, a statement, piece of machinery, a process are lost. By looking only at them at their internal properties, you cannot decide if they are true or false, efficient or wasteful, costly or cheap, strong or frail. These characteristics are only gained through *incorporation* into other statements, processes and pieces of machinery…
>
> The presence or the absence of references, quotations and footnotes is so much a sign that a document is serious or not that you can *transform a fact into fiction or fiction into fact* just by adding or subtracting references…A paper that does not have references is like a child without an escort walking at night in a big city it does not know: isolated, lost, anything may happen to it. (*Our emphasis*).

As members of a particular society, culture, and social class, none of us can avoid our subjectivity no matter how hard we try. Information and design consultant Richard Saul Wurman (2001:31) also notes that: "Facts in themselves make no sense without a frame of reference. They can be understood only as they relate to an idea." He describes a situation in which 15 reporters are assigned to cover the same event and file 15 *different* stories, because each reporter provides information based on his or her personal understanding of the world. As Wurman says: "Accuracy, in itself, is not the means to making things understandable. Once you realize that absolute accuracy is impossible, you can be more relaxed and comfortable with your own choices as to the level of detail and to the point of view. The key to understanding is to accept that any account of an event is bound to be subjective, no matter how committed the recounter is to being accurate and objective."

E-Rhetoric and the Drive-Thru Reader

The drive-thru reader has an urgent need to gain knowledge because, in the global community, there is not one truth, but many different truths. In this situation, every text becomes a form of persuasion. Although writing researchers Aviva Freedman and Peter Medway (1994:5) are describing print documents in *Genre and the New Rhetoric*, their comments apply equally to those on the Web: "…the composing of texts traditionally regarded as containers of knowledge comes to be seen, far more dynamically, as part of the social process by which that knowledge, 'the world, reality, and facts' are made." Let's take a Web example. You're interested in the drug Viagra, which gained renown in the late 1990s as an antidote for male impotence. You search for information about Viagra on the Web, using search engines/directories. The hit results during March 2001 were:

Google—693,000

AltaVista—207,515

Lycos—468,254

Excite—328,710

Northern Lights—421,535

And if you searched through these hits, you'd find a variety of sites about Viagra. The intention of all these sites is to persuade you that *they* have the truth about Viagra, that is, to create "the world, the reality, and facts"—all within their own particular texts. Of course, not all of them succeed as well as others. Table 4.1 demonstrates some examples of these sites and what, we suggest, are their rhetorical credibility.

Table 4.1   Viagra Sites and Rhetorical Credibility

TYPE OF SITE	SUGGESTED CREDIBILITY RATING
Government health site	High
Physician's advice column	High
Men's health forum	Medium
Pharmaceutical company	Medium to Low
Mail-order pharmacy	Low
Testimonials (a sales site)	Low

Being an E-rhetorician is not, essentially, different from the work you've done in other media. However, in this case, you won't be able to fall back on the rhetorical advantages provided by other media, such as the linearity of printed material, or the focus of the camera which creates a film's narrative, or the singular space of the stage which provides cohesion for a play's language and action. Instead, you'll need to develop rhetorical strategies that take advantage of Web characteristics such as the information architecture, navigation, and visuals. To do this, you'll need to understand user reading and navigation behaviors.

> You've been a rhetorician in other media.

The Web with its mix of media and instantaneous linking is a highly complex communications environment. And, because it is undergoing constant change as a result of technological advances, its possibilities are unknown. Nevertheless, we believe that there are rhetorical strategies for making online text persuasive—strategies that will remain stable and enduring regardless of technology.

The Four C's of Quality Web Content

The textual area of rhetoric will be the one you're most familiar with, because it's likely that you've written intentionally persuasive texts in print-based media—texts such as brochures, booklets, press releases, advertising copy, speeches, and so on. As you know from these experiences, every word choice is a rhetorical strategy. However, there are some macro-textual areas that require special consideration as you write/edit for the Web. Credibility, clarity, conciseness, and coherence are elements of text that contribute significantly to a document's ability to persuade readers that it has the "right stuff."

Presenting a Complex Argument on the Web

As a print writer, I was accustomed to developing concise and extremely coherent arguments of logical persuasion. In essence, I was holding the reader's hand from the start and never letting go. But the Web makes this a very difficult task since you don't know at what point the reader will enter your argument. How can you make a lengthy, complex argument compelling to the Web's short-attention-span skimmers? And how will they understand an issue if they don't read all the supporting arguments? Recently, I had to write a persuasive Web piece on an important social and political issue. My client didn't want the text in a .pdf file, so I divided the argument into idea-sized chunks, put each on a separate Web page, and added a lot of links. Another part of the solution was to place a mind map graphic on every page that showed readers where they were in the argument.

Steve Clason, Writer
Top Dog Strategy
www.topdogstrategy.com

NOTE

A .pdf file is a method of delivering content through a software called Adobe Acrobat Reader that allows viewers to see a text as if it were in a print format.

Credibility

> *cred·i·bil·i·ty Noun: 1. The quality, capability, or power to elicit belief.*
>
> THE AMERICAN HERITAGE DICTIONARY

In a world where there is no one truth, and everyone is hunting for information, credibility is a highly valued commodity. Credibility is, of course, in the eye of the beholder, because beliefs are based on an individual's cultural, spiritual, and personal experiences. Everyone has a different mix of beliefs which, in turn, engender differing opinions and attitudes. For example, what is believable to one person may seem hypocritical to another, or what feels like proselytizing prose to one user may appear to be credible information to another.

Librarians Janet E. Alexander and Marsha Ann Tate (1999:10-14) present five criteria for evaluating the quality of information on the Web and demonstrate why online content poses such problems regarding credibility.

- **Authority**: "Authority is the extent to which material is the creation of a person or organization that is recognized as having definitive knowledge of a given subject area." Establishing authority is particularly important on the Web because anyone can become a Web publisher.

- **Accuracy:** "Accuracy is the extent to which information is reliable and free from errors." In print, we can expect reputable publishers to provide accurate material through use of editors, peer-reviewers and/or fact-checkers. Unfortunately, "the steps that contribute to the accuracy of traditional media are frequently condensed or even eliminated on the Web."

- **Objectivity:** "Objectivity is the extent to which material expresses facts or information without distortion by personal feelings or other biases." Although "no presentation of information can ever be totally free of bias," our knowledge of who published material, and why, can help us evaluate objectivity. "However, because the Web so easily offers the opportunity for persons or groups of any size to present their point of view, it often functions as a virtual soapbox."

- **Currency:** "Currency is the extent to which material can be identified as up to date." Copyright dates provide information about print publications, but Web dates are confusing because they can be "variously interpreted as the date when the material was first created, when it was placed on the Web, or when the Web page was last revised."

- **Coverage and intended audience:** "Coverage is the range of topics included in a work and the depth to which those topics are addressed. Intended audience is the group of people for whom the material was created." Print documents usually come with prefaces, tables of content, introductions, and/or indexes—all elements that provide readers with knowledge of the content and whether they form the appropriate audience. Web sites, on the other hand, lack these elements and, therefore, coverage and intended audience aren't immediately obvious. If the site doesn't include a good site map, users are compelled to surf the site to find out what it includes.

Credibility within text is the combination of words and phrases that a writer/editor uses to persuade the reader that the intentions of the document are sincere and honest. And current research demonstrates that online credibility is strongly affected by writing style. A study done by John Morkes and Jakob Neilsen (1997) demonstrates that sites with a "promotional style of writing (i.e., 'marketese,'), which [contain] exaggeration, subjective claims, and boasting, rather than just simple facts" detract significantly from usability. In other words, users are often turned off by language that seems to be selling them something. Take, for example, the opening paragraph from a page on the Internal Revenue Service (IRS) Web site Source (www.irs.gov/ind_info/index.html).

> Writing style affects online credibility.

The tone of this paragraph is sales-oriented, designed to convince taxpayers that the IRS is a benign, friendly organization whose sole purpose is to make the tax-filing process more user-friendly.

> You'll be glad you've landed on the Tax Info For You page. Because here you'll find tax tips for individuals—for folks just like you. Find out about exemptions. Learn how to estimate tax liability. Or, discover all the latest changes and reminders regarding your taxes. In case you don't have a pre-printed envelope, there's even a map to help you find out where to file. So, now that you've got exactly what you need, things will definitely go a whole lot smoother.

We suggest that the writers/editors of this text should have asked themselves a number of questions after creating this paragraph, such as:

- Are people, other than accountants and tax lawyers, ever glad to be dealing with tax information?
- Do citizens like to be called "folks just like you"?
- Why write, "So, now that you've got exactly what you need," when users will not have even started the process? And will these words truly convince them that the Web page will, in fact, provide them with the necessary information?

- How effective is colloquial terminology such as "things will definitely go a whole lot smoother" in convincing people that the complex process of tax-filing will actually be easier?

- In trying to avoid complicated tax jargon, has the text been "dumbed down" too far?

To demonstrate how promotional this text is, we have re-written it, eliminating subjective evaluations and hyped facts, and used bullets for easier reading.

> The "Tax Info For You" page is designed to help you through the process of filing your federal income tax. In it, you will find many useful tax tips, including information about:
>
> - Exemptions
>
> - Tax liability
>
> - Recent changes in taxation policy and legislation
>
> - Reminders regarding filing
>
> - Where to file your tax forms if you don't have a pre-printed envelope

Every Web site is trying to sell something, and a site's credibility depends not only on words, but also on who is providing the information and why, its visuals and navigation, and how often the information is updated. Nevertheless, the paradox that you face as a Web writer/editor of informational sites, other than those of e-commerce, is to develop content that "sells" the user without appearing to sell anything. Table 4.2 includes useful tips to help you develop textual credibility.

Clarity

The ability to write and edit text so that it will be clear and easily readable are skills you should already have under your belt. The most important issue with regard to clarity is that its greatest enemy, on the Web, is a strongly expressed personal writing style. Strunk and White (1959:66), in their classic text *The Elements of Style*, describe style as "an increment in writing" and that "every writer, by the way he uses the language reveals something of his spirit, his habits, his capacities, his bias." As a Web content developer, you must suppress any inclination you have to reveal any of the above. The user is not interested in you, but in the information you have to offer. Table 4.3 includes useful advice to achieve clarity.

Write/edit plain, functional text.

Table 4.2   Tips to Developing Online Credibility

TEXTUAL ASPECT	YOU SHOULD...
Tone	■ Avoid marketing language, particularly adjectives that inflate or exaggerate claims. Present information as factual, relevant, and accurate. ■ Although language on the Internet is generally more conversational than print documents—for example, the use of "you" is frequent—avoid being overly chatty and intimate. ■ Avoid convoluted syntax that makes it difficult for users to sort fact from fiction. Easy reading contributes to credibility. Writing that creates obfuscation makes people suspicious. ■ Avoid humor as some readers may get the joke while others may not. Remember, you may be writing/editing for an international audience. ■ Be careful with the use of adverbs that indicate a personal stance and, therefore, undercut objectivity. Such adverbs include *of course, obviously, clearly, unfortunately,* and *certainly.*
Presentation	■ Have a logo or other information on every Web page to identify the site owner(s) or author(s). ■ Ensure clean, well-presented text whose visuals are also clear and consistent regarding tone, color, and graphics. This demonstrates that the site owner(s) take pride in the content. ■ Eliminate typos, grammar mistakes, and other errors—they suggest that the content may also be erroneous. ■ Put the date of publication on every Web page, particularly if the site has the type of information that must be kept current to be relevant to users.

Writing with clarity is often referred to as using *plain language*—a term which means making text understandable, particularly government documents that are used by the public. Communications specialist Beth Mazur (2000:206), noting that plain language movements exist in North America and Europe, says: "Proponents assert that documents created using plain language techniques are effective in a number of ways. A recent plain language resource (Baldwin, 1999) lists the following reasons:

■ Readers understand documents better.

■ Readers prefer plain language.

- Readers locate information faster.

- Documents are easier to update.

- Documents are cost-effective.

However, it's important to remember that clarity is not the same as simplicity. As information designer Nathan Shedroff (1999:281) explains:

> ...if the message is about a complex relationship, it may necessitate presenting a large amount of data. This complexity can be

Table 4.3 Tips to Clarity in Online Writing

TEXTUAL ASPECT	YOU SHOULD...
Structure	▪ Keep sentences short—no more than one or two clauses.
	▪ Keep paragraphs short and discuss only one topic per paragraph.
	▪ Ensure that the first sentence of the paragraph states the theme. Many users will skim first sentences only.
Words/Phrases	▪ Use the active voice such as *The CEO held a meeting,* not *The meeting was held.*
	▪ Use phrases that are specific and concrete such as *we transformed the text,* rather than abstractions such as *the transformation of text.* Long, abstract nouns require concentration to read and understand.
	▪ Do not use adverbs unless you deem it necessary.
	▪ Avoid puns and other jokes that will not be understood by a global audience.
Presentation	▪ Use a Web page title that condenses and explains the page's content.
	▪ Use short and informative headers frequently.
	▪ Put spaces between paragraphs for easier reading.
	▪ Highlight key words either through bolding or italics. However, be careful not to overdo highlighting as it will detract from readability.
	▪ Put captions both above and below tables and figures. Remember that users often scroll fast and use the PgUp and PgDn buttons. Putting captions above and below helps users identify content easily.

made clear through effective organization and presentation and need not be reduced to meaningless "bite-sized" chunks of data, as simplifying it usually does. Clarity is best accomplished by focusing on one particular message or goal at a time and not attempting to accomplish too much all at once. Simplicity, on the other hand, is often responsible for the "dumbing down" of information rather than the illumination of it.

Conciseness

Be brief, for no discourse can please when too long.

MIGUEL DE CERVANTES

Drive-thru readers don't provide Web content developers with much time to establish their credibility and build a persuasive argument. Therefore, conciseness is an important quality of Web text. Being concise means having the skill to present a topic in the most economical manner possible, that is, using as few words as you can but still meeting the user's need for information.

> Be brief but thorough.

The amount of economy required of Web text depends on *where* the text is on the site and *how* the reader will use it. For example, pages that are primarily about navigation (providing links to other pages) require very condensed, tight text. On the other hand, pages that carry the main information of the site can be longer and more complex, depending on the type of content involved. (For a more detailed discussion, see Chapter 7, "Writing/Editing *for* the Web Page; Writing/Editing *to* the Web Screen.")

Reducing Verbiage

However, no matter what type of content you are writing/editing, you must never underestimate the value of concise text. In his book, *Designing Web Usability*, Jakob Neilsen (2000:105) discusses a test that he performed with collaborator, John Morkes, to test concise text on the Web. Table 4.4 demonstrates the results of this text and how a paragraph's readability can be improved through conciseness along with non-promotional writing and the use of bullets. The researchers took a sample paragraph and used it as the experimental control, rating it as having 0 percent in terms of usability improvement. They then

Table 4.4　Test of a Paragraph's Readability in Four Different Versions

TYPES OF TEXT	SAMPLE PARAGRAPH	USABILITY IMPROVEMENT RELATIVE TO THE CONTROL CONDITION
The Original Version	Nebraska is filled with internationally recognized attractions that draw large crowds of people every year, without fail. In 1996, some of the most popular places were Fort Robinson State Park (355,000 visitors), Scotts Bluff National Monument (132,166), Arbor Lodge State Historical Park & Museum (100,000), Carhenge (86,598), Stuhr Museum of the Prairie Pioneer (60,002), and Buffalo Bill Ranch State Historical Park (28,446).	**0%** = the control
Concise Text (50% of word count)	In 1996, six of the best-attended attractions in Nebraska were Fort Robinson State Park, Scotts Bluff National Monument, Arbor Lodge State Historical Park & Museum, Carhenge, Stuhr Museum of the Prairie Pioneer, and Buffalo Bill Ranch State Historical Park.	**58%** better
Scannable Text (same word count but use of bullets)	Nebraska is filled with internationally recognized attractions that draw large crowds of people every year, without fail. In 1996, some of the most popular places were: ■ Fort Robinson State Park (355,000 visitors) ■ Scotts Bluff National Monument (132,166) ■ Arbor Lodge State Historical Park & Museum (100,000)	**47%** better

Table 4.4 (Continued)

TYPES OF TEXT	SAMPLE PARAGRAPH	USABILITY IMPROVEMENT RELATIVE TO THE CONTROL CONDITION
	■ Carhenge (86,598) ■ Stuhr Museum of the Prairie Pioneer (60,002) ■ Buffalo Bill Ranch State Historical Park (28,446)	
Objective Text (using neutral words but no bullets)	Nebraska has several attractions. In 1996, some of the most-visited places were Fort Robinson State Park (355,000 visitors), Scotts Bluff National Monument (132,166), Arbor Lodge State Historical Park & Museum (100,000), Carhenge (86,598), Stuhr Museum of the Prairie Pioneer (60,002), and Buffalo Bill Ranch State Historical Park (28,446).	**27%** better
Combined Version (concise, scannable and objective)	In 1996, six of the most-visited places in Nebraska were: ■ Fort Robinson State Park ■ Scotts Bluff National Monument ■ Arbor Lodge State Historical Park & Museum ■ Carhenge ■ Stuhr Museum of the Prairie Pioneer ■ Buffalo Bill Ranch State Historical Park	**124%** better

Source: Material excerpted from *Designing Web Usability* by Jakob Neilsen (2000). © by New Riders Publishing. Used with permission.

altered the paragraph in four different ways to gauge how its readability was enhanced.

However, it's important to remember that not all text can or should be bulleted. The paragraph in Table 4.4 particularly lends itself to bulleting because it includes a list of items. When considering how text should be presented, you must constantly consider the readability needs of users. Some text won't work as bullets. As well, the decision to use a sentence/paragraph structure versus a list depends primarily on what you want to emphasize and the visual effect. Bulleted lists with short items are easier to read and, therefore, draw the eye. That's why they're extremely useful for highlighting important information. On the other hand, a page that only contains bulleted lists is confusing for users because all of the text appears at an equal level of importance. Your job as a writer/editor is to provide a judicious, balanced mix of sentences/paragraphs and bulleted lists.

Advice for Shrinking Text

The revisions of the CIA site in Chapter 2 (see Figures 2.1 and 2.2) and the "Tax Info for You" paragraph in this chapter are examples of how text can be edited down to make it more concise and, therefore, more readable for users. M.D. Morris (2001:21), writing in *Intercom*, the magazine of the Society for Technical Communication, provides useful tips for "shrinking any written product to scale."

- Determine precisely what the document wants to tell you, that is, the theme.
- Select key words or thoughts that would be the basis of major headings in your revised document.
- Build sentences applicable to the theme around the key words.
- Only use one or two key thoughts per sentence. Put those sentences in a logical sequence to convey the narrative of the document.
- Add some transitional words to make the abbreviated text flow smoothly. (You'll find a list of these words under "Conjunctions: Those Old Standbys" in this chapter.)
- Continue to rewrite until your text achieves these four goals:
    1. You've reduced principal concerns to the fewest words possible.

2. You've provided a comprehensive view of the situation.

3. You've ensured that the concepts of cause-and-effect are clearly differentiated wherever they occur in the text.

4. You've retained a clear sense of substance and quality in your document.

Coherence

In Chapter 2, we described text as a place where writers/editors and readers are dealing with a *situation-in-hand*, rather than just a series of sentences, one after the other. A defining characteristic of this situation is its coherence. All parts of the text connect together in clear and logical ways, enhancing its ability to persuade readers. Although Web content does not appear to readers in the same linear way that print content does, users must still experience a coherent situation or they will become disoriented, frustrated, and annoyed. Textual coherence occurs through three inter-related elements: the structure of information; the ties that hold text together; and use of the reader's background knowledge.

> Minimize users' cognitive work.

The Structure of Information and the Myth of NonLinearity

When you write/edit print material, you are constantly aware of the structure from the macro- to micro-levels. For example, if you're developing a staff newsletter, you consider four levels of structure: what content will appear on the front and subsequent pages; how content is organized on each page; the order of paragraphs within each article; and the structure of each sentence. If an article is split between pages, you have to indicate this to readers through an instruction such as "continued on next page" or through use of an arrow icon.

As a writer/editor coming to the Web from print, you are likely to be most concerned with the Web's lack of linearity. Users can enter a site on any page and, once they've arrived, can link around to their heart's content. How can you make sure that they follow a useful flow of information? What tricks can you learn that will help you guide them through the information in the right way? These questions have two underlying assumptions:

- Users' Web behavior is significantly different from readers' behavior in print.

- There is a right and wrong way to go through information to make it coherent.

Let's look at the first assumption. Do print users behave differently than Web users? Do they actually follow the linear path of information that you've so carefully structured in your print publications such as textbooks, training manuals, and how-to books? Patrick Lynch (2000), a specialist in new media design, says: "How many non-fiction reference books have you ever read straight through from cover to cover? There's nothing unique about the 'non-linear' way we use Web pages; readers have bounced from one content point to another in reference documents since the dawn of writing." Computer scientist and futurist Steven Holtzman (1998:171) describes a common way we read newspapers:

> You visually sweep a paper's front page to capture a sense of what's happening in the world. You absorb a picture, headline, caption, and some text in a glance. You spread the paper over your desk and read what catches your eye or intrigues you, skipping from one article to another, not necessarily completing any of them. There is no fixed beginning or end; you select a beginning when you jump straight to the business or sports page, and the end whenever you put the paper down. You scan a story, turn pages for more and turn back easily to the beginning. You skip to the paragraph that summarizes the conclusion. As with a mosaic, you build an image of the day's news from various pieces of information.

There is no right or wrong way to read text.

In other words, in print publications, readers use tables of content, indexes, and skimming and scanning strategies to determine what content they actually want to read. In fact, we suggest that the only print text that readers follow from page to page is fiction, and even then we've met readers who check out the ending of a novel before they start it!

The second assumption—that there is a right and wrong way to go through information to achieve coherence—is no longer correct if the first assumption is not accurate. If readers can approach print information in a nonlinear fashion and still experience coherence, the variety of ways they can approach Web content should not present as much of an obstacle as you may think. "Hold it," we can hear you saying. "At least readers can see the way a print document is structured. All they have to do is leaf through the pages." We agree that the visible linearity of a text provides writers/editors with two important advantages in developing print content:

- Readers can, from the "look-and-feel" of a publication, figure out immediately what kind of text it is—for example, a promotional brochure, a report, or a dictionary.

- They can also view entire pages at a glance, enabling them to absorb a great deal of content structure right away.

In fact, it is these two characteristics of print that allow writers/editors to create headers that are provocative, rather than just informative. Take, for example, the first ambiguous header of Chapter 2, *The Bubble Syndrome*. It works in print, because you have the book in hand and know what the content is about. As well, you've been trained through years of education that the reading payoff will come when you apply your concentration to reading the text. Now, imagine yourself surfing the Web and entering a site on a page called "The Bubble Syndrome." You've no idea what this means and, therefore, you're already annoyed. You may try, from the navigational information, to figure out what the site is about. You may, in your rush to get information, skim the text to see if it's useful to you. But chances are, because you can't figure out the site, you'll leave as quickly as you arrived.

> Ambiguity doesn't work on the Web.

Research in human-computer interaction (HCI) shows that Web users try to visualize or get a handle on the overall context as they read site content. Experiments by cognitive psychologist Peter Foltz (1996) demonstrate that reading a hypertext is:

> Not just a reading process, but also a process of problem solving...The strategies used by the subjects show evidence for the dominance of global comprehension in reading. The subjects used a rational approach to reading, maintaining an order of reading that was consistent with the macrostructure of the text. Even when the structure of the text had been modified from its linear form, they chose paths through the text that would flow coherently. This is consistent with the readers' goals to form a coherent macrostructure. Thus, readers of a hypertext are opportunistic. They look for the cues that will lead them to the most coherent path through the text.

Coherence in the structure of content on a site depends on three important elements that we discuss in this book:

- **Well-built information architecture** in Chapter 3, "Organizing a Web Site: 'Elementary, My Dear Watson.'"
- **Internal links that make logical sense** in Chapter 6, "Logic, Links, and the Layered Reader."
- **Web pages that can stand alone as rhetorical units of information** in Chapter 7, "Writing/Editing *for* the Web Page; Writing/Editing *to* the Web Screen."

When this type of content coherence is supported by equally strong coherence in design and navigation, users gain confidence in their ability to understand what the site is about and how it will meet their needs.

The Ties That Bind: Holding Text Together

When you write/edit print material, you continually make use of rhetorical strategies to ensure that the text presents a clear flow of information and readers won't get lost as they follow the text. One such strategy is the use of cohesive ties.[1] These are equally useful on the Web, but you must re-think how they work on the Web where readers scroll and move from page to page. Table 4.5 demonstrates the positive and negative effects of using print cohesive ties on the Web.

What Readers Know and the Importance of Prediction

As a writer/editor, you've taken, consciously or unconsciously, advantage of readers' background knowledge when you develop content. In this book, we have made many assumptions about *your* knowledge of writing/editing and *your* experiences in different media. As well, we've counted on your experiences as Web users so that, for example, when we mentioned *scrolling* in Table 4.3, we didn't have to actually describe what this action entails. Our use of your background knowledge is an important strategy that we've used to create coherence in this book.

To create coherence, readers can combine the text and their prior knowledge in four ways:

- **Genre recognition:** They recognize the kind of text that they are reading—for example, conversation in a Web chat room.
- **Understanding of conventions:** They understand the conventions of a text—for example, that underlined words are links.

Table 4.5 Print Cohesive Ties and Web Content

COHESIVE TIES	EXAMPLES	AS APPLIED TO WEB WRITING
Repetition: When the same words or words with similar meanings are used in a text.	*Your resume is an important tool. When building a resume, start with your work objective.*	Repetition is the most powerful cohesive tool that you have to connect text within a Web page and among Web pages. The repetition of a word in titles and headers and throughout the site is like a strong glue holding the content together.
Synonyms: When a word that is different but similar in meaning occurs in the text.	*The audience clapped, and the performer bowed to acknowledge the applause.*	You may find that you're using the same word too often. If that's the case, then a synonym is your best device.
Collocation: When words that are related in topic re-occur in the text.	*The child played with a toy at the day care center.* *The soldiers wore uniforms when they were on parade.*	Building a collocational chain throughout a Web site is an important means of holding the content together.
Reference: When words in the text refer back to previous words. For example, use of pronouns—*it, he, she*—that connect back to a regular noun or name.	*Sharon hit the ball. She hit it hard.* *Ernest Hemingway was a famous writer. Papa was known throughout the world and won a Nobel prize.*	Can be used within a single sentence, a single paragraph, or in the bullets following a sentence/paragraph. However, do so with caution. Users who are scrolling may not be able to look back easily if the reference confuses them. Cannot be used at all among Web pages. Take the second example. If a user enters the Web site on a page where Hemingway is only referred to as *Papa*, he/she is likely to have difficulty understanding the content.

continues

Table 4.5 Print Cohesive Ties and Web Content (Continued)

COHESIVE TIES	EXAMPLES	AS APPLIED TO WEB WRITING
Conjunction: When a word is used to connect clauses and sentences together. English has hundreds of words that perform this function.	*consequently* *therefore* *in other words* *on the other hand* *in addition*	Extremely useful for connecting text—sentences and paragraphs—together on a Web page, as long as this type of tie is not overused.
Ellipsis: When the reader is able to presuppose something because of what is left out of the text.	*"Did you go to the store?"* *"No."* (The full, non-ellipsed answer would be "No, I didn't go to the store.")	Ellipsis occurs primarily in dialogue which occurs rarely on information-based Web sites. Use with caution.
Substitution: When the reader understands a word because it is a substitute for something else.	*When buying oranges, make sure you pick out <u>ones</u> that are ripe.*	Can be used within a single sentence, a single paragraph, or in the bullets following a sentence/paragraph. However, use with caution as users who are scrolling may not be able to look back easily if the substitution confuses them.

Source: *An Introduction to Functional Grammar: Second Edition* by M.A.K. Halliday (1994).

- **Language knowledge:** They have prior knowledge of the rules of language, that is, how words come together to make meaning.

- **Background knowledge:** They bring their knowledge of the world based on their personal experiences, education, thoughts, feelings, emotions, and values.

Although all of these types of knowledge contribute to coherence, as a Web writer/editor, you must pay particularly close attention to types of texts and conventions of text, because this knowledge plays a significant role in users' ability to make pre-

Predicting Text

Being able to predict text is based on a phenomenon of language that's called *redundancy* which creates information overlap so that the messages we send
are received appropriately. For example, when you see a
"Q," you know that it is followed by a "u." In essence, the
"u" is redundant. The same thing applies to sentences
and paragraphs. They're filled with redundancies such as
words like "a" and "the," and repetitive elements. We
generally read very quickly—from 200 words a minute up to
600 words, depending on the type of text. We don't look at
all these words, but sample as we go. Redundancy plays
an important role in increasing the capacity of our short
term memory by allowing us to predict what's coming and
not have to read every single word.

**Dr. Alice Horning, Professor of Rhetoric and
Linguistics
Oakland University, Rochester, Michigan**

dictions about what they will be reading. Prediction is as strong a component of coherence as the use of cohesive ties. Remember the problems of the user who clicked on that fictitious Web page, "The Bubble Syndrome"? The annoyance and frustration created by that title were caused by the user's inability to predict where it would lead in terms of useful information. Good content, on the other hand, helps users understand Web genres and conventions.

The Web has been, and will continue to be as it evolves, an environment for new kinds of texts and conventions. Consider all the new forms of reading that have become commonplace in the past few years such as informational sites, online newspapers, e-zines, e-books, chat rooms, ListServs, and newsgroups. The Web has also created certain conventions such as the "Home" page and the "Top of Page" icon and/or text. When developing Web content, you can't take it for granted that users fully understand these kinds of text and conventions. They are too new and too transient. Table 4.6 provides useful strategies for ensuring coherence.

Table 4.6 Tips to Building Online Coherence

ASPECT OF COHERENCE	TIPS
Signals of Predictability	■ Make sure the content clearly explains what the site contains.
	■ Check that navigation information indicates how the site is structured.
	■ Ensure that each Web page reinforces the identity of the site through text, design, and main navigation links.
	■ When making changes to an existing Web site, consider all users—whether previous or new visitors—as first-time readers who must learn the new "signals."
Conventions	■ Help the designer understand that the rules of well-known Web conventions shouldn't be broken. (We have, for example, come across Web text that is underlined, but not a link. We have also worked with a designer who decided that links should be in a different color than the main text, but not underlined. Because Web design research is still relatively new, it will be a long time before conventions are tested, evaluated as efficient, and become so well-established that they no longer can be changed.)
	■ When setting up a new convention, work with the production team to ensure its clarity.

The Small Stuff Counts

As we mentioned earlier, every word you use is a rhetorical choice. This micro-aspect of writing is crucial in Web content development in three areas: microcontent, conjunctions, and the decision to bold or italicize a word/phrase for visual impact.

Make Microcontent Meaningful

Microcontent is a term we use in this book to refer to small bits of text such as titles, headers, and labels. Jakob Neilsen, who coined this term, also uses it to refer to links, but because links have a different function than titles and headers, we don't find

Table 4.7 Web Page Titles as Rhetorical Strategies

HIT/PAGE TITLE	A GOOD RHETORICAL STRATEGY?
Viagra Talk— With Dr. Brian McDonough	Good: Users can immediately understand the purpose of this site—a medical discussion forum about the drug.
Viagra World-Wide	Poor: The title gives no real hint what this site does, which is offer information on sales, information, news links, and discussions about the drug.
Viagra Jokes + Humor Section	Good: We get it!
Consumer Information about Viagra	Poor: This site is hosted by the Food and Drug Administration (FDA) which is, theoretically, the most credible of all information sites about drug issues in the United States. Unfortunately, the only way users can tell who owns this site is if they look at the Web address which begins with *www.fda.gov* and know what *fda* stands for.

it useful to group all these items together in one category. However, we do agree with Neilsen's (1998) comment that microcontent must be "pearls of clarity," because, as we've noted throughout this chapter, Web readers intensely dislike ambiguity. Drive-thru users want to know immediately what the content is about and why they should continue reading. Another reason for creating clear and concise microcontent is that titles can play an important role in how a site appears as a hit on a search engine. Table 4.7 demonstrates how rhetorically effective some Viagra Web pages were when they showed up on the Google search engine.

> Microcontent must be "pearls of clarity."

When considering title choices, it's important to remember that Web search engines are all different, using a variety of criteria for bringing up hits. They are also affected by how a site owner identifies keywords and uses metatags. (In Chapter 8, "Content + Technology: A Surprising Alliance," we discuss how Web writers/editors can help clients make good decisions with regard to titles and keywords so they can achieve more effective search engine results.)

Conjunctions: Those Old Standbys

Good, persuasive argumentation works because it helps readers sort through information. Research shows that readers form hierarchical frameworks, known as schemata, in their minds in order to understand content. They first determine what's the most important bit of information, what comes next, and so on. As part of this cognitive work, readers seek to identify the relationships among items of content. Technical communications researcher Jan Spyridakis (2000:366) notes that: "...studies suggest that the more an author does to order information in ways that will orient readers and help them follow connections, the better off the reader will be."

Traditional rhetorical strategies for building a persuasive argument include:

- The introduction that sets out the topic.
- The discussion that builds the argument through facts, examples, citations, and examples.
- The conclusion that sums up the evidence.

The introduction, discussion, and conclusion are, in turn, made up of facts which are the "meat"of the argument and conjunctive words/phrases, such as *nevertheless* and *on the other hand*, which are the connective "tissue." Conjunctions help readers understand rhetorical relationships—how and why X fact is related to Y fact. For example, here are four such facts:

Conjunctions help users sort through information.

- I eat oranges after dinner.
- Oranges are sweet.
- Apples can be tart.
- Navel oranges are the sweetest.

These facts could be connected in a variety of ways depending on the rhetorical argument that you are presenting. Table 4.8 demonstrates how these facts can be connected through three types of conjunctions and provides you with a good inventory of conjunctions to ensure your text is not overly repetitive.

Not all rhetorical conjunctions work well on the Web because readers don't follow a linear path through pages and are often forced to scroll down a single page to get the information they want. Avoid conjunctions that will cause problems, because they refer back to text that the users can't see or access easily. Such conjunctions include:

- As noted above
- As mentioned on the previous page
- In reference to our earlier discussion
- As we noted earlier

Table 4.8 Useful Rhetorical Conjunctions

RHETORICAL STRATEGY	CONJUNCTIVE WORDS/PHRASES
Elaboration The second sentence/clause further specifies or describes the first. For example: *Oranges are sweet. In fact, navel oranges are the sweetest.*	In other words For example/instance At least Incidentally In any case Actually In particular/fact/short/conclusion
Extension The second sentence/clause extends the meaning of the first by adding something new. For example: *Oranges are sweet. On the other hand, apples can be tart.*	Also Moreover As well In addition However On the other hand/the contrary Instead Alternatively
Enhancement The second sentence/clause qualifies the first by reference to time, place, manner, cause, or condition. For example: *Oranges are sweet. For that reason, I eat oranges after dinner.*	Next Afterwards At the same time Before that Finally Until then Meanwhile At this moment/point Likewise Similarly In a different way Thereby Consequently Therefore As a result For that reason/purpose In that case/event Otherwise Yet Still Despite this Nevertheless In this respect

Source: *An Introduction to Functional Grammar: Second Edition* by M.A.K. Halliday (1994).

To Boldly Go...?

Be cautious when highlighting Web text.

The Web designer generally determines the font type, size, and characteristics for titles, headers, and subheaders. But within the text itself, you, as the writer/editor, will determine if and when words/phrases should be highlighted by bolding or italicizing the font. Given the number of possible visuals on Web screens—icons, navigation bars, graphics, links—it is clear that, if you decide to bold or italicize text, you will have to do so cautiously. Too much and your text will be *screaming* at readers and *fighting* with the other visuals for their attention. On the other hand, little or no bolding or italics may mean that you're missing opportunities to signal important information to users.

So how can you decide when and if text should be bolded or italicized to provide rhetorical clues to readers? The answer lies in the context of your Web site and page. Mindy McAdams, a professor of online journalism, says that: "Bolding online text is like using a yellow highlighter to alert readers to something that could be meaningful to them which they might otherwise miss. It emphasizes or hints at a significant idea within the content." Figure 4.1 is text from one Web page that appeared in an online scholarly article, *Hypertext*, written by McAdams and her collaborator, Stephanie Berger (2001). The authors have chosen to bold certain words and phrases that they feel are important flags for the reader. Take the opportunity to read through it and see if the bolded material enhances your understanding of the text. For an even better analysis of the effect, read the text online at www.press.umich.edu/jep/06-03/McAdams/pages/threads.html.

To Sum It Up

As you research the area of Web content development, you'll discover many rules of thumb. Some rules are general—for example, one such rule suggested by Jakob Neilsen (2000:101-102) is to "write 50 percent less text." Other rules are more specific—a common one is to use more headers. These rules are useful, but our approach is to ask "Why?" every time we come across one. And we feel the answer—that people scan text on the Web because it's hard to read online—is only part of the

A "thread" is a path that the reader follows through an article. A typical written-for-print article has a single thread, from beginning to end, which the writer expects the reader to follow. The construction of this thread lies at the core of the craft of writing.

The **absence of a unilinear thread** marks the most obvious difference between hypertext and the typical printed text. The responsibility of constructing threads remains with the writer, but the writer acknowledges that hypertext form requires multiple threads — not just one.

If the writer provides access to all the components from the very start of the hypertext (by linking them there), and maintains that same complete access in each component, then the reader can construct a thread almost at will — **whatever path the reader takes** will become the thread for that reader.

Making all the components equally available is practical in smaller hypertexts. With a small number of components (six or fewer), the reader can **evaluate** the links to all of them and **choose** one, without too much difficulty. In such a hypertext, all the threads are reader-built threads.

With a larger number of components, the writer must construct a **hierarchy** so that the reader will not be burdened with confusing decisions about where to go next. This hierarchy opens particular pathways (or threads) and closes off others. The possible pathways are author-built threads.

Figure 4.1   An example of bolding within online text.

story. Therefore, the purpose of this chapter has been to help you put those rules of thumb into the larger context of rhetoric and the increasing need for persuasive text in modern society. We hope that understanding this context will help you thoughtfully build your own rhetorical practices and apply the rules in a knowledgeable and effective way.

Resources for This Chapter

Books

Dynamics of Document Design: Creating Texts for Readers by Karen Shriver. Although primarily aimed at developers of print documents, this book highlights rhetorical principles that are relevant to Web development. (John Wiley & Sons: 1997)

Visual Explanations: Images and Quantities, Evidence and Narrative by Edward R. Tufte. A fascinating look at how graphs, charts, and other visuals succeed or fail in convincing readers. (Graphics Press: 1997)

Secrets of User-Seductive Documents: Wooing and Winning the Reluctant Reader by William Horton. Although written for technical communicators, this book has good advice for all Web writers/editors. (Society for Technical Communication: 1997)

Web Wisdom: How to Evaluate and Create Information Quality on the Web by Janet E. Alexander and Marsha Ann Tate. Includes useful checklists for developing and/or evaluating different types of Web sites. (Lawrence Erlbaum Associates, Publishers: 1999)

The Electronic Word: Democracy, Technology, and the Arts by Richard Lanham. Informative and thought-provoking essays about writing, rhetoric, and electronic technologies. (University of Chicago Press: 1993)

The Attention Economy: Understanding the New Currency of Business by Thomas H. Davenport and John C. Beck. Why information delivery and management is crucial in a time when human attention is in such short supply. (Harvard Business School Press: 2001)

Advertising and the World Wide Web edited by David W. Schumann and Esther Thorson. A collection of papers that look at persuasive text from the point of view of advertising and promotion. (Lawrence Erlbaum Associates, Publishers: 1999)

Web Sites

Thesaurus.com (www.thesaurus.com). An excellent resource for finding alternative words. Also includes useful links to grammar and writing resources.

Plain Language Network (204.254.113.22). Provides information and links about improving communications from government to the public.

A Glossary of Literary Terms and a Handbook of Rhetorical Devices (www.uky.edu/AS/Classics/Harris/rhetform.html). A database of terminology and definitions as well as an introduction and self-test.

Silva Rhetoricae (humanities.byu.edu/rhetoric/silva.htm). An overview of the history of rhetoric plus a list of rhetorical terms.

American Communication Association (www.uark.edu/~aca/index.html). A virtual professional association for practitioners and academics with many articles and useful links to other resources. Membership is free.

Endnotes

1. This summary of print cohesive ties is based on the work of linguist, Michael K. Halliday who developed a new way to think about grammar. Until his work, formal grammars focused on how words fit correctly within clauses and sentences, regardless of when and how people *used* those clauses and sentences. Halliday's theory of systemic functional grammar took an entirely new approach, examining how words function within clauses and sentences to create meaning as people use them within the context of social situations.

CHAPTER 5

Is Seeing Believing?
The Art of Visual Rhetoric

What's Inside:

- How to build your "visual" vocabulary
- Visuals and human perception
- Images and icons
- Interaction between visuals and text
- Design tips from designers

There are painters who transform the sun into a yellow spot,
but there are others who, thanks to their art and intelligence,
transform a yellow spot into the sun.

PABLO PICASSO

Visual design is as important as text in creating persuasive Web sites. Whereas text depends on the credibility, conciseness, clarity and coherence of words as rhetorical tools, Web design relies on creating a consistent and coherent look-and-feel. However, it's important to remember that text and visuals don't exist separately from one another. Rather, they must work together rhetorically in what information designer Robert Horn (1999:27) calls *visual language:*

> Visual language is defined as the tight coupling of words, images, and shapes into a unified communication unit. "Tight coupling" means that you cannot remove the words or the images or the shapes from a piece of visual language without destroying or radically diminishing the meaning a reader can obtain from it.

The rhetoric of online visual language, within the constraints of technology, should represent the site's identity and goals, and work to ensure that the drive-thru reader will stop long enough

Visuals and text work together rhetorically.

to find out what the site has to offer. As Web design specialist Patrick Lynch (2000b) notes: "A strong and consistent enterprise identity can aid in establishing or legitimizing institutions, creating trust and authority. All long-lasting forms of group identity must be ritualized and symbolized, with titles, graphics, customs and other visual and functional evidence of social cohesion and purpose."

The area of visual rhetoric falls within the expertise of the Web designer. However, most graphic designers are facing the same problems as professional writers/editors in adapting print-based skills to a Web environment. As professor of communications design Katherine McCoy (1999:8) says: "Most of the pioneering graphic designers who specialize in new media today have had to acquire this knowledge informally, largely through trial and error, in the context of professional design practice." For designers, this means trying to create pleasing aesthetic experiences within the limitations posed by the computer environment. Visual designers Kevin Mullet and Darrell Sano (1995:11) describe it this way:

> Good design defuses the tension between functional and aesthetic goals precisely because it works within the boundaries defined by the functional requirements of the communications problem. Unlike the fine arts, which exists for their own sake, design must always solve a particular real-world problem. Functional criteria govern the range of possibilities that can be explored; aesthetic possibilities that are not compatible with this minimum standard of usability must be quickly discarded, if they are considered at all.

Figure 5.1 demonstrates the difficulties that graphic designers face in creating effective graphical user interfaces (GUIs) for the Web.

As part of the Web production team, you'll find yourself interacting with a designer(s) on a regular basis. The client and/or designer may want your opinion on design, or you may not like the way a design affects text, or you may have a design idea that you think would be effective. In any case, the more you understand how visuals act rhetorically, the more valuable you'll be to the production team.

It's also useful when thinking about design to consider the quality of graphics on the Web site, such as photographs, clip art, and illustrations. Low-quality artwork has the same adverse effect on credibility as text presentation that has typos, grammatical mistakes, spacing inconsistencies, and spelling errors. High-quality visuals suggest a commitment to excellence that contributes to strong credibility.

The Web Design Challenge

Trial-and-error learning

+

Functionality versus aesthetic appeal

+

Constantly changing technologies

+

User/client needs

Constant experimentation
with no right or wrong answers.

Figure 5.1 Web design is in a state of constant experimentation with no right or wrong answers.

We can't cover the vast scope of design and graphics issues regarding the Web in this book. Nor is it our intent to analyze in this chapter the integration of audio, video, and animation as part of a site's multiple media mix. If you want to explore these areas of specialization, you'll find many books, both academic and professional, on these topics. Rather, our intention is to provide you with different frameworks to think about how people perceive and react to visuals, specifically graphical images and how they are arranged and displayed. As a result, you'll have words for talking about design that extend far beyond: "It just doesn't appeal to me"—a statement that won't help either the client or designer on your production team. At the end of the chapter, we also provide you with a table of useful graphical tips culled from our work and readings on Web design.

> You need a "visuals" vocabulary.

"A Picture Is Worth a Thousand Words"

In Chapter 2, we noted that seeing is an innate skill that enabled our species to survive. We know how to look at something and grasp what it's about in a glance. Text, on the other hand, is not something we can decipher immediately. We have to read it first. Information designer Yvonne Hansen (1999:204) explains why "A picture is worth a thousand words":

> The advantage of fusing graphics along with words and phrases is being able to see relationships and structure among the data that are obscured in a text-only situation. Detecting patterns, which are visual phenomena, in a field of text is virtually impossible. In addition, reading and analyzing page upon page of text requires a powerful memory and the ability to absorb, store, categorize, and retrieve information. However, when information is presented in graphic form and concepts are given shape, relationships among the various elements are easier to see. And, as the graphic representation is further enriched with visual information, long-term memory is triggered and even more information and perceptions can be added, enabling viewers and oneself to detect new patterns, processes, and other phenomena.

Communicating through visuals is an economically efficient way to get messages across to users, particularly on the Web where screen real estate is at a minimum. The problem is, however, that although we can all agree about the subject of an image, that is, it's a house, a landscape, an animal, and so on, our individual perceptions about that image may be very different.

What Is an Image?

Online graphic visuals—color, background, icons, illustrations, and photographs—are powerful tools for communicating with users and equal to text in delivering persuasive messages. McCoy says that visuals can act on their own or interact with text, supporting, enhancing, or detracting from it. Visuals can underscore a particular message or provide a counterpoint to it, thereby creating new meaning beyond what is in the text. "Images are visual words," she notes, "and visual communications is a tightrope act between the visual and the verbal."

An image is an icon, index, or symbol.

McCoy points out that all images—from those found in comic strips to those in photography—fall into one of three categories: iconic, indexical, or symbolic.[1]

The Image as Icon

An image is iconic if it bears a similarity or resemblance to what we already know or conceive about an object.[2] For example, a map, painting, and photograph are icons. A familiar icon on the Web, shown in Figure 5.2, is the house on a navigational bar as a link to the site's home page.

Figure 5.2   The image as an icon.

The Image as Index

The indexical image is recognizable, not because of any similarity to an object or person, but because we understand the relationship between the image and the concept that it stands for. A weathervane, for example, has no resemblance to any aspect of weather, yet it stands for the concept of wind. A standard Web indexical image is the upward-pointing arrow on a scrollable page. Indexical images are often only understood within a cultural context. As Figure 5.3 demonstrates, some indexical images may require text in order to make them more understandable to a variety of audiences. In this case, the two pens holding hands is not sufficient to explain that the image stands for penpals.

The Image as Symbol

In this case, the image has no visual or conceptual connection to an object or person. We only know the meaning of the image because of convention, that is, it's something that we've learned.

Figure 5.3   The image as an index.

Indexical Signs and Deduction

I think of indexical signs as the Sherlock Holmes class of signs, because deductive reasoning and life experience can help you figure out a great deal of information. For instance, a plume of smoke means fire near its base. A footprint in the sand is the effect of a foot landing there. With a basic amount of cognition, you can tell the direction of the walker, as well as his or her relative size and if he/she were walking or running. It takes more life experience to know that measles' blisters indicate the presence of a disease, and some education to know that it would show up in a blood sample under a microscope. And you'd have to live in a certain geographical location to know that rust on a used car in Los Angeles indicates that it has been in the upper Midwest or Northeast, where they use salt on the roads. There's always a strong cause-and-effect relationship between the indexical sign and its meaning.

Katherine McCoy, Designer and Lecturer
High Ground Tools and Strategies for Design
www.highgrounddesign.com

A word, for example, is a symbol because it doesn't resemble what it stands for, nor does it have any relationship to what it signifies. Take the word *rose*. It doesn't look like a rose or bear any relationship to the concept of a rose. A standard Web symbol, shown in Figure 5.4, is the line beneath a word or phrase used to indicate a link.

Images, whether iconic, indexical, or symbolic, help users in the cognitive processing of information. Human-computer interaction researchers Eric Wiebe and Julie Howe (1998:226) say that images: "...can increase the size of the information chunk to be processed: The same [mental] resources used to process a single sentence of a paragraph can be used to process a graphic that

This is a link

Figure 5.4   The line beneath the word is an image as symbol.

Table 5.1 Seeing Versus Reading

SEEING IMAGES	READING TEXT
Visual	Verbal
Intuitive	Rational
Holistic	Linear
Simultaneous	Sequential
Experimental	Intellectual
Right brain	Left brain

Source: Katherine McCoy, 2001.

summarizes the entire paragraph." However, as Table 5.1 demonstrates, we process images differently than we process text.

It's also important to understand that our minds sometimes *read* images and *see* text. McCoy notes that we tend to *read* visual codes such as icons, indexes, and symbols in much the same way that we read text. And, we also tend to *see* text first as graphical images. This is significant for Web writing/editing when you consider how quickly users run their eye over a Web page trying to decide if they want to stay or leave. They're not reading the text at this point, but viewing the text as an image and getting an holistic impression of it. They *experience* it in a quick glance. Short chunks of text, supported by headers and surrounded by white space, will have a different visual impact than large chunks of text without breaks. How users feel about text from a graphical point of view, particularly in an environment that causes quick eye fatigue, has a strong effect on their willingness to shift from seeing it as a graphic to reading it as a text.

What Do We Really See?

Although the ability to see is innate, each user reacts to graphics differently. Visual communications and advertising researcher Ann Marie Barry explains that what we see as individuals varies significantly because of our individual needs and experiences. At the same time, there are significant and deep similarities in the way we respond to visuals. Barry says that each act of perception involves four elements:

- **Visual stimuli:** First, we receive visual stimuli from our environment, initiating the process of perception.

- **A gut-level reaction:** We become aware of the perceptual process as an immediate emotional response to the visual stimuli, according to basic perceptual laws developed through brain evolution. In essence, self-preservation makes us look for patterns that help us understand how the world works, and these patterns then serve as maps to understand new stimuli and events. For example, certain colors, shapes, and even facial expressions are pan-cultural and universally understood because they're so deeply rooted in our evolutionary psyche. Researchers in this field have shown, for example, that similar patterns in facial expressions reveal the same basic emotions across cultures. And visual experts point to the ability of basic shapes to evoke emotional states, such as a diagonal or triangular shape to create tension and movement, a square to suggest stability, and a circle to create a sense of security and community.

- **Reactions based on our current needs:** What we want or need at the moment also affects how we see. If, for example, we've decided to purchase a new piece of clothing, fashion pictures will take on more conscious significance than usual, but we may also be more susceptible to fashion images if we're anxious about our social position. When we purchase advertised products, we use their advertising images to *re-advertise* to others who we are and which groups we are part of.

- **The ongoing development of mental templates based on our past experiences and memories:** These templates are the result of emotional learning built by past social and cultural experiences, and they're etched more deeply each time we see an image and fit it into its appropriate context. This etching is not conscious on our part. It's an unconscious process that results in the feeling that something we've seen feels right or not, depending on the exactness of its fit into these templates. Different images, therefore, have different cultural, and even generational, impacts.

These templates are extremely powerful in the overall process of perception. For example, the appropriate body shape for women in Western society has been determined, not by any rational principles, but by the continual re-etching of our mental templates through the portrayal of women in

> Each of us "sees" differently.

various media. Barry (2001) describes the evolution of this template:

- **1965:** British model Lesley Hornby, known as Twiggy, was ridiculed by the American edition of *Vogue* for her thinness and lack of feminine shape. She was five feet, seven inches tall and weighed 92 pounds.

- **1967:** By now, Twiggy had taken the international fashion world by storm and provided a role model for a new generation of young women who began to starve themselves in ever-increasing numbers.

- **1980:** The term *anorexia nervosa* first made its appearance in the American Psychological Association's *Diagnostic and Statistical Manual* (DSMII), which recognizes psychiatric disorders.

- **1984:** A *Glamour* magazine survey reported that 75 percent of respondents between 18 and 35 years of age believed they were fat, while only 25 percent actually were overweight. Significantly, 45 percent of women who were underweight still believed they were too fat.

- **1987:** The average fashion model reportedly weighed 23 percent less than the average American woman.

- **1996:** A study of 2,379 preadolescent girls by the National Heart, Lung and Blood Institute found that 49 percent of nine- and ten-year-old girls were trying to lose weight.

- **Today:** Eating disorders are more rife than ever before and, in the United States and Great Britain, anorexia has the highest death rate of any mental illness.

Don't Let Gestalt Get You Down

When you become involved in Web design issues, you may begin to hear about Gestalt theory without getting a clear idea what it's about. Essentially, Gestalt is a general psychological theory, developed in the late 1890s and early 1900s, that described the whole of anything as greater than its parts. This theory evolved in reaction to other psychological movements of the time that attempted to analyze mental experiences in a piecemeal fashion, that is, separate from their context and broader meaning for the individual. As psychologist Peter Grey

The Emotional Basis of Perception

We're all victims of perception. The way our brains respond initially to an image is based on primitive, neurologically based perceptual laws that establish unconscious attitudes and motivate action. Essentially, we acquire visual wisdom about what's "right" and "wrong" from an emotional base, rather than a rational one. This means that to work most effectively, designers must develop an understanding of how people receive information below the surface of awareness, and learn to integrate the whole design into a coherent and psychologically appropriate pattern, rather than to merely "decorate" with particulars. A novice designer might add colors simply because they are personally appealing or because they are trendy, instead of analyzing the underlying psychological impact of those colors in relation to a design or marketing function.

A red context, for example, excites us and makes time seem to slow down; a blue context keeps us calmer and less aware of time passing. Large amounts of white space immediately upscale a product, while clutter will downscale it considerably. I suspect that the great visual artists have always understood how the brain works by sensing their own emotional responses to the subtleties of shape, lighting, color, texture, and space. They seem to know instinctually how to use visual elements to create the impact of a whispered "Listen!" around their commercial products, fine art works, and environmental designs.

Dr. Ann Marie Barry, Professor of Visual Communications Boston College, Chestnut Hill, Massachusetts

explains (as quoted in Moore and Fitz, 1993:138) the basic premise of Gestalt psychology:

> ...was that the mind must be understood in terms of organized wholes, not elementary parts. A melody is not the sum of its individual notes, a painting is not the sum of the individual dots of paint, an idea is not the sum of elementary concepts that make up the idea. The meaningful units of consciousness are whole, organized constructs—whole melodies, whole scenes, whole ideas—that cannot be understood by analyzing elementary judgments and sensations.

The Gestalt Principles

Gestalt psychological theory had a major influence on the study of human perception. When applied to art and design, Gestalt theorists emphasized the overall structure or pattern as the primary way we perceive form. Human-computer interaction researchers William Marks and Cynthia Dulaney (1998:32) explain that: "In processing visual displays, some aspects are perceived as figure, or that which is attended to, and other aspects are considered background, or that which is unattended to. Several principles of organization facilitate processing the components of a visual display into meaningful figures or units." The Gestalt principles are *figure-ground segregation*, *proximity*, *similarity*, *continuity*, and *closure*.

> Gestalt principles explain some visual reactions.

Figure-Ground Segregation

We always perceive visual objects against a background. In other words, without an existing background, we wouldn't be able to perceive an object. Figure 5.5 plays with our perceptions of figure-ground segregation by creating two different visuals. Either we perceive the image to be two faces looking at one another against a white background, or a vase with handles against a black background.

A secondary principle of figure-background segregation is that of *area*. As Figure 5.6 demonstrates, when two figures overlap, we see the smaller as the figure with the larger as the background.

Figure 5.5   The Gestalt principle of figure-ground segregation.

Figure 5.6   The Gestalt principle of area and figure-ground segregation.

This is a smiley face.

Figure 5.7 The Gestalt principle of proximity.

Proximity

We perceive visual objects closest together as a group, even if such objects are not similar in shape or function. Figure 5.7, an emoticon, appears as a smiley face because its individual objects —the colon, dash, and bracket—are together and separated from the rest of the words in the sentence by spaces.

Why we perceive this group of items as a *face* doesn't have anything to do with Gestalt principles. Cartoonist Scott McCloud (1993) has an interesting theory that we, as human beings, are so inclined to make the world over in our own image, that we can't avoid seeing faces in any object whose elements could be interpreted as facial. For example, even an object as seemingly unambiguous as a wall socket has three plug holes configured in such a way that they can be construed as eyes and a mouth.[3]

Similarity

We perceive visual objects that appear alike in terms of form, size, color, and so on as a group of objects that belong together. Objects that don't fit within the grouping will be seen as separate entities. In Figure 5.8, we see two different groups of boxes because of the size difference between them.

Continuity

We perceive visual objects that continue a pattern or direction to be grouped together as part of the same pattern. For example, in Figure 5.9, we see the object as two lines crossing rather than four lines meeting at the center.

Figure 5.8 The Gestalt principle of similarity.

Figure 5.9   The Gestalt principle of continuity.

Closure

If we see an object that is not a complete shape, we attempt to organize that object into a closed structure. For example, in Figure 5.10, we see the object as a circle rather than two independent brackets.

How You Can Help

As Barry says, "The Gestalt principles are hard-wired into our brains." This means that when a Web design violates these principles, it adversely affects what the site is trying to communicate. Instructional designer Bonnie Skaalid puts it this way: "The Gestalt principles help people focus in a holistic way that can't be divorced from usability." Knowing the Gestalt principles may help you understand why you react to a visual in a negative way. For example, in most projects, a designer will provide several different concepts for the look-and-feel of the graphical user interface (GUI). Figure 5.11 is a replication of one such concept that we encountered during a project.

We found that this design forced us to look left to the monitor screen away from the content, rather than back towards the center where the text was contained. Essentially, the arrow shape was forcing our eyes left because of the Gestalt principle of continuity. According to this principle, we're compelled to visually follow the vector of an object, even beyond the boundaries of that object.

Figure 5.10   The Gestalt principle of closure.

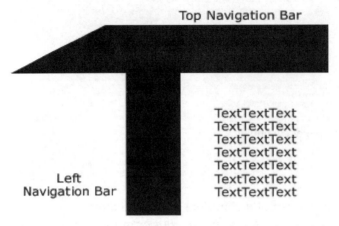

Figure 5.11 A GUI design that misuses the Gestalt principle of continuity.

Knowledge of this principle gave us the vocabulary to explain to the client why we felt this GUI concept design wasn't as appropriate as others the designer had provided.

The Psychology of Art

Vision and perception are different.

Rudolf Arnheim, building on the tradition of Gestalt psychology, was one of the most important researchers to promote a psychological approach to perception and aesthetics. Working after World War II, he made a major contribution to understanding art by separating the concept of "seeing" from that of "perceiving." In doing so, he set forth a number of principles that are useful in understanding how we react to Web design and navigation.

Perception as Cognition

We are not passive receivers of a visual scene, but actively work to perceive what is before us. As Arnheim (1969:15) says: "The world emerging from this perceptual exploration is not immediately given. Some of its aspects build up fast, some slowly, all of them are subject to continued confirmation, reappraisal, change, completion, correction, deepening of understanding." For most of our visual experiences, perception as cognition happens unconsciously, or we would spend an inordinate amount of time just thinking about what we are seeing. However, if you've ever sat before the "Home" page of a poorly designed Web site, trying to conceptualize what it is all about, you've experienced the interaction of perception and cognition in a conscious and likely painful and/or frustrating way.

Richard Johnson-Sheehan, a researcher of language and rhetoric, and Craig Baehr, a technical writer and Web page designer (2001:22) compare the cognitive issues of reading text in print versus on the Web: "…the basic linearity of the text defines how users conceptualize their place in the document. They still see themselves somewhere on a line between the beginning of the text and the end. In contrast, hypertexts urge users to think visually as they orient themselves in the text-space and determine where they might travel in the site." As a new medium, the Web presents users with new cognitive challenges that they must face in order to achieve their information goals.

Vision Is Selective

Arnheim (1969:20) reminds us that our eyesight evolved as a biological necessity for survival and, for this reason, it wouldn't be functional for us to focus on everything in our visual field with equal concentration. Rather, we focus only on select items that are meaningful to us—primarily things that change in our environment. "When something appears or disappears, moves from one place to another, changes its shape or size or color or brightness, the observing person or animal may find his own condition altered: an enemy approaching, an opportunity changing, a demand to be met, a signal to be obeyed." However, if change is repetitious, we lose interest in it—again a biological aid. We've figured it out and are ready to move on to the next interesting visual item.

> Motion and change attract the eye.

To take advantage of our selective vision, Johnson-Sheehan and Baehr (2001:24) suggest that: "Any changes on the screen should reflect new information [which] should appear in predictable places on the screen…" In other words, altering navigation design so that changes occur in different places detracts significantly from usability. As well, our selective vision explains why users become bored and irritated by repetitive on-screen movements such as those found in Web site animation, banners, and *screen candy*—often images with one continually moving part and pop-ups that appear and disappear.

Fixation Solves a Problem

Arnheim (1969:23-26) notes that the human species, which is at a "biologically higher level" than other species, has a greater ability to choose stimuli and react to them. These choices reflect the cognitive behavior of problem-solving because it allows us to determine our visual focus: on what, where, and how long. Although the field of our acute vision is limited to a narrow area, he notes that: "This limitation, far from being a handicap, protects the mind from being swamped with more information than it can, or needs to, handle at any one time. It facilitates the intelligent practice of concentrating on some topic of interest and neglecting what is beside the point of attention."

Users arrive at a Web screen, seeking answers to information problems. Arnheim's (1969:35) description of how a viewer approaches a work of art is applicable to how they approach the look-and-feel of a Web site:

> ...the observer starts from somewhere, tries to orient himself as to the main skeleton of the work, looks for accents, experiments with a tentative framework in order to see whether it fits the total content, and so on. When the exploration is successful, the work is seen to repose comfortably in a congenial structure, which illuminates the work's meaning to the observer.

This concept—that a viewer can have a successful exploration of a work of art—applies to a user's exploration of a Web site. A GUI that we call *intuitive* is one that allows us to immediately grasp the meaning and overall information structure of the site without a struggle of comprehension. The rhetorical goals of Web design must be to facilitate, not hinder, this process. For example, very cluttered design makes it difficult for viewers to concentrate on any one item. On the other hand, design that is too spare means that users may not have enough information to understand what the site is about and, also, may decide that the site doesn't supply enough information. This issue regarding Web design is beginning to be a major part of usability testing and research.

Discernment in Depth

Focus reflects visual choice.

When our eyes fixate on an object, our field of focus is very narrow. If we're looking at something close-up, the background is blurry. If we look at the background, closer items become blurry. As we focus, we make choices about what is relevant to us. However, as Arnheim (1969:27) states: "This strategy of thought may be hampered at its very foundation when the visual range of the situation to be contemplated is incorrectly chosen...Since reasoning about an object starts with the way the object is perceived, an inadequate percept may upset the ensuing train of thought." Consider what happens when you arrive at a Web site. Suppose you focus on a visual first. Everything around it will disappear from your vision as you stare at it. What happens if you can't figure out what it means? Or if it sets you on the wrong track of thought? Would you stay? Chances are, you'd act like most drive-thru readers and leave immediately, searching for some other site where the information will have more clarity.

In Chapter 4, we discussed text from the IRS Web page, "Tax Info For You." Figure 5.12 shows the first screen of that Web page. Notice the graphic items at the top: a tabletop jukebox and a blender. How precisely are these objects connected to the United States federal income tax? What do they have to do with taxpayers? What do they have to do with one another? The text in the top banner:: "We'll help you select what you need. And you won't get mixed up in the process," verbally sets up two obscure visual-conceptual relationships: 1) choosing music from a jukebox with selecting the right tax forms, and 2) mixing food in a blender with not getting mixed up while filing taxes. The choice of objects in this figure creates rhetorical confusion in meaning and a resulting lack of clarity between design and text that is, unfortunately, not uncommon on the Web.

Shapes Are Concepts

Arnheim (1969:27) says that we define the shape of an object based on the concept of the shape that we hold in our mind, as opposed to the actual object itself. "The full moon is indeed round, to the best of our viewing powers. But most of the things we see as round do not embody roundness literally; they are mere approximations." In other words, as we view objects, we

Figure 5.12 What happens when the choice of objects doesn't rhetorically enhance text. ?

March 30, 2001 (www.irs/gov/ind_info/index.html)

fit them to mental templates that make it easy for us to identify and classify them. Johnson-Sheehan and Baehr (2001:26) describe good visual rhetorical strategies with regard to shapes on the Web:

> On the screen, visual elements should be simple, consistently used, and familiar. Strange or unfamiliar shapes will slow the users' reading process down considerably, because the users will either 1) need to reform these abnormal shapes into pre-established conceptual categories, or 2) create a new conceptual category into which they can place the unfamiliar shape. To help the user be more efficient, simple and consistent shapes should dominate the design. Strange shapes should be used only when the designer *wants* the users to slow down.

Consistency in shapes and other design features is often a problem on both the Internet and Intranet sites of large organizations where there is no centralized Web team, and different departments publish independently of one another. The result can often be chaotic and disorienting for users.

Perception Takes Time

As we noted earlier, people "read" graphical images. Arnheim says that, although we can see by instinct, perception is a learned skill, developed through time and based on our cultural, educational, and personal experiences. Arnheim (1969:31) notes that: "What is rational for one group, will be irrational for another, i.e., it cannot be grasped, understood, compared or remembered." Graphic design expert and architect Roger Whitehouse (1999:107) provides an example of a cultural difference that demonstrates this principle:

Perception is cultural.

> In Western culture the environment abounds in straight, and frequently parallel lines: the facades of buildings, streets and sidewalks, railroad tracks—our world is constructed of beams, blanks, and panels whose very essence is to be parallel. Moreover, an environment of parallel lines is one rich in natural perspective—the lines of the curb, street, or highway converge toward a point on the horizon.

> People in other cultures, such as the Zulu of Africa, see far fewer straight lines. Linear perspective is rarely experienced and so is typically not a developed attribute of their perception. Instead, they inhabit a landscape of plains, hills, and meandering rivers inhabited by trees and animals. Their immediate environment is of circular huts, pots, and baskets. Instead of the linear perspective

with which we are familiar, they inhabit a free-form world of organic shapes. As a result, their perceptual experiences tells them, size is the clue to distance; perspective is of little consequence.

When given distortion-illusion tests, the Zulu react only slightly to the effects of perspective. By contrast, in industrially developed cultures, the effects of perspective very strongly affect our perception.

Such cultural differences have important implications for clients who want their Web sites to reach a global audience. (See Chapter 9, "Keep CALM: Content and Logical Management" for an in-depth discussion of Web development and international audiences.)

How You Can Help

It's important to realize that, if you're having difficulties with the look-and-feel of a site, the problem isn't necessarily you. It's very likely that other users may encounter the same problems. Here are some suggestions for working with your production team to enhance the site's visual rhetorics based on Arnheim's principles:

- Work with the designers to ensure that major design elements remain consistent throughout the site.

- If the site isn't intuitive for you, ask the production team to consider the design from Arnheim's principle that fixation solves problems, that is, the user will study the look-and-feel with a goal in mind. This may help focus the team on user needs and get an arm's length distance from the novelty, imaginative, or creative elements of the Web page design to which team members may have become attached.

- Discuss usability issues with regard to visuals such as banners and repetitive animation. See if the team can develop alternative design strategies.

- Try to make the subject of illustrations, photographs, mouse roll-overs, and other visual highlights such as color changes and distinguishing lines part of team discussions. Ask questions such as:
  - Are these elements as appropriate as they could be?
  - Do these elements enhance the text or detract from it?
  - How long will it take users to download these elements?

- Will these elements work in the two most commonly used browsers, Internet Explorer and Netscape?

- Will users understand what they mean at a quick glance or will they have to spend time figuring them out? What will happen if they're not immediately comprehensible?

- Have we taken into consideration accessibility and cultural issues? (For more information on these topics, see Chapter 9, "Keep CALM: Content and Logical Management.")

- Are there other choices we could make that would be more effective?

Visual Semio-What?

Current researchers of culture, noting the increasing use of visuals in all forms of media—from more photographs in newspapers to multimedia on the Web, believe that viewers need to be more critically aware of how and why images are produced, and the ways they affect us, emotionally and cognitively. Barry (1997:6), pointing to the use of digitized images which can be easily manipulated, says : "Today, so ubiquitous is the impact of the visual on our lives, so dire are the consequences of actually believing what we see, that even visual 'literacy'—with its sense of simply understanding what we see and being able to converse in a similar language—is not enough."

How, then, can viewers be more visually literate? In Chapter 2, we discussed a field of research, known as social semiotics, that explores how people make meaning out of the language, actions, and objects in their lives. In the past, social semioticians focused their analyses on language in documents and conversation. During the 1990s, the increasing use of multiple media in print and on the Web led a number of researchers to study visual semiotics in order to develop a theoretical framework that would explain how images interact with print to make meaning in social and cultural contexts. Discourse analysts Gunther Kress and Theo van Leeuwen (1996) provide one such framework that describes how people react to visuals in Western cultures.

> An image's meaning reflects its cultural context.

The Image Act

The next time you look at an illustration, photograph, or painting, examine the participants in it and ask: Where are the participants in an image looking? At each other, into the distance, directly at the viewer? And how do these different portrayals affect me? According to Kress and van Leeuwen (1996:122-125), there are two types of image acts.

- **Demand:** When the participant in an image looks directly at the viewer, that is, "a visual form of direct address."

- **Offer:** When the participant looks elsewhere, either outside the picture or at another participant in the image.

Figure 5.13 is an example of a visual *demand*. It's a photograph on a prototype Web site we developed for SEVEC Youth Exchanges Canada to help teachers and others organize home-stay exchanges for young people. Note how the participants in the photograph are looking directly at the user. When this occurs, Kress and van Leeuwen (1996:122) say that the producer of the image "uses the image to *do* something to the viewer...the participant's gaze...demands something from the viewer, demands that the viewer enter into some kind of imaginary relation with him or her."

Also, notice the happy smiles on the faces of the participants in Figure 5.13. Put yourself in the place of a teacher or other orga-nizer. How would those smiles make you feel about this organi-zation? As one that would help you create happy, successful experiences for your students? The use of smiles and other expressions as well as gestures in an image are visual rhetorical

Figure 5.13 The image act as a demand.

Copyright SEVEC Youth Exchanges Canada 2001. Published with permission.

strategies. Kress and van Leeuwen (1996:122-123) describe it this way:

> [Participants] may smile, in which case the viewer is asked to enter into a relation of social affinity with them; they may stare at the viewer with cold disdain, in which case the viewer is asked to relate to them, perhaps, as an inferior relates to a superior; they may seductively pout at the viewer, in which case the viewer is asked to desire them. The same applies to gestures. A hand can point at the viewer in a visual "Hey, you there, I mean you", or invite the viewer to come closer, or hold the viewer at bay with a defensive gesture, as if to say: stay away from me. In each case the image wants something from the viewers—wants them to do something (come closer, stay at a distance) or to form a pseudo-social bond of a particular kind with the represented participant.

Visual *offers*, on the other hand, provide users with objects to contemplate in an impersonal manner. Figure 5.14, a page from the Web site of the U.S. National Parks Service (NPS), is about United States history. Note how every object in the photographic collage is like a specimen in a museum display case, including the human face whose eyes are looking somewhere else. The designer created this collage to reinforce NPS's public image as the collector and protector of the American past. He or she didn't

Figure 5.14 The image act as an offer.
June 13, 2001 (www.recreation.gov)

want any particular item to be more important than another. Had the face demonstrated a demand, it would have dominated the image, pushing the other items into the background.

Social Distance

Every one of us has a sense of personal space around our bodies that is, generally, culturally determined. If someone, usually not an intimate, steps too close, we feel uncomfortable because that person has, as we say, "invaded our personal space." In visual media, personal space is determined by how the producer uses close-ups, medium shots, and long shots of participants. (This camera terminology is applicable to techniques in drawing and painting.) The field of study that analyzes how spatial distances between individuals affect their behavior, culturally and cognitively, is called *proxemics*, a term coined by Edward Hall (1966). According to the theory of proxemics, we can "feel" personal space in images.

> Social distance is about intimacy.

- **Intimate distance:** We can see the head and face only.
- **Close personal distance:** We can see the head and shoulders.
- **Far personal distance:** We can see participants from the waist up.
- **Close social distance:** We can see the whole figure.
- **Far social distance:** We see the whole figure with space around it.
- **Public distance:** We see torsos of several people.

Kress and van Leeuwen (1996:133) use proxemics to describe how we react to participants in images with respect to how close or far away they seem to us. "The relation between the human participants represented in images and the viewer is once again an imaginary relation. People are portrayed as *though* they are friends, or as *though* they are strangers."

Look at the three people in Figure 5.15, a page from a U.S. government site about nutrition. You can see everyone, roughly, from the torso up. There is space around the figures and, if this group of people wasn't designed to seem like a family, the image could almost be described as a small crowd shot.

All three participants are at a public distance. Also, notice that not one of the participants is making a visual demand. In fact, the closest figure, the boy, is looking down so you can't even see his face. This Web site is about good nutrition for all Americans,

Lifecycle
Issues

Figure 5.15 The figures are at a public, arm's length distance from the viewer.
June 13, 2001 (www.nutrition.gov)

and the producer of the image wants you to view this group of people as representative. If you got too close to, or too involved with, the image's participants, you might begin to see them as individuals who don't represent you at all. Although we consider this photograph to be a poor choice because, in fact, it portrays only a white, middle-class group, its "public distance" does support the rhetorical strategy of the site.

Perspective and Angles

Perspective represents the image-maker's point of view with regard to the overall image. Kress and van Leeuwen (1996:135-139) note that, prior to the Renaissance, art works were generally part of locations such as frescoes or mosaics in a church. Such images did not have a single, centralized viewpoint, but were tied to their environment. It wasn't until an artwork became:

> ...an autonomous object, detached from its surroundings, movable, produced for an impersonal market [that]...a frame began to separate the represented world from the physical space in which the image was viewed: at this time perspective was developed, pictures began to be framed precisely to create this division, to mark off the image from its environment, and turn it into a kind of "window on the world".

Figure 5.16 is an example of the image of a house drawn *without* perspective. Figure 5.17 is an image of a house drawn *with* per-

Figure 5.16 An image without perspective.

Figure 5.17 An image with perspective.

spective. In the latter, the producer uses three-dimensional depth to accentuate certain features of the house and make it, overall, a much more engaging picture.

Perspective enables image-makers to make rhetorical choices about what to highlight within an image and what to play down. By doing so, they impose upon us their view of the world. Figure 5.18 is the main page of the U.S. Supreme Court's Web site. The photograph of the Supreme Court building is taken from an ant's-eye perspective. It allows the photographer

> Perspective reflects point of view.

Figure 5.18 Glorifying the U.S. Supreme Court through perspective.
June 2, 2001 (www.supremecourtus.gov)

to glorify the Court by emphasizing the grandeur of its architecture and its classical elegance. Note, for example, how the perspective elongates the columns and makes the portico more imposing. As well, the photograph places the building at a high vertical angle from the viewer so that we must look up at it—a statement about the pre-eminent power of the Court. (For more information on the depiction of power in images, see *Vertical Angles and Power* later in this chapter.)

It's important to remember that the producer of this Web page had other photographic choices. For example, we could have seen the Court from a bird's-eye viewpoint, putting it within the context of its surroundings and giving us the higher angle. Or we could have had a photograph of the building taken on its steps so that we would be looking toward the interior—more of a medium angle that would imply some equality between citizens and the judicial system.

Horizontal Angles and Involvement

The horizontal angle is one in which the image-maker manipulates the frontal view of an object so that we see it directly facing us or at an oblique angle to us. Kress and van Leeuwen (1996:143) say that these different horizontal angles affect the viewer's relationship to the participants in an image. "The horizontal angle encodes whether or not the image-producer (and hence, willy-nilly, the viewer) is 'involved' with the represented participants or not."

- **The frontal view creates involvement.** "The frontal angle says, as it were: 'what you see here is part of our world, something we are involved with.'" In other words, the person in the image becomes one of us. In Figure 5.13, the participants in the SEVEC group are in frontal view. When you add that angle to the demand presented by the image act and their happy smiles, you receive a strong invitation to become part of the experience of that group.

- **The oblique view creates detachment.** "The oblique angle says: 'what you see here is not a part of our world; it is their world, something we are not involved with.'" In other words, the person in the image becomes another or in a group of others. Figure 5.19 shows the use of oblique horizontal angles to separate us, the viewers, from the intimacy of the couple in the image.

Figure 5.19   Oblique horizontal angles exclude the viewer.

It's important to consider, when analyzing the horizontal angle, how it can interact in interesting ways with the image act and social distance which we discussed above. For example, Kress and van Leeuwen (1996:144) take particular note of the double message that can be sent when an oblique horizontal angle is mixed with either a demand or an offer.

> The body of a represented participant may be angled away from the plane of the viewer, which his or her head and/or gaze may be turned towards it—or vice versa. The result is a double message: "although I am not part of your world, I nevertheless make contact with you, from my own, different work"; or "although this person is part of our world, someone like you and me, we nevertheless offer his or her image to you as an object for dispassionate reflection."

Vertical Angles and Power

Two types of vertical angles are important in analyzing visuals because they reflect the image-maker's messages about power among people in an image and between the viewer and the people in the image:

- **Vertical angle among participants within an image:** One or more participants look up to, directly at, or down at, one or more other participants.

- **Vertical angle between the participant(s) in the image and the viewer:** The image is designed so that we look up to, directly at, or down at one or more participants.

Figure 5.20 Vertical angles and power relationships in an image.

In either case, the angles have the same meanings:

- A high angle represents greater power. In Figure 5.20, the individual standing over the others and looking down at them is clearly the powerful figure in the setting.

- A medium angle represents equality. The seated individuals in Figure 5.20 are all at the same vertical angle to one another, suggesting a team of employees all holding similar positions within the organization.

- A low angle represents less power. The seated individuals in Figure 5.20 must look up at the standing figure, implying that they are positioned lower in the organization's hierarchy.

How You Can Help

When presented with images, some members of your production team are likely to make visual judgments almost instantaneously. Remember—we're all visual experts. However, they may not be able to articulate the reasons behind their likes and dislikes. Visual semiotics can help you describe your insights about images. Some important questions you can ask the team are:

- What messages do we want to send users through the visual impact made by this image?

- Does this image send those messages effectively? What criteria can we use to judge when an image is effective or not?

- Are there aspects of the image that might detract from its message such as the image act, social distance, perspective and angles?

- How does the image affect our thoughts and feelings? Will it affect users the same way?

- Are there other choices of images or a different organization of elements within the image that would make it more effective rhetorically?

Design Tips from Designers

Designers and users may not have an identical view of a Web site, because browsers and individual monitors can alter the appearance of Web pages. Therefore, designers must work within an environment where their choices are affected by circumstances outside their control. Despite this problem, the design community seems to be in agreement about some practical methods to enhance Web usability, particularly regarding text (see Table 5.2).

Visit this book's Web site to view different design choices.

Table 5.2   Design Tips

AREAS OF DESIGN	GENERAL TIPS FOR IMPROVED USABILITY
Fonts	■ Use san serif typefaces such as Arial or Helvetica. ■ Use 12- to 14-point type for continuous text. ■ Avoid putting text in all caps. ■ Avoid overuse of bold and italicized text. ■ Limit the number of different typefaces and sizes.
Words, Lines, and Spacing	■ Don't hyphenate words. ■ Type for extended reading should be flush left, ragged right. ■ Non-bulleted lines of text should be no shorter than 40 characters and no longer than 60. ■ Provide extra space between lines of type. ■ Put spaces between paragraphs. ■ Spacing between words and sentences should be consistent. ■ Use center spacing cautiously.

continues

Table 5.2   Design Tips (Continued)

AREAS OF DESIGN	GENERAL TIPS FOR IMPROVED USABILITY
Color in General	■ Use color for emphasis. ■ Overuse of color detracts from usability. ■ Colors should be used consistently to create relationships among objects. ■ Colors are affected by brightness and surrounding colors. ■ Keep contrast high by not putting text, backgrounds, and graphics in the same lightness.
Color and Eye Effects	■ Saturated colors—those that are bright and un-mixed with any other color—cause eye fatigue. ■ The eye can't see blue as well as other colors so it works best as a background, rather than a text color. This is a problem that increases with aging. ■ Consider how people with color-blindness problems will view the site.
Background	■ Create a clean look-and-feel by avoiding distracting backgrounds such as those with patterns. ■ Ensure that watermarks are not too strong. ■ White backgrounds provide the best contrast and aren't affected by browsers or monitors. ■ Light blue is a good color for backgrounds. ■ Make sure the background color doesn't interfere with link color.
Images	■ Make sure images are large enough to be seen and understood, but still are balanced within the context of the screen. ■ Create iconic images that are simple and distinct, and based on real-world objects so that users can draw on background knowledge to understand them. ■ Use a common style for all iconic images. ■ Don't mix visual metaphors. (A good example is that of the two unrelated icons in the "Tax Info For You" graphic in Figure 5.12.) ■ Add text labels to images to enhance understanding if necessary. Text can be inserted into the graphic or displayed through a mouse roll-over.

To Sum It Up

As a professional writer/editor, you have a high level of verbal skills and a heightened sensibility to words. These characteristics are essential to success in your field. However, you may not have had to consider visuals in your work before. In general, the more you wish, or are compelled, to get involved in Web site production, the more you'll have to hone your visual skills, your sensitivity to how such images interact with your text, and your ability to convey your reactions effectively to others. You'll also need to remember that your interpretations of visuals and those of the client and other team members are highly personal, affected by age, gender, education, and life experiences. In the projects we've worked on, we've found that this variety of individual preferences combined with innovative designers and a smoothly working team can result in highly satisfying results— text that is enhanced by graphics and more accessible and pleasing to users.

Resources for This Chapter

Books

The Icon Book: Visual Symbols for Computer Systems and Documentation by William Horton. A look at the wide variety of icons and how they are used by designers and perceived by users. (John Wiley & Sons: 1994)

The Essential Guide to User Interface Design: An Introduction to GUI Design Principles and Techniques by Wilbert O. Galitz. A good resource for GUI design and visual impacts. (John Wiley & Sons: 1997)

Visual Intelligence: Perception, Image, and Manipulation in Visual Communication by Ann Marie Seward Barry. Provides a discussion of the neurological and emotional bases of perception. (State University of New York Press: 1997)

Designing Visual Interfaces: Communication Oriented Techniques by Kevin Mullet and Darrell Sano. Describes the fundamental techniques for good graphic design within the context of communications. (Sun Microsystems Inc.: 1995)

Visual Intelligence: How We Create What We See by Donald D. Hoffman. A cognitive scientist's approach to how we perceive line, color, depth, and motion. (W.W. Norton & Co.: 1998)

Reading Images: The Grammar of Visual Design by Gunther Kress and Theo van Leeuwen. A seminal work for people interested in the theory of in visual semiotics. (Routledge: 1996)

Web Sites

Web Design for Instruction (www.usask.ca/education/coursework/skaalid/index.htm). Provides an excellent and easy-to-read overview of design theory, including the Gestalt principles.

Multimedia Design Bibliography (www.arts.uwaterloo.ca/~ipederse/index.html). Provides a thorough list of readings in visual theory and design with short descriptions of each entry.

Visual Intelligence: How We Create What We See (aris.ss.uci .edu/cogsci/personnel/hoffman/vi6.html). A selection of animations to demonstrate how we see visual motion.

Color Matters (www.colormatters.com). Explores color from the perspectives of psychology, philosophy, and art. Includes a section on "Color & Computers."

Colors for the Color Blind (www.toledo-bend.com/colorblind). Although designed to help users with color deficiencies, this site provides useful information, including color charts, for those interested in making the Web more accessible.

International Visual Literacy Association (www.ivla.org). For artists, educators, and researchers interested in different modes of visual communications.

Visual Literacy Bibliography (www.ivla.org/news/rdocs/vlbib/index.htm). A comprehensive list of resources for people who wish to delve deeper into theory.

Visual Information, Intelligence & Interaction Research Group (www.eng.auburn.edu/csse/research/research_groups/vi3rg/vi3rg.html). Provides readers with an idea of the type of academic work being done in this area of research.

Endnotes

1. McCoy's discussion of images is based on the work of American Charles S. Peirce (1839-1914) who is recognized today as an intellectual of extraordinary breadth with interests in areas such as mathematics, logic, and linguistics. He is considered a co-founder of the field of semiotics.

2. A very famous example of the image as an icon is René Magritte's painting of a pipe with *This is not a pipe* written below it.

3. In *Understanding Comics: The Invisible Art,* author Scott McCloud explains how cartoons and comic strips make meaning and examines a variety of different types of cartooning from American action/adventure comic strips to those that appear in different cultures. What makes this book a good read is that it is entirely written as a comic strip itself.

CHAPTER 6

Links, Logic, and the Layered Reader

What's Inside:

- **Associative thinking and hypertext**
- **Different types of Web links**
- **The writer/editor as content arranger**
- **Creating departures and arrivals**
- **A case study in associative linking**
- **Tips to effective linking**

The term, *hypertext*, has a history that is almost as old as the first computer system. It was coined by visionary Ted Nelson in the early 1960s. As he explains in a 1996 radio interview:

> I had done a great deal of writing as a youth, and re-writing, and the intricacy of taking ideas and sentences and trying to arrange them into coherent, sensible, structures of thought struck me as a particularly intricate and complex task, and I particularly minded having to take thoughts which were not intrinsically sequential and somehow put them in a row because print as it appears on the paper, or in handwriting, is sequential.

> There was always something wrong with that because you were trying to take these thoughts which had a structure, shall we say, a spatial structure all their own, and put them into linear form. Then the reader had to take this linear structure and recompose his or her picture of the overall content, once again placed in this non-sequential structure…you had to take these two additional steps of deconstructing some thoughts into linear sequence, and then reconstructing them.

> Why couldn't that all be bypassed by having a nonsequential structure of thought which you presented directly? That was the hypothesis—well the hyperthesis really—of hypertext, that you could save both the writer's time and the reader's time and effort in putting together and understanding what was being presented.

Hypertext is content connected by links.

Hypertext, as Nelson foresaw, is a nonlinear way of presenting information. Using links to and from Web pages, readers can move around a site according to their own inclinations, constructing a text that is all their own. In Chapter 4, we provided an extensive discussion on what writers/editors must do to ensure users have coherent reading experiences in a hypertext environment. But what about the act of *creating* hypertext? What form of creation is it exactly? And what strategies can writers/editors use to create meaningful links for readers? As cognitive psychologist Peter Foltz (1996) notes: "...in hypertext, information can be represented in a semantic network in which multiple related sections of the text are connected to each other...[However], the effectiveness of various features that can be used in hypertexts can vary greatly depending on the domain and content of the text and the goals of the reader. Up to this point, no standards or definitive rules exist on how to develop an effective hypertext."

In Chapter 3, we discussed the role of links in the context of information architecture and navigation of main site sections. In this chapter, we provide a new framework for linking, arising from the concept of hypertext, that goes beyond main navigation. This framework is designed to provide you with a rhetorical strategy, unique to the Web, for developing persuasive text and helping users layer information so that they can build knowledge.

Brain Links: From Apples to Muffin Tins

I have found power in the mysteries of thought.

EURIPIDES

Linking mirrors the way we think.

Users like links. "The first thing I look at on a page," one user told us, "are the links in the text. I want to see if there will be interesting things ahead." The idea that human beings are curious and enjoy novelty is not new, and it's one reason why they find links appealing. Another reason is that linking reflects thought patterns called *associative thinking*—a discontinuous process in which our minds hop around from one topic to another, one idea to another, one concept to another.

Russian psychologist Lev Vygotsky studied the development of thought from childhood to maturity. In his influential work, *Thought and Language* (1934/1986), he described how the chatter of children—that out-loud thinking of preschoolers—progresses into the inner speech of the adult. This inner speech, however, is not really language, but is comprised of pure meanings that are stimulated by language. In other words, although we don't think in words, words make us think. As Vygotsky (1934/1986:244) explained: "The sense of a word…is the sum of all the psychological events aroused in our consciousness by the word." In Vygotsky's terms, associative thinking would work like this:

- You see a fruit to which you give the word *apple.*

- This word makes you think about the old adage, "An apple a day keeps the doctor away."

- The word *doctor* leads you to thoughts about your last doctor's visit where you were advised to go on a diet.

- The word *diet* makes you think about last night's dinner when you ate too much cheesecake.

- *Cheesecake* leads you to thoughts of calories, and you decide to not have a muffin today at lunch.

- *Muffin* reminds you that you need to buy a new muffin tin…and so on.

Associative thinking is not linear—it only appears that way in retrospect if you take the time later to connect all the lines of thought to the dots where you landed for brief seconds. And, more importantly, associative thinking is not chaotic, because we organize the ideas, memories, and facts that arise during this type of thought. We layer information into hierarchies in order to create meanings for ourselves. If we didn't do this, every bit of information would be equal, and we wouldn't be able to distinguish between what was important and what was not. As digital communications researcher Edward Barrett (1989:xvi) notes: "Advanced thinking is more than the sum of its parts. We cannot merely collage strings of objects together to attain a richer meaning or understanding."

Here's an example. A friend has told you things about a used car you're interested in purchasing—its price, condition, color, mileage, age of its tires, and its off-again, on-again air-conditioning system. Each of these facts stimulates various paths of associative thinking within you. The price may lead you to thoughts of your bank account. The tires may spark a memory of a blowout. You don't mentally churn all these facts and thoughts together to make a decision. As Figure 6.1 shows, in the process of developing knowledge to make your decision, you put the information into layers of importance, creating relationships among them that have meanings for you. Perhaps the

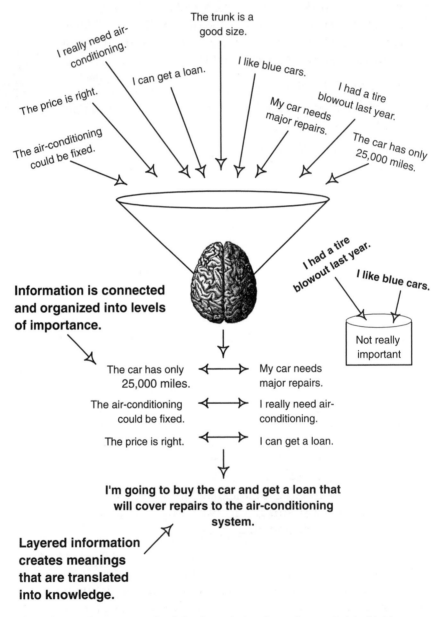

Figure 6.1 The process of gaining knowledge through associative thinking.

price and condition of the car are more important to you than its tires. Perhaps you absolutely require air-conditioning. Eventually, these meanings come together in an overall knowledge about the car and your desires that guides your decision regarding its purchase.

The Web Site: A Network of Associations

When visitors click to different links within a Web site seeking information, they're performing actions that mirror associative thinking. The major difference, however, is that associative *thinking* is based on self-generated mental links and nodes, while associative *linking* is based on online connections created by someone else. However, just as with associative thinking, a Web site's hypertext links have to be organized into a hierarchy. In an article on information strategy, Dow Jones Reuters Business Interactive Limited (2000) notes that: "…information does not equal knowledge, and as the quantity of information mushrooms, the gap between these two entities widens. Disorderly or poorly managed information actually impedes knowledge, rather than increasing it." Philosopher David Kolb (1997:31-32) puts it this way: "Every node cannot demand equal attention to itself, or attention will fail. If everything has equal emphasis, nothing has much emphasis. A hypertext must be more than a sequence of random associations."

As a developer of hypertext within a Web site, your role regarding information is akin to that of a music composer or arranger who organizes the way a piece of music is presented. Kolb continues the analogy:

> Investigations in music indicate that sequences of randomly chosen notes do not hold the listener's attention. Sequences ("brown music") where the choice of each note is somewhat constrained by neighboring notes sound better, but still lack the attraction of more composed music...Hypertext suffers this problem when the horizon of reading is too close. Musical compositions go beyond this kind of linkage to create rich and complex temporal and formal and thematic connections to other sections of the piece in many different levels and sizes. Hypertext could do the same with sequences and nodes that are not just influenced by their immediate neighbors. There should be large structures, echoes, returning themes, transformations and recapitulations and variations…

The Writer/Editor as Arranger

Some writing and literacy researchers, particularly those in the early days of hypertext development, lamented the new role of writer/editor as arranger. For example, literacy researcher Myron Tuman (1992:64) notes: "If any text is, like a hypertext, no more than a collection of fragments, the author becomes no more than that personage charged with collecting and arranging the material."

Others, however, foresaw potential. Hypertext theorist George Landow (1991:82-83) states that the: "…emphasis upon inter-connectedness (or connectivity) provides a powerful means of teaching sophisticated critical thinking, particularly that which builds upon multi-causal analyses and relating different kinds of data." Barrett (1989:xiv), says that:

> The most supple hypertext, therefore, would be one that does more than provide mere navigational guides through an already chartered database of text-objects…A muscular hypertext, an active system rather than a passive one, would support the social construction of meaning that characterizes understanding and communication in the larger world beyond the computer screen

Arranging content requires creativity.

In other words, the more you can help users connect information within a Web site, the more you provide them with the means to create knowledge for themselves. Although readers *do* create a personalized text through link choices, *what* you've written and the *way* you've written it will linger in their minds. As users, we don't read one Web page in isolation from the last. Every text leaves an imprint in our minds—a new fact, a new twist on an old fact, a fresh perspective—that affects the way we read the next text, which, in turn, impacts on the next text, and so on. Language researchers call this phenomenon, *intertextuality*. As the writer/editor—the person most knowledgeable about the arrangement of content within the site—you're in a position to play a creative and influential role in helping readers layer information, through intertextuality, in order to gain knowledge.

Macroarranging: The Main Navigation Links

If you work with the client and production team in designing the information architecture, you will help determine the site's main navigation links. As you do so, you will also be creating the possibility of associations, depending on users' purposes in clicking on the link. For example, if users click back to the

Let's Speak the Same Language

When researching for this book, we found chaos when it came to the naming and defining of Web site links. To help you (and us!) better understand how links work, we have used terms that already exist, but created new definitions based on how the links function for users and their placement in a site. When reading these definitions, it's important to understand that links can have more than one function and, therefore, fall within more than one category.

Navigation Link. A link that provides a path for users as they seek ways to travel on the Web. All links are navigational in nature even if they have other functions.

Internal Link. A link that allows users to travel within a Web site.

External Link. A link that allows users to travel off a Web site.

Associative Link. A link used for the purposes of gaining information as opposed to simply traveling. Such links are often *embedded* in the text.

Embedded Link. A link within the body of the text as opposed to being on a navigation bar or sub-menu. Includes *drill-down links* that move users vertically through the site and *lateral links* that move users horizontally through the site.

"Home" page for the purpose of accessing "About Us," their purpose has been purely navigational. However, if users click back to the "Home" page to refresh their memory about the site owner, their purpose is to gain more information and create additional meaning for themselves.

The main navigation links are those that link to the site's major Web site sections. (For more information on developing main navigation links, see Chapter 3, "Organizing a Web Site: 'Elementary, My Dear Watson.'")

Microarranging: Embedded Links

Embedded links are those found within the body of the text. They're navigational (as all links are) and usually internal, but their *primary* function is associative because users click on them

> Embedded links show textual relationships.

to gain additional knowledge. For example, in the sentence, "Content development requires <u>specific skills</u>," the underlined words, *specific skills*, is an embedded link leading users to further information about those skills. Professor of online journalism Mindy McAdams and her colleague Stephanie Berger (2001) describe the work of creating embedded links as: "Inventing connections: The writer does this by determining what structure the hypertext will have by building a hierarchy of threads, and finally, by creating the links…If a reader finds that links confuse or disappoint, lead to irrelevant material, or fragment the text without reason—look to the decisions made by the writer."

Determining main navigation links usually involves the entire production team. However, as the Web writer/editor, you're the person most familiar with content and most likely to choose embedded links. There are two different types of embedded links: drill-down links and lateral links.

Drill-Down Links

As you're writing/editing, you decide that a Web page is too long and will require too much scrolling. You determine that certain information needs to be distributed among other Web pages. Figure 6.2 shows what happens when you decide to break up the information that's on a single page. In this example, the result is four pages—one page whose text now has some of the information from the original page plus three bulleted links, and three pages (each connected to a bulleted link) that are one vertical step down from the original and all at the same hierarchical level.

Lateral Links

As you're writing/editing, you may decide that there are words/phrases within a sentence that should be linked to other text(s) on the site—text(s) that does not or will not exist on pages directly below the original page in the site's hierarchy. For example, in Chapter 2, we revised text from the CIA Web page to read:

> The Intelligence Community serves a broad range of clients from the President, Cabinet, and Congress to military forces deployed in the field.

Suppose that you were responsible for the content on this site. You could decide that it would be useful for interested visitors

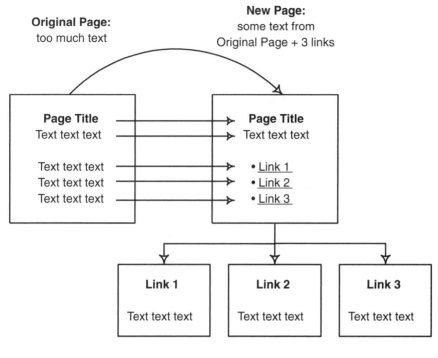

Original Page:
too much text

New Page:
some text from
Original Page + 3 links

3 Lower-Level Pages:
text from Original Page now
accessible through links on
the New Page

Figure 6.2 An example of drill-down linking.

to understand more about the CIA's clients. Therefore, you create a new page for each client and place these pages in a different site section of the site—perhaps a new section such as "Our Clients." You then create embedded, lateral links, using the symbol of the underline to indicate their function:

> The Intelligence Community serves a broad range of clients from the <u>President</u>, <u>Cabinet</u>, and <u>Congress</u> to <u>military forces</u> deployed in the field.

Or, you could choose to put the links into a list:

> The Intelligence Community serves a broad range of clients.
> - <u>President</u>
> - <u>Cabinet</u>
> - <u>Congress</u>
> - <u>Military forces</u> deployed in the field

The decision to embed links in a sentence or use a list depends primarily on what you want to emphasize.

A Balancing Act

When developing embedded links, either drill-down or lateral, you must consider the visual effect of underlining on readability of the text as a whole. Technical communications specialist Jan Spyridakis (2000:370) warns about having too many embedded links: "…links embedded in the middle of a sentence can disrupt the reader's processing of overall sentence syntax." Usability authority Jakob Neilsen (2000:55) notes that the length of the embedded link can be a problem: "If too many words are used for a link, the user cannot pick up its meaning by scanning. Only the most important information-carrying terms should be made into hypertext links."

As we discussed in Chapter 4, an important aspect of your work as a Web writer/editor is to provide a visually balanced Web page with regard to sentences/paragraphs and bulleted lists.

Embedded Lateral Links: Choice and Context

I call links within the body of a text *contextual links*, because my choices depend entirely on the context—the genre I'm writing in and the content I'm developing. The same term can mean different things in different contexts. Editing in a Web site about publishing text is not the same as editing in a Web site on producing videos. Or, for instance, I could be writing about different *kinds* of editing in the site on publishing text. Then a link like editing wouldn't be meaningful because it wouldn't be specific enough. I might then choose links such as editing for style and editing for factual errors. When you're choosing these links, you have to try to anticipate your users' goals in reading the content. Your links have to be relevant to both the context and their needs and desires.

Mindy McAdams
Knight Chair, Professor of Journalism
University of Florida, Gainsville, Florida
Mindy.McAdams.com

The same applies to embedded links. If there are too many on one Web page or they're too long, the user will hardly be able to follow the flow of the text. Again, your task will be to maintain a judicious balance—this time, between text and links.

The Rhetoric of Departure and Arrival

In theorizing about hypertext, Landow (1991:82-83) described it as "…a medium [that] conveys the strong impression that its links signify coherent, purposeful, and above all *useful* relationships." Users, therefore, arrive to, and depart from, links with high expectations and, if these expectations are disappointed, they will be annoyed, frustrated, and likely to dismiss a site as a waste of time.

Departures: The Art of Politeness

The rhetoric of departure is about courtesy. The reader is on a page and has to be sent on to another. You do this politely by providing the appropriate introductions as you lead the reader to the new bit of information and/or technology that he/she is about to encounter. Therefore:

Create courteous departures.

> **A link's words or phrases must clearly tell users where they are going and why they should go there.**

Sometimes a single word/phrase is sufficient because it is self-explanatory, such as the links in:

> The Intelligence Community serves a broad range of clients from the <u>President</u>, <u>Cabinet</u>, and <u>Congress</u> to <u>military forces</u> deployed in the field.

In other instances, you may decide that a link requires an accompanying explanation so that users can understand the relationship that you're creating. In the following example, also taken from the rewritten CIA text, the titles of the Act and, particularly, the Executive Order don't give sufficiently strong cues as to what the links will contain. Therefore, the links require additional information.

> The legal authority for our activities is based on:

> ■ <u>The National Security Act of 1947 </u>(as amended) which provides the basic organization of the U.S. national security effort.

- Executive Order 12333 which provides current guidelines for the conduct of intelligence activities and the composition of the Intelligence Community.

You'll find many inappropriate links in Web text—links that are unnecessary, useless, and/or illogical. For example, on the Stanford University "Home" page (www.stanford.edu), the zip code for the university is a link. We clicked on this out of curiosity. What could a zip code link to? Other zip codes? A directory of zip codes? In fact, this link leads users to an important list, *Frequently Needed Phone Numbers and Addresses*. Such ambiguous departures create confusion, annoyance, and resentment in users.

Poorly titled links create a similar problem for users. Human-computer interface researchers Jose Borges, Israel Morales, and Nestor Rodriguez (1998:145) studied users' ability to predict 50 links randomly selected from ten commercial Web sites based on the links' titles. They found that approximately 25 percent of the time, "…the link names suggested a wrong idea about the content of a page." Many books on Web content describe this as a design problem, because link titles have, in the past, been the responsibility of Web designers. This is one reason why you, as a professional with a sensitivity to language and its effects on others, can make such a contribution to the development of Web content. Table 6.1 provides you with tips to better link titles.

How you title a link depends on what users will find after they click on the link. You must be as specific as possible and keep the title short. Look at the following example:

> Content developers must deal with other people on the production team whose opinions may affect the process.

This link is clearly too long, and it's also unpredictable. Will users find themselves linked to people, to opinions, or to the process? Table 6.2 shows alternative ways to improve this link, assuming that the writer's/editor's purpose is to inform users about the *process* of content development.

NOTE

A .pdf file is a method of delivering content through a software called Adobe Acrobat Reader that allows viewers to see a text as if it were in a print format.

Table 6.1 Tips to Creating Link Titles for Polite Departures

WHEN...	YOU SHOULD...
Creating the Title	■ Be informative. Ensure that the title provides users with some means of predicting what's ahead of them if they click on the link.
	■ Be concise. A good rule of thumb is "less is better." Aim for five words or less.
	■ Consider the effects of translation, if applicable. French, for example, adds 25 to 30 percent more text to the original. (For more information on translation issues, see Chapter 9, "Keep CALM: Content and Logical Management.")
Adding Information	■ Provide a brief explanation, if necessary, to flesh the title out, but don't underline this information.
	■ Indicate if the link will lead users off the site into another text format, such as .pdf, or if they're moving into audio or video content.
	■ If a link leads to a .pdf file or other format, consider creating an additional link to the appropriate plug-in/player download page, such as Adobe Acrobat Reader, Shockwave, or RealPlayer. This is useful if you think it likely that your users won't have that plug-in or player. (For more information on plug-ins/players, see Chapter 8, "Content + Technology: A Surprising Alliance.")

Table 6.2 Text Alternatives and Links

RHETORICAL SITUATION	APPROPRIATE TEXT AND LINKS
The text needs to link to one page describing the process.	Content developers must deal with other people on the production team whose opinions may affect the process.
The text needs to link to several different pages about the process, or the text is at the top of an internally linked, scrollable page with "Back to Top" buttons. (For more information on internally linked, scrollable pages, see Chapter 7, "Writing/Editing *for* the Web Page; Writing/Editing *to* the Web Screen.")	Content developers must deal with other people on the production team whose opinions may affect the process of: ■ Consulting on the concept. ■ Advising on information architecture and navigation design. ■ Writing/editing. ■ Copyediting the Beta product.
The text needs to link to a format other than the Web page.	Content developers must deal with other people on the production team whose opinions may affect the process (.pdf file).

Arrivals: Creating Safe Landings

Arrivals must fulfill a user's expectations about where they thought they were going. This involves two separate issues: destinations and titles. Getting users to the appropriate destination involves the technologies of programming. Within your own site, you can ensure that your link goes to the right page or section of text. However, external links can cause problems such as:

- **Broken links**—Web pages that no longer exist or have been moved.

- **Inaccessible pages**—Certain Web site formats, such as those with frames, that make it difficult to put the user on the exact page where the information exists.

When problems arise with inaccessible pages, you'll have to add travel information to your link to help the user get to the exact information. Here's an example of a situation we encountered when trying to create a link to the "Youth Entrepreneurship Financing" page for the Business Development Bank of Canada (BDC). This is a frames-based site, driven by databases, in which the Web address for every page is the same: www.bdc.ca/bdc/home/Default.asp. The result was that the programmer on our site couldn't create a link to the BDC page we required. Adding to our difficulty was the fact that the BDC doesn't have a "Home" page that provides users with an intuitive grasp of the site's contents. However, because the link was important for our site, we had to include it. Our final solution was:

> Youth Entrepreneurship Financing. This link brings you to the Business Development Bank of Canada. Click on the "Site Map," indicated in the top navigation bar, and a pop-up window will appear. Select "youth business."

But, consider the predicament of users who may not remember these instructions after clicking on the link. There's almost no chance that this trip will result in a safe and happy landing. This story also serves as a reminder that, if your client wants his or her site to be link-friendly, it must be configured to make information accessible to other site owners who want to connect to it.

The second issue involved with creating safe arrivals is that of titles. Have you ever clicked on a link and been transported to a page whose title either doesn't match that of the link title, or is an abbreviated or mangled version of the link title? This problem can disorient users who think that the link has taken them to the wrong place. Table 6.3 provides useful tips to ensure that users don't feel lost upon landing.

Table 6.3 Tips to Titles for Safe Arrivals

TYPES OF LINKS	TIPS
Internal Drill-Down Links	Be extremely careful to ensure an exact match with Web page titles. The more you do this as you write/edit, the easier your proofing tasks will be during later stages. Proofing all linkages for title consistency can be a daunting and difficult task on a large site.
Embedded Lateral Links	When creating embedded links within a sentence, ensure that the word/phrase that you've chosen is included somewhere in the title of the page to which it links. For example, "Use active verbs when writing your resume" should link to a page whose title includes the phrase, *active verbs*—for example, "Active Verbs for Your Resume." Otherwise, users will get that "I'm-lost-again" feeling.
External Links	Be equally careful to use the exact title of the other site or linked page. Periodically check these links because other sites are likely to change their content.

Types of Associative Links

As we noted earlier, each link on a Web site is navigational in nature, but it also has the potential to be associative, depending on the intent of the user. Associative links are those that users click on to obtain more information. These links mimic associative thinking and create relationships among information and data. Table 6.4 summarizes the seven types of associative links that we've identified based on their function for users.

Authorizing

The authorizing link provides the legal, formal policies and/or contact information that helps to authenticate the site and its information. Some typical examples of authorizing links are:

Authorizing links enhance credibility.

- "About Us" or "Company Profile."

- "Privacy Policy" or "Security/Privacy Guarantee."

- "Legal Notices" or "Disclaimer."

- "Terms and Conditions of Use."

Table 6.4   Summary of Associative Links

LINK	FUNCTION	EXAMPLES
Authorizing	Describes the legal, formal policies and/or contact information that authenticate the site and its content.	■ About Us ■ Customer Service Policies
Commenting	Provides opinion about the site and/or its content.	■ Press Releases ■ Testimonials
Enhancing	Provides factual information by either offering more detail or painting the bigger picture.	■ Guidelines for Membership ■ Site Map
Exemplifying	Provides a specific example of content within a broader category.	■ Future Events ■ Today's Horoscopes
Mode-Changing	Moves users from the reading mode to one that requires a different kind of activity.	■ Online Survey ■ Shopping Cart
Referencing/Citing	Provides information that "informs" the site's content.	■ Bibliography ■ Related Links
Self-Selecting	Allows users to narrow a search by making choices based on their age, sex, geographical location, life situation, personal interests, and so on.	■ For Seniors Only ■ Your Local Chapter

Other types of authorizing links are those that create authenticity by providing the legal or legislative basis for an organization's activities—for example, the links to "The National Security Act" and "Executive Order" in the revised CIA site discussed earlier, or the "By-laws and Articles of Agreement" link that may be found on a non-profit organization's site. Links to an organization's workplace policies such as those found on Intranets also serve to demonstrate and validate authority.

NOTE
A link may have more than one associative function.

Although authorizing links can act rhetorically to enhance a site's credibility, it's important to remember that these links must *not* be written in a promotional style. Users don't visit a site to read about organizational back patting. On the other hand, clients are inclined to feel strongly about this information. Most are becoming more Web savvy, but we still meet clients who want the CEO's picture and the mission, vision, and values of the organization on the "Home" page. Your role, as the writer/editor, is to tactfully remind the client that, to attract users, the site must focus on their needs and concerns, and that such information is more useful when incorporated as a link.

Commenting

The commenting link is one that provides opinion, either obvious or subtle, about the site and/or its content. Examples of commenting links are:

> Commenting links are opinions.

- The "Read Messages" link on an online discussion forum, which is a Web site essentially devoted to commentary.

- A link such as "Press Releases" on a corporate site that connects users to documents that provide commentary about the business and its recent activities.

- A link to an expert's or consumer's review of a company's products or services.

- Links to opinion articles on non-news sites.

- Audio or video links to people discussing/presenting the content.

Commenting links can be both verbal and/or visual. For example, Holiday-Rentals.com (www.holiday-rentals.co.uk) has a site section devoted to testimonials from people who've used their services to rent out condominiums, villas, ski chalets, and so on. These testimonials are accompanied by photographs of beautiful interiors and exteriors, lavish landscapes, and panoramic views.

The difference between whether a link functions as commenting (opinion) or enhancing (factual) exists in the mind of the user. What some people consider opinions, others believe are facts, and vice versa.

Enhancing

The enhancing link layers information for the user either by *zooming in*, that is, adding more detail, or *zooming out*, that is, providing the bigger picture. This type of link has two important characteristics.

- **Function:** Readers use the link to find factual, objective information. (For a discussion of factual information, see Chapter 4, "E-Rhetoric: A New Form of Persuasion.")
- **Location:** Where the user is located on the site determines whether the link enhances through detail or the bigger picture.

Users who link to enhance through detail are usually drilling down through the site's information architecture, moving from the general to the increasingly specific. Enhancing through detail includes any link that leads users to how-to or resource information, guidelines, descriptions, or explanations. An interesting example of this type of link is on the Web site for the U.S. Federal Emergency Management Service (FEMA). This site (www.fema .gov/library/photo.htm) has photos from different crisis areas. For example, the link, "Mississippi Tornado Photos," provides visuals from this particular emergency with each picture accompanied by a short descriptive note. These photos enhance a user's knowledge about the emergency from a visual perspective.

On the other hand, users seeking the bigger picture must usually link in reverse, moving from the specific to the more general. For example, if your search engine drops you on the Web page containing the photos from the Mississippi tornado, you'd have to click on either "Home," "Site Help," or the "Site Index" to figure out where you were and the purpose of the page.

Other types of associative links that frequently act as enhancing are those that authorize, exemplify, and refer. However, their primary function depends on the users' intent.

Exemplifying

The exemplifying link is the online equivalent of the print phrases *for example* and *for instance*. When users are looking within general categories and then click to find specific content as examples within that category, the link has an exemplifying function. You will find many exemplifying links on the Web such as those that connect users to:

- Individual products or services on an e-commerce site.
- Job openings on corporate sites and job posting sites.
- Recipes on a cooking or gourmet site.
- Books on publishers' sites.
- Events on sites such as professional associations, museums, and nonprofit groups.
- Audio or video interviews with people providing examples.

Exemplifying links generally function as either commenting or enhancing links, depending upon whether the examples are opinions such as the testimonials on the Holiday-Rentals.com site or facts such as the photos and text from the FEMA site.

Mode-Changing

The mode-changing link moves users from the reading mode to one that requires a different kind of activity such as:

- Taking a quiz.
- Completing an online survey.
- Filling out a form.
- Undertaking an e-commerce transaction.

We consider these links as associative, because they also help users gain knowledge. In some cases, as in quizzes and other online educational tools, users are provided with interactive methods for learning more about a specific content. In such cases, these links also act as enhancing links. However, filling out forms and undertaking e-commerce transactions are somewhat different. Although participants in these activities are achieving goals not related expressly to gaining information, they're learning other things about a site. For example, if their experiences go smoothly, they'll believe in the site's competency and efficiency—all aspects that have a significant impact on credibility. If their experiences are bad ones, they'll likely never return.

> Mode-changing links teach Web functionality.

We suggest that these particular types of links build another kind of knowledge as well. In modernized cultures, we learn how to fill out printed forms and shop at stores at a very early age—so early, in fact, that they seem almost second nature to us. However, to accomplish these activities online is a learning experience for users who must adapt to rapidly changing technologies, deal with the lack of well-established conventions, and handle fears about privacy and security. These mode-changing links help users build an overall understanding about the relationship between their actions and the Internet.

Referencing/Citing

> Referencing/citing links provide information backup.

The referencing/citing link allows Web site developers to refer to information that backs up or informs their content. "Related Links" is a very common way for site owners to demonstrate a solidarity with similar subject matter sites. Referencing/citing is frequent on scholarly sites. For example, a site on postmodern thought may provide an overview of the topic and then list numerous links to articles and books on the subject. Library and information researcher Deborah Shaw describes such links as: "…paying homage to pioneers, giving credit for related work…, providing background reading, and providing links to poorly disseminated, poorly indexed, or uncited work" (Garfield, as cited in Shaw, 2001). Citing is a subset of referencing and occurs when a researcher posts an article, whether individually or in an online journal, and provides bibliographic citations that link to other online articles. A referencing/citing link is almost always an external link.

Self-Selecting

> Self-selecting links narrow choices.

This link allows users to narrow their search for information by making choices based on their age, sex, geographical location, life situation, personal interests, and so on. This type of link creates the logical "If…then" relationship. For example, "If you are over 65 years of age, then click here," "If you're interested in printers for home office use, then click here," or "If you're ready to purchase, then click here." Sometimes, self-selecting links are only visuals such as the shopping cart icons used on some e-commerce sites. These links, whether textual and/or visual, occur in a wide variety of sites. Some examples are:

- Children's sites with links such as "Parents" and "Teachers" that provide educational advice and information on products.

- E-commerce sites that provide links to different categories of products.

- Links to special interest groups (SIGS) on a professional association's site.

- Sections of e-commerce sites that allow transactions such as an airline's online reservation service where users narrow choices by clicking on different destinations, times, and so on.

Self-selecting links generally function as enhancing when users are seeking further information or as mode-changing when they wish to undertake transactions.

Intranet E-Orientation: A Case Study in Associative Links

In 2000, the Canadian Imperial Bank of Commerce (CIBC)—a financial institution with more than 40,000 employees located in Canada, the United States, Europe, and the West Indies—decided to create an online employee-orientation program, *Discover*CIBC (see Figure 6.3), and asked us to organize and write the content.

This project presented two major challenges. First, the product had to be both a Web site and in CD-ROM format because not all employees worldwide would have access to the company's Intranet. Therefore, the program had to be as self-sufficient as possible, that is, we couldn't rely on outside links to help users gain required information. Secondly, the client wanted an interactive structure that would allow users to learn according to their own inclinations, rather than a program of sequential learning modules that would compel them to go through information in a preorganized format. However, new employees had to learn the content within a three-month period. This combination of requirements—self-sufficiency, a nonlinear structure, and must-learn content—meant that linking material laterally across the site was as rhetorically important as linking it vertically. Embedded links would serve as continual reminders for users about information they needed to know as they moved around the site according to their own preferences.

> The project had major challenges.

We organized *Discover*CIBC into six main site sections. Four sections contained *hard* content—material that employees had to know about the company and industry. These sections were:

- **CIBC: The Inside Story**—the bank's history, policies, and organizational structure.

- **Employee Benefits**—specific programs within the bank.
- **Employee Support Programs**—initiatives within the bank.
- **Know Your Industry**—information about the financial industry developed by the Canadian Banking Association. (This unit was a standalone, separate from the rest of the content.)

The remaining two main sections contained *soft* content—material that employees should know about themselves in relation to their work, workplace, and co-workers. These sections were:

- **Starting Out**—work issues in the first day and weeks of employment.
- **Building Your Career**—topics involved with career management.

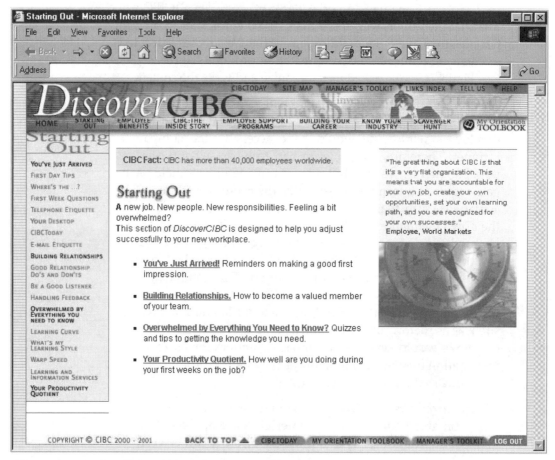

Figure 6.3 The "Starting Out" page for *Discover*CIBC.

Copyright CIBC, 2001. Published with permission.

Highlighting Employee Policies

Many of the lateral embedded links in the orientation program served as authorizing links, connecting text about workplace behavior to internal employee policies. For example, the client wished to emphasize CIBC's strong policy against harassment. Therefore, in the site section, "CIBC: The Inside Story," we created a Web page, *Harassment in the Workplace,* that provided official guidelines regarding this policy. It included:

> Authorizing links supported internal policies.

- A definition of harassment.
- The consequences of harassment.
- How CIBC employees were expected to conduct themselves in the workplace.
- A quote from the CEO about adverse effects of harassment.

This page was long and written in legalese—not conducive to easy reading. It was, however, an important page that required emphasis throughout the program. As Table 6.5 shows, we created lateral embedded links in other main site sections that would link to this page.

Building a Learning Culture

Like many organizations in today's workplaces, CIBC wanted to emphasize the importance of learning to its employees. Its new

Table 6.5 Authorizing Links to *Discover*CIBC's Harassment Policy Page

SITE SECTION	WEB PAGE TITLE	LATERAL LINK
Starting Out	*E-Mail Etiquette*	"Don't use e-mail for any statement or joke that could be considered as offensive or perceived as a form of <u>harassment</u>."
Employee Support Programs	*Employee Relations Support*	"Employee Relations Support is a confidential, consulting service designed to help you resolve workplace issues and handle concerns relating to support in areas such as discrimination, <u>harassment</u>, and workplace accommodation."
Building Your Career	*Professionalism*	"**Workplace Behaviour.** We will not engage in <u>harassment</u>, discrimination, or violence."

Embedded links created awareness.

employees had to learn a great deal of information in a short amount of time, and all its personnel had to understand that life-long learning was a significant aspect of career management.

To address these issues within the orientation program, we set ourselves two goals.

- **Goal 1:** We wanted to create Web pages wherever possible to make employees aware of good learning practices and learning opportunities. Table 6.6 shows these pages and where they appeared in the program's different site sections.

- **Goal 2:** We wanted to develop a network of embedded links, both drill-down and lateral, that would maintain the user's awareness about the importance of lifelong learning. Table 6.7 shows the interlinking that we created across the program.

Table 6.6 Web Pages about Learning in *Discover*CIBC

SITE SECTION	WEB PAGE TITLES AND CONTENT
Starting Out	*Overwhelmed by Everything You Need to Know?* A page with drill-down links to:
	■ *Learning Curve "True or False"*: A quiz to build a more positive attitude toward learning.
	■ *What's My Learning Style?*: A quiz to help users determine whether they're visual, auditory, or tactile learners.
	■ *"Warp-Speed" Learning Strategies*: Tips for learning based on learning styles.
	■ *Your Development Plan*: Applying your learning style to developing on-the-job knowledge.
Employee Benefits	*Learning and Information Services*: CIBC's in-house library and learning programs.
Employee Support Programs	*Global Tuition Assistance Policy*: CIBC's program to help employees achieve learning goals.
Building Your Career	*Learn From Mistakes:* Tips to building on experiences.
	Get Accredited: Courses that provide employees with professional designations.

Table 6.7 Network of Embedded Links about Learning in *Discover*CIBC

SOURCE PAGE	LINK	DESTINATION PAGE	PURPOSE(S) OF LINK
Overwhelmed by Everything You Need to Know?	Learning Curve "True or False"	*Learning Curve "True or False"*	Mode-changing/ Enhancing
Overwhelmed by Everything You Need to Know?	What's My Learning Style?	*What's My Learning Style?*	Mode-changing/ Enhancing
Overwhelmed by Everything You Need to Know?	"Warp-Speed" Learning Strategies	*Warp-Speed Learning Strategies*	Enhancing/ Exemplifying
Overwhelmed by Everything You Need to Know?	Your Development Plan	*Your Development Plan*	Enhancing
Learn from Mistakes	"Ask yourself what you could have done differently. What do you need to learn in order to try again?"	*Learning and Information Services*	Authorizing/ Enhancing
Get Accredited	"If you are a full-time or part-time employee, you can apply under the Global Tuition Assistance Policy to take courses offered by professional associations."	*Global Tuition Assistance Policy*	Authorizing/ Enhancing
Career Opportunities	"Determine what you need to learn to get where you want to go. Check out learning and information services."	*Learning and Information Services*	Authorizing/ Enhancing
Lifestyle Benefits	Global Tuition Assistance Policy.	*Global Tuition Assistance Policy*	Authorizing/ Enhancing
Productivity Strategies	**"Learn from your successes and mistakes.** If you've done well, analyze your actions, know why you were effective, and congratulate yourself. If you've made a mistake, take steps to make it a learning experience."	*Learn from Mistakes*	Enhancing

continues

Table 6.7 Network of Embedded Links about Learning in *Discover*CIBC (Continued)

SOURCE PAGE	LINK	DESTINATION PAGE	PURPOSE(S) OF LINK
Productivity Strategies	**Commit to lifelong learning.** Today's workplace is undergoing constant change. To keep up, you'll need to continually upgrade your skills. CIBC offers a variety of <u>learning programs</u> to help you achieve your goals.	*Learning and Information Services*	Authorizing/ Enhancing
Your Development Plan	Determine activities to address your development needs (e.g., on-the-job learning, buddy coaching, <u>learning programs</u>).	*Learning and Information Services*	Authorizing/ Enhancing
Your Development Plan	Find out your <u>learning style</u>.	*What's My Learning Style?*	Mode-changing/ Enhancing
Your Development Plan	Explore <u>learning strategies</u> that would suit you best.	*Warp-Speed Learning Strategies*	Enhancing
Your Development Plan	Don't be afraid to ask questions. Learn from your <u>mistakes</u>.	*Learn from Mistakes*	Enhancing

The Manager's Orientation Toolkit

In addition to the main program, the site had a special, stand-alone section, "The Manager's Toolkit," which was designed to assist managers in orienting employees during their first days and weeks on the job. The message in this section was: "Create great beginnings for new employees," and the client wished to emphasize the importance of providing a welcome to newcomers. We, therefore, created a page (see Figure 6.4) called *What's in a Welcome*.

To reinforce the message, we used enhancing links elsewhere in the Toolkit to link back to this Web page whenever possible (see Table 6.8 on page 198).

The Launch

CIBC launched *Discover*CIBC in spring 2001. In addition to the program's interactivity, the final product included video

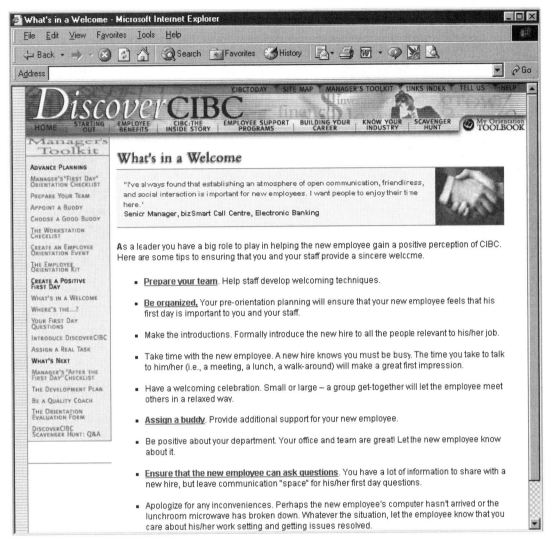

Figure 6.4 *What's in a Welcome* Web page from "The Manager's Orientation Toolkit."
Copyright CIBC, 2001. Published with permission.

Webcasts that allowed company executives to speak directly to employees.

Tips to the Process of Linking

In this chapter, we've developed a framework to help you develop links, particularly embedded lateral links, in a thoughtful way. Some will be obvious; while others will require analysis

> Keep track of
> link creation.

Table 6.8 Enhancing Links to *What's in a Welcome* Page

TITLE OF WEB PAGE	EMBEDDED LINKS
Create a Positive First Day	"<u>What's in a Welcome?</u> What kind of celebration do you intend? Tips to making people feel at home with you and your team."
Prepare Your Team	"Explain that you want staff to make the new employee feel <u>welcome</u> and part of the team."
Advance Planning	"Your well-organized plans for a new employee's first day can have a great payoff. ■ Makes the new employee feel important and welcome."
Manager's "First Day" Orientation Checklist	"Before the new employee's first day: ■ Plan <u>welcoming</u> activities."

A Successful Start

The response to *Discover*CIBC has been very positive. Orientation can set the tone for long-term employment, and this program is one step to ensuring that every new employee has a good early experience and the potential to build a successful career. New employees tend to get a lot of information all at once, and they just can't absorb it. In fact, the information available in *Dis-cover*CIBC would take them months to find on their own. Now, they can visit the site as often as they like, choose information that suits their needs, and learn at their own pace. The Webcasts of the "Welcome" from the Chairman and other senior executives have been particularly effective. One person commented: "I felt as if the Chairman was speaking just to me." "The Manager's Toolkit" has also been especially well received. Managers and business units are finding it valuable in building their face-to-face sessions.

**Judy Winestone, Consultant, Enterprise Learning Initiatives
CIBC Knowledge Network, CIBC
www.cibc.com**

on your part. If you're creating the information yourself, you're likely to have an instinctual feel for where meaningful links for readers can occur. If you're editing content, you'll have to develop an in-depth knowledge of the material before you'll be able to consider linking. In either case, keeping all the content in your head and trying to conceive of possible links are difficult tasks. Because adding embedded lateral links in a Web site requires extra work and costs in programming, you may have to justify such linking to your client. Table 6.9 provides some suggestions for lateral-link creation during the process of Web site development.

NOTE
In Chapter 7, "Writing/Editing *for* the Web Page; Writing/Editing *to* the Web Screen," we describe how to indicate linking information to programmers.

Table 6.9   Tips to Embedded Lateral Linking

WRITING/EDITING STAGES	TIPS
Designing Information Architecture and Main Navigation	■ Consider the possibilities of links across the main site sections. As you develop text, constantly ask yourself: "Would this word or phrase make a good associative link to X, Y, or Z?" and "If I create this link, will it help readers layer information?" ■ Keep a notebook with one page per site section and jot down your link ideas.
Writing/Editing Content	■ Create links as you go, considering *why* you're creating the link and how it will be meaningful for users. ■ Keep track of your links per site section by using a Lateral-Linking Table that notes source pages, linking text, destination pages, type of links, and dates of link creation. (You'll find a downloadable table on our Web site at www.wiley.com/compbooks/hammerich.)
Copyediting/Proofreading	■ Print out all Web pages so that you have the complete text of the Web site in hard copy.

continues

Table 6.9   Tips to Embedded Lateral Linking (Continued)

WRITING/EDITING STAGES	TIPS
Copyediting/Proofreading (continued)	■ As you copyedit and proofread, also look for linking possibilities. The larger the site, the more likely it is that you'll find possible links that didn't occur to you or the original writer/editor. ■ Create another Lateral-Linking Table for these additional links or expand your previous table.
Managing Content	■ Use this stage to add links that were missed during the prelaunch period. ■ When updating content, see if new links can be created. ■ Continue to update your Lateral-Linking Table.

To Sum It Up

In our experience, developers of informational sites have not taken full advantage of associative linking and its potential for helping users gain knowledge. Most clients' priority is to get the information architecture, navigation design, and GUI in place. Embedded lateral linking is, essentially, below their radar. It is, however, the kind of task that is second nature to professional writers/editors. If you've ever done the following —used a sub-header to connect two pieces of text, or used collocation (a chain of similar words throughout a text) to link ideas, or followed the tenets of the persuasive essay: "Tell them what you're going to say; tell them; and then tell them what you've said,"—then you've made meaningful connections for readers. Embedded lateral linking is different in the medium of the Web, but the same in principle. In fact, we suggest that once you begin to use your skills to create this type of linking, you'll find it one of the most challenging, innovative, and fascinating aspects about developing online content.

Resources for This Chapter

Web Sites

Writing Effectively Online: How to Compose Hypertext (corax.cwrl.utexas.edu/cac/online/01/troffer/htintro.html). A useful overview of hypertext writing from *Computers and Composition: An International Journal for Teachers of Writing* (Spring, 2001).

Hypertext (www.press.umich.edu:80/jep/06-03/McAdams/pages). An easy-to-read scholarly article—presented in purely hypertext format—about the practical uses of hypertext.

Web Publishing Paradigms (www.hoshi.cic.sfu.ca/~guay/ Paradigm/Paradigm .html). An examination of different paradigms regarding interactivity on the Web.

Hypertext Semantics (academic.brooklyn.cuny.edu/education/ jlemke/webs/hypertext/tsld001.htm). Social semiotician Jay Lemke provides a new academic perspective on how hypertext creates meaning.

Writing/Editing *for* the Web Page; Writing/Editing *to* the Web Screen

---

What's Inside:

- The Web page as a rhetorical unit of content
- The Web screen as a flexible unit of space
- Navigation pages vs. destination pages
- Building a Web page persona
- Screen scrolling and alternatives
- How to develop an editorial style guide

---

*What is written without effort is
in general read without pleasure.*

SAMUEL JOHNSON

You've reached the writing/editing stage of content development. You may have helped define the goals of the Web site, analyzed the target audience, consulted on information architecture and navigation, and been part of discussions on GUI design. You have a fairly good idea of what the content should be Web page by Web page, but you may still have flexibility to create other pages depending upon how the text develops. Now you either face a blank word-processing screen, content submitted by a subject matter specialist, or online material that needs revision. Where do you start? What factors should you consider? What principles can guide you?

In our experience, writers/editors must keep two separate concepts in their mind as they work—that of the Web page, and that of the Web screen. Although many people use these terms interchangeably, the fact is that they require different writing/editing strategies. In essence, you will write content *for* the Web page, but *to* the Web screen. Why the distinction? Drive-thru readers can enter your site at any point, and will read your content using their own computer equipment. Therefore:

- You must write/edit *for* a Web page that stands alone, completely separate from the rest of the site.

- You must write/edit *to* a Web screen whose space is flexible, depending on users' individual monitor resolutions.

The Web is unique in presenting writers/editors with this double-edged challenge. In every other media, content is fixed in place. Every reader of a particular publication sees the same content in exactly the same way; every television watcher sees the same picture even if the size of their television sets differ; and every audience member hears the same speech no matter where he or she sits in the room. Because Web content is not fixed in a spatial sense, and users can access pages unpredictably, you must be able to create coherent, persuasive text *for*

Let's Speak the Same Language

As we noted above, many people use the terms *Web page* and *Web screen* interchangeably, although they are different concepts. To ensure standardization of terminology, we've built the following definitions, based on the concept of the Web page as the basic unit of a Web site.

Web site: A collection of Web pages arranged into hierarchical levels of grouped information, connected by navigation design, and presented through graphical user interface (GUI).

Web site section: A part of the site whose Web pages are grouped together because they hold related content—for example, the "About Us" section of a corporate site. A Web site section is sometimes referred to as a *key content area*, a *channel*, or a *theme/stream*.

Web page: A rhetorical unit of content that may be visible on one Web screen or may require scrolling.

Web screen: A unit of space that holds whatever Web page content appears on an individual user's monitor at a given time.

the Web page and, at the same time, *to* a screen whose viewing space you can't predict.

Is a Web Page Really a Page?

The page, in Web terms, is a metaphor taken from the world of print and is, therefore, misleading. The print page can come in a variety of widths and lengths, but it has size limits. We must be able to hold it comfortably in our hands and be able to grasp its content in a glance. If it doesn't fit within those parameters— very small or very large—it turns into a novelty item. A Web page, on the other hand, can theoretically be of enormous width and length because of the possibilities of scrolling from left to right and from top to bottom.

Web page is a metaphor from print.

In practice, developers limit Web pages in width, because it is far too difficult for users to read horizontally while scrolling from left to right at the same time. (Also, mouse manufacturers enhance vertical scrolling by incorporating scrolling wheels.) However, Web pages frequently require scrolling in the vertical, and one Web page can contain the equivalent of many print pages. It isn't unusual, for example, for an academic to post research papers that, when printed, are 40 to 50 print pages long. So is a Web page really a page? The answer is no, but the metaphor has stuck. What's important is that you understand its potential and limitations for delivering content to users.

Starting with a Splash

On any given site, you'll find different kinds of Web pages— from the front-end "Splash" page to the depths of its archives. Table 7.1 (on the next page) provides a summary of the different types of Web pages.

Navigation Pages versus Destination Pages

Table 7.1 provides separate definitions for navigation and destination pages based on functionality. However, both types of pages contain the same kind of material—content and links. How can you determine whether a page is truly a navigation or destination page? Wouldn't there be cases in which the differences may be ambiguous? You may find it useful to think of the purely navigation page and purely destination page as opposites on a continuum (see Figure 7.1) with hybrids in the middle.

Table 7.1 Types and Functions of Web Pages

TYPE OF WEB PAGE	FUNCTIONS
"Splash"/Welcome Page	The front end of a Web site that usually provides site identity through a title, graphics, and/or animation. Is common on informational sites that appear in more than one language where users need to choose a language preference.
"Home" Page	The site's first real content page. It usually contains brief information about the site, provides users with a first understanding of the site's navigation through the GUI, and may include links within the text.
Navigation Page	A page designed primarily for navigation. May also contain some content.
Destination Page	A page designed primarily to inform. May also contain some links.
Archival Page	An online storage location for historical information or data that can be generally retrieved by topic, date, or author. Such content is usually deep down in the site's hierarchy.

A Navigation Page with Some Content

The deeper users go down into the hierarchy of the site, the greater their expectation of reaching content. As we noted in Chapter 3, usability is improved when deeper level pages are not just menu pages of links. Figure 7.2 shows the text of a navigation page we created while working on a career site.

When building this site, we considered this page, "Cover Letters That Work," as a navigation page because its primary purpose was to lead users to the four other pages that contained the

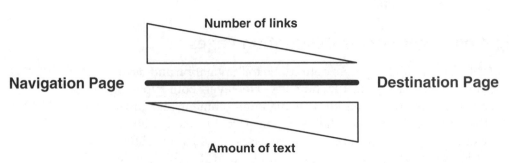

Figure 7.1 Many Web pages fall on a continuum between purely navigation and purely destination.

Cover Letters That Work

The cover letter is attached to your résumé and it's the first thing an employer reads. Think of it as your "Hello," handshake and smile. It has to:

• Be polite, positive and appealing.

• Make the employer want to know more about you.

• Inspire the employer to read your résumé carefully.

> **Career Tip:** Why is a cover letter so important? Because it's your first chance to "speak" directly to an employer about how your qualifications match the job.

• Cover Letter Content and Sample

• Cover Letter Do's and Don'ts

• More Sample Cover Letters

• Employers Talk About Cover Letters

Figure 7.2 Text from a navigation page that contains introductory content.
May 17, 2001 (www.worksearch.gc.ca/english/index.pl?tid=57)

main content on this topic. However, because this page already occurs three clicks from the site's "Home" page, we didn't want users to feel that they were engaged only in a drilling-down exercise. Therefore, we provided useful introductory information as well as links. Figure 7.3 shows where "Cover Letters That Work" would fall on the continuum, based on the fact that its four links contain a great deal more content.

Two Types of Destination Pages

Destination pages—those that contain primarily content as opposed to navigation—can be divided into two types.

■ **Primary:** Pages that contain the main content of the site. For example, the primary pages on an e-commerce site are those devoted to products or services for sale.

■ **Secondary:** Pages that contain information not directly connected to the main purpose of the site. For example, the

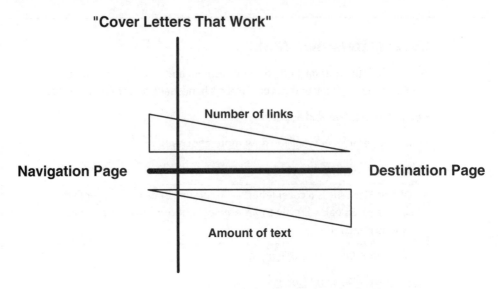

"Cover Letters That Work"

Number of links

Navigation Page **Destination Page**

Amount of text

Figure 7.3 "Cover Letters That Work" is a hybrid navigation-destination page.

same e-commerce site might include sections on corporate information, privacy policies, and so on.

Primary and secondary page types usually require different presentations of content and may require different styles of writing/editing. Table 7.2 shows the types of content found on primary and secondary destination pages by informational site.

How Many Screens Does It Take?

To count screens, use the PgDn button.

Web pages consist of one or more Web screens. In theory, every Web page can have as many screens as it has lines of text—a possibility if a user were to scroll through the page, pausing as each top line disappeared. Another way to judge the number of screens is to start at the top of the Web page and use the PgDn button. Count the first screen as number one and the rest consecutively each time you hit the button. Although there is still some overlap of information using this method, it does provide a useful gauge for counting the number of screens on a Web page.

The rule of thumb is little or no scrolling, but Web sites frequently break the rule. For example, Amazon.com, an e-commerce site, flaunts this rule consistently on its pages on books. On a monitor with an 800 x 600 resolution (the most commonly used resolution), one recent bestseller had 18 screens that included:

Table 7.2 Types of Content on Primary and Secondary Destination Pages

TYPE OF SITE AND TARGET AUDIENCE	PRIMARY DESTINATION PAGES	SECONDARY DESTINATION PAGES
Type: Government **User:** Average Citizen **Example:** Nutrition.gov (www.nutrition.gov)	■ Dietary supplements ■ Food labels ■ Foodborne illnesses ■ Home canning ■ Lifestyle issues for men	■ Research centers ■ Grant opportunities ■ Funding agencies
Type: Museum **User:** Visitor **Example:** Metropolitan Museum of Art (www.metmuseum.org)	■ Egyptian art collection ■ Drawings and prints ■ Upcoming exhibitions ■ Visitor information ■ Guided tours	■ Endowment ■ Libraries and study centers ■ Products from the museum store
Type: Professional Association **User:** Member **Example:** Society for Technical Communication (www.stc.org)	■ Special interest groups ■ Jobs database ■ Member directory ■ Annual conference	■ Past presidents ■ Marketing communications resource committee ■ Sustaining organization program
Type: E-Commerce **User:** Shopper **Example:** Sephora (www.sephora.com)	■ Individual beauty product information ■ Gift suggestions	■ Articles and reviews ■ Personal shopping account ■ Store return policy
Type: Job Bank **User:** Job hunter **Example:** Monster Board (www.monster.com)	■ Individual job postings	■ Individual companies ■ Career development and work search strategies ■ Writing cover letters and resumes

- Information on the price of the book and its different editions.
- Other book picks by customers who had also ordered this bestseller.
- Editorial reviews.
- Customers' reviews of the day.
- Links to all customers' reviews.
- Other authors chosen by customers who had ordered this bestseller.

- Sections devoted to different kinds of links that might appeal to readers.
- Ordering information.

Why can Amazon.com break the scrolling rule? We've posed this question at Web writing workshops and the answer is always: "Book readers like to read." We think this only partially answers the question because book readers, like all other Web users, are drive-thru readers—impatient, ruthless, and goal-driven. The paradox with regard to Amazon.com's book pages is that users are willing to do more than simply skim and scan; they're actually willing to read intensively online. The reason for this involves the nature of the Web page, and what it must contain to satisfy users.

The Web Page: A Rhetorical Unit of Content

Print documents have different kinds of pages, all of which serve a rhetorical function. For example, a how-to book is likely to have:

- "Table of Contents" pages to give readers an at-a-glance perspective of the author's depth of knowledge.
- Preface pages to explain the importance of the book.
- Content pages to convince readers that the writer is, indeed, an authority.
- Index pages to ensure readers that the author has covered the topic in detail.

Although these pages have other purposes such as helping the reader access information, their primary function is essentially to persuade readers that the author is an expert on a significant topic and, therefore, worth reading.

Web pages are no different. Their primary purpose, as we explained in Chapter 4, is to persuade users that their Web site speaks the truth amidst the great cacophony of other voices on the Internet also claiming equal credibility. However, unlike a print page that resides within documents or books that already give it a certain authority, the Web page exists in isolation, floating, so to speak, in cyberspace. It must, in only a few seconds, convince users

Web pages are isolated in cyberspace.

that its content is credible and, at the same time, persuade them to keep on reading and visit other parts of the site.

Credibility Basics

A Web page must first establish an identity in the mind of the users, and this is accomplished, at first glance, by the GUI design. Electronic media researcher Margaret Turner (1999) says that: "...It is a designer's task to provide 'hand holds' for the surfer. These handholds can be colour, background design, motif, a visual metaphor. Importantly, they need to be standard across the site to reinforce the visitor's sense of being in one place and to enhance the quality of holding that allays anxiety."

Although a pleasing GUI creates presence, it isn't sufficient to ensure credibility. As a rhetorical, stand-alone unit, every Web page must also include:

> Credibility depends on many factors.

- A short page title that informs users about that page's content.

- An organizational title or logo so the user knows who owns the site.

- Navigational information that tells users how to get to the "Home" page.

- A description of the site owner(s) through a link such as "About Us."

- A contact address for feedback and questions—this can be done through a link to "Contact Us."

- A date indicating when the content was written or revised. This allows users to place the content within a chronological context and to know if it's current.

(For more information on credibility and writing style, see Chapter 4, "E-Rhetoric: A New Form of Persuasion.")

The Page as Persona

As we discussed in Chapter 2, writing is not a one-way trip of content from the author to a reader. Rather, it's a two-way exchange to which each player brings knowledge and, thus, creates meaning. Cognitive theorist Walter Kintsch (as reported in Mary Coney and Michaël Steehouder, 2000:328) notes that readers have three different ways of building representations of text in their minds.

- **Surface:** A verbatim representation based on the letters, words, and sentences.

- **Semantic:** A representation of conventional meanings based on the knowledge of words and syntax.

- **Situational:** A mental mode representation in which readers gain an image of the text's reality but then actively integrate it with their own prior knowledge, beliefs, needs, preferences, and cultural assumptions.

Technical communications researchers Coney and Steehouder (2000:328) conclude that content developers must recognize that content can't be separated from context, or text from the author or the audience. "When we analyze a text, whether it is printed or electronic, we should...study all these factors, particularly *their relationship to each other*, to predict how effective a document will be for its intended audience."

> You're the host of a party.

To put it in a different way, as the Web page writer/editor, you should consider yourself the host of a party—one that must be re-created on each and every single Web page. Each page must have its metaphorical balloons and streamers, food and drinks, smiles and welcomes. Each user is an invited guest, although a stranger to you. His or her arrival requires an interaction—the textual equivalent of a social engagement. In this metaphor, every word you write or edit is part of a conversation in which you must put your best foot forward. The party will only take place if you can convince each and every visitor to join in the festivities.

Users and Parasocial Interaction

The term *parasocial* refers to social interaction that is not direct, but mediated through a persona. In the past, researchers have studied parasocial interaction as it relates to television viewing behavior, and examined the types of relationships built up between viewers and television personalities such as soap-opera characters, news anchors, hosts of shopping channels, and so on. Research demonstrated that this type of parasocial interaction is based on how much the viewer relates to, and identifies, with the persona. Elements such as physical appeal, perceived similarity, empathy, and likeability all contribute to building the parasocial relationship.

Web advertising researcher John Hoerner (1999:138) decided to see if Web sites also created parasocial interactions with users. Hoerner tested four commercial Web sites—two that were hosted by actual personae, and two that were not. Adapting the parasocial interaction scale used for testing television viewers, he asked users to indicate their agreement or disagreement with the statements in Table 7.3.

> Parasocial interactions don't involve actual people.

Hoerner (1999:145-146) discovered that: "Parasocial interaction with web sites does not appear to be dependent on the presence of a persona….The design metaphor, flow of the web experience, and styles of textual and graphic presentations of the information all become elements of a web site persona and encourage parasocial interaction by the visitor/user with that persona." In other words, as a writer/editor, you can have a sig-

Table 7.3   A Parasocial Interaction Web Site Scale

A PARASOCIAL INTERACTION WEB SITE SCALE

- This Web site adds credibility to the information it provides me.
- I would tell my friends about this Web site.
- I feel sorry for this Web site when there are mistakes or problems with it.
- This Web site is interested in my opinions and comments.
- I feel as if I am part of a close-knit group when I visit this Web site.
- Visiting this Web site helps me form opinions about the topics and issues presented at this site.
- I would visit this Web site again.
- The personality of this Web site is friendly and down-to-earth.
- I can trust the information I get from this Web site.
- Visiting this Web site made me relax and have fun.
- I wanted to say something to this Web site.
- I got mad at this Web site when it didn't work properly.
- The personality of this Web site makes me comfortable, as if I am with friends.
- I felt the time I spent visiting this Web site was worth it.
- This Web site was considerate and didn't overload my computer's technical capabilities.

Source: Adapted from "Scaling the Web: A Parasocial Interaction Scale for World Wide Web Sites" by John Hoerner (1999).

nificant impact on helping users develop an affinity to, and a relationship with, a Web site.

Role-Playing Online

As a professional writer/editor, you've had experience massaging text to have it present a persona to the reader. Perhaps you've written reports designed to be highly objective and authoritative, advertising copy that's been conversational and friendly, or speeches and dialogue that aim for immediacy and intimacy. When you've done this, you've given the text a persona by playing a role in the text, that is, the authority figure, friend, or close acquaintance.

At the same time as you're acting in an online role, you're giving users roles to play as they read your text. For example, as you develop content from a teaching perspective, users must take on the role of learners/students for the site to be successful. Similarly, if you're marketing a product, users must be willing to become shoppers. Coney and Steehouder (2000:329-330) state:

> It is very important to realize that the real visitor and author can be very different from these roles...The Web site creates roles that

People Create Credibility

A Web site doesn't have credibility on its own. It's just a vehicle for getting a message from A to B. The organization that creates the Web site doesn't necessarily have credibility either. An organization is just a *thing*, a third party. So who's really credible? People—people who give a voice to the site. And the Web isn't some shiny, brave, new world where the old communications rules don't apply. A lot of people think the Web is completely different from print but, in fact, Web writers and editors face the same challenges as if they were writing a brochure. You have to ask yourself questions like: "Who is the audience?"; "Is this format appropriate?"; and "What level of language should I use?" These are all elements of good communication which create credibility for users.

Linda Jorgensen, Manager, EEI Press
EEI Communications
www.eeicommunications.com

define the content, the tone, the way of communicating within the site. The communicative effect depends on the degree to which the author role is attractive and trustworthy to the real readers, and whether the real readers are able and willing to play the role attributed to them.

However, what happens if the page persona doesn't meet the needs of users?

> The effects of poorly conceived or constructed roles cannot be mitigated by well-designed graphics and navigation, or well-crafted text. If we as users don't like who we are allowed—sometimes required—to become as we enter a particular site, we are not likely to stay for long. And if the authorial persona we are expected to engage with is offensive, condescending, confusing, inconsistent, or just plain boring, few sites can hold us for long.

And how different is role-playing on the Web as compared to print? Coney and Steehouder (2000:32) suggest that the Web's interactivity enhances the rhetorics of role-playing. When users become active browsers of informational sites as opposed to passive readers/viewers of information, they play roles that are: "…more visible, more flexible—indeed, more dramatic than in traditional media…" Online functions—surveys, activities such as quizzes, and hypertext links—that help users build knowledge, can create dynamic parasocial interactions between Web sites and users.

How can you learn more about online role-playing? Figure 7.4 provides you with a checklist of questions you should ask when you explore other sites and when you're developing content for your own site.

Creating Page Personalities

> *If you would win a man to your cause,*
> *first convince him that you are his sincere friend.*

> **ABRAHAM LINCOLN**

As the host of the textual party, you're in charge of creating a credible page persona for your visitor. As in any social engagement, the relationship created will be highly sensitive to the language used and the social skills it reveals. For example, writer Nick Usborne (2001) notes that Web sites can listen as well as talk:

If your site is loud and pushy, there's a clue that you don't want to listen too much. If the tone is arrogant and all-knowing, there's another clue. If you hide your feedback button, if you fail to reply to inbound emails, and if you have no phone number on your site—

---

1. Surf similar sites and ask yourself:

☐ What role is the writer/editor assuming?
☐ What role am I expected to take on?
☐ Am I willing to take on this role or not?
☐ What elements of the text affect my response?
☐ What elements of the graphics and look-and-feel affect my response?

2. On your site, what role do you intend to play?

☐ Authority
☐ Teacher/Instructor
☐ Counselor
☐ Peer
☐ Friend

3. What role do you want users to assume?

☐ Shopper seeking bargains or high-quality goods/services
☐ Students/learners
☐ Advice-seekers
☐ Peers
☐ Friends

4. What's an appropriate tone for your text?

☐ Authoritative/objective
☐ Cool/clever
☐ Wise/kindly
☐ Warm/friendly
☐ Intimate/cozy

5. Examine the graphics* and look-and-feel of your site.
Ask yourself how the visuals make you feel:

☐ What is my perception of this site at first glance?
☐ Do I get a sense of distance or intimacy? Why?
☐ How are people portrayed in photographs: friendly, aloof, inviting, creative, stern?
☐ How do the colors and shapes affect my emotions?

6. Now, try to anticipate the questions that users will ask when arriving on any Web page of your site for the first time. Ask yourself:

☐ Will they immediately recognize the role they're asked to assume?
☐ Will they be willing to assume that role?
☐ How do I know this?

*For help with analysis of visuals, see Chapter 5, "Is Seeing Believing? The Art of Visual Rhetoric."

Figure 7.4 A role-playing checklist.

these are all signs that you really aren't that interested in listening to your site visitors…What's the point in building your business within a uniquely interactive business environment if you have no interest in interacting?

You must ensure that *every Web page* on your site has a pleasing personality that demonstrates strong social skills. This means having meaningful content on every Web page, even if it's only one or two sentences. This content should be:

> Put meaningful content on every Web page.

- Relevant to the needs and wants of your visitors.

- Factual and accurate, not promotional and self-serving for the organization.

- Friendly and inviting, without being overly intimate and cloying.

"We" versus "You"

Many languages, such as Spanish, don't use personal pronouns except for emphasis. In English, however, we place personal pronouns in every sentence except a command where the *you* is implied. Our use of personal pronouns is often subtle and

A Calm, Capable, Reassuring Personality

I was brought in to help a small company in the computer hardware business who wanted to add a satellite site for a new product line. The clients had no idea who they were writing to, and their content had been created by committee. It had all different styles and points of view. The sales people had written fluff; the engineer's material was incomprehensible; and the marketing specialist's content was "Me, Me, Me." This was a pinball method of message creation, and it didn't create any kind of branding for the company. They needed text that was capable, calm, and reassuring throughout. I had to convince them, tactfully, that none of their perspectives had considered the user's needs.

Anne Tengler, Content Strategist
Cornerstone Content Services
www.cornerstonecontent.com

nuanced, and can have a powerful effect on readers. This is particularly true of *we* and its other grammatical forms, *us, our* and *ours*, and *you* as well as its other forms, *your* and *yours*. These pronouns play a significant role in creating intimacy or distance. Table 7.4 provides you with some tips for using these pronouns.

As we've noted earlier, text on the Web tends to be less formal than that in print. Professor of sociology and anthropology Rob Shields (2000:148) provides a reason by suggesting that the terms, *Web* and *Internet*, are metaphors that control the way we think about this medium and, therefore, affect how we use and contribute to it. "In the case of 'the Net,' this overall vision offers us the illusion of mastery of the Internet; the global and hugely scaled is represented as a tool, as a simple object. The Internet comes represented as a 'landscape before us' awaiting our instructions." Added to this notion of the Internet as something we can manipulate for our own purposes is the concept of a Web: "While our experience of such a social network is only of interaction and sociability with those we interact with immediately, we have the social understanding that our interactants relate to others whom we may or may not know. Thus, what we say may indeed be conveyed to others. The idea that networks may stretch beyond our own localized interactions is a familiar one that offers a sense of possibility." Only the Web provides us with this potential; all other public media have gatekeepers— for example, the editors who choose what gets to be published

Table 7.4 Tips for Using "We" and "You"

WHEN USING...	CONSIDER...
We, Us, Our, Ours	■ Using the "exclusive" *we* when you wish to maintain a distance between the site owner(s) and the audience—for example, *We have a strong privacy policy* and *Our site is designed for readability.*
	■ Using the "inclusive" *we* to create equality and intimacy—for example, *All of us must decide to act.*
You, Your, Yours	■ That commands, such as *Click to...*, imply *you.* If this implied *you* only occurs in commands, you'll achieve a formal, distancing effect.
	■ Using *you* in the text if you wish to achieve a conversational tone—for example, *If you prefer other colors, you'll find the shirt in green, blue, and yellow.*

The Mariachi Syndrome

When I teach my students how to apply for a job, I warn them about the *mariachi syndrome*—every sentence starts with the first-person pronoun, so you end up with "I, I, yi-yi." While the people paying for most corporate Web sites have generally taken business-writing courses like mine, they seem to suffer from terminal mariachi syndrome. Their sites are monuments to self-worship, and the role of the visitor seems to be to sit slack-jawed before the splendor of the corporate ego. Better to say "you" four times for every time the pronoun "we" appears and to emphasize the reader's interests and concerns. Our visitors have paid us a huge compliment by arriving on our site. If we want to return the compliment, we owe them the kind of personal attention we would give them if we were thinking of marriage... or least a really serious love affair.

Crawford Kilian, Instructor of Communications
Capilano College, Vancouver, British Columbia

and the television/film producers who decide what can be seen. The Internet/Web, on the other hand, has no filters or structure. The result is a paradox—a vast and yet intimate medium.

The Web Screen: A Flexible Unit of Space

If you've worked in print, you were developing text knowing that it would reach readers in a conventional, well-known format. In fact, if you were also part of a print production team, you knew exactly how the text would appear in the lay out—the location of certain headers and words, how paragraphs would break between pages, and so forth. The Web is different. As an online writer/editor, you must constantly write *to* a screen that you can't see and whose boundaries are unknown because you can't predict how the user will view your content.

Those Baffling Browsers

Browsers have a major effect on what users see on their monitor screen. First, a wide variety of browsers are in use, and each affects what can be viewed onscreen. Secondly, users have different browser versions and operating systems which also affect on-screen visuals. Finally, users can alter browser defaults and change what appears on a screen in a variety of ways. For example:

> Browsers affect onscreen viewing.

- Task bars can be visible or not visible.

- Images and banners can be turned on or off.

- Functionality elements such as Java can be switched on or off. This can be done by users or as part of an Intranet system with firewalls to prevent the use of certain technologies/functionalities in the workplace.

- Accessibility design doesn't allow for some functions.

Like Web designers, you'll assume that users' browsers are in default format but, in reality, you must be aware that your best intentions for viewing text may not be realized when that content reaches users. (For more information on browsers, see Chapter 8, "Content + Technology: A Surprising Alliance.")

Users' Monitor Technology

In an ideal world, all users would have the same monitors and *resolution* settings—settings with regard to number of pixels, color density, and vertical/horizontal orientation. However, the Web world is less than ideal. Older monitors may have only one resolution; new monitors may allow users to choose a wide variety of resolutions. The three common resolutions, based on pixels per square inch, are:

- **640 x 480**—older monitors.

- **800 x 600**—most commonly designed standard for desktop computers since 1998.

- **1024 x768**—generally designed for laptop computers and larger monitors.

Differing monitor resolutions have an equivalent in print media. Imagine a book that comes in three sizes—a mass-market paperback, a hardcover edition, and a large-print version for visually impaired readers. Although each type of book contains the exact same text, the size and number of its pages will be different. The result will be that any given page, say, page 42, will not have the same text as would appear on page 42 in the two other versions. However, this analogy can only go so far. Print media provides users with traditional navigation and sufficient text on a page—no matter what the size, thereby ensuring a smooth and coherent reading experience.

The three monitor resolutions affect how much of a Web page that a user will see on his or her screen. Figures 7.5, 7.6, and 7.7 show how the first screen of the "Cover Letters That Work" page appears in three resolutions.

As these figures demonstrate, how content is presented on the first screen of a Web page will have a major effect on users. The title of your Web page and the first few lines of text will be crucial in helping users predict what's ahead and decide whether they will continue reading.

Can You Count on Word Count?

You may be familiar with using word count as a means of determining how much text you need to write. For example, a newspaper columnist may have to fill a 300-word column; a magazine

Word count varies considerably.

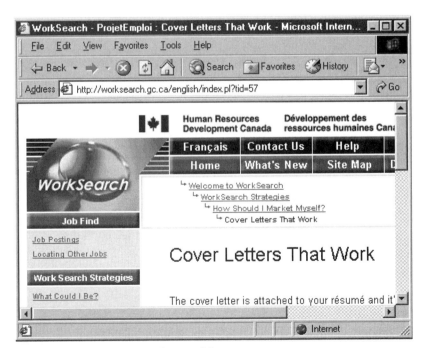

Figure 7.5 "Cover Letters that Work": 640 x 480.

May 17, 2001 (www.worksearch.gc.ca/english/index.pl?tid=57) Human Resources Development Canada; reproduced with the permission of the Minister of Public Works and Government Services Canada, 2001.

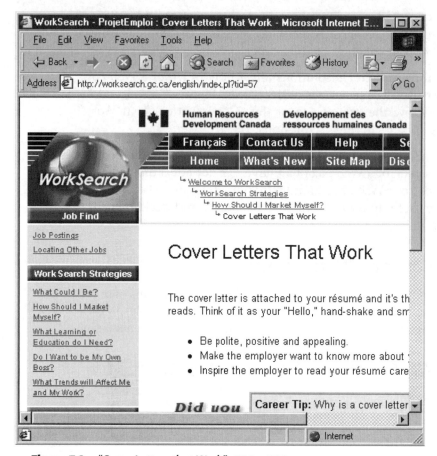

Figure 7.6 "Cover Letters that Work": 800 x 600.

May 17, 2001 (www.worksearch.gc.ca/english/index.pl?tid=57) Human Resources Development Canada; reproduced with the permission of the Minister of Public Works and Government Services Canada, 2001.

writer may be commissioned to complete an article of 2,000 words. Even writers who don't write for print media use word count to assess content. Speechwriters, for example, consider that the average speaker will use 100 words a minute so a 15-minute speech should run 1,500 words.

Let's say that your client assumes that most users will have a monitor resolution of 800 x 600 and that the onscreen font size will be the customary 10 or 12 points—a size that is variable, depending upon the site's programming and the user's browser setting. Can you use word count reliably to determine how much you can write to a screen with that resolution? The answer

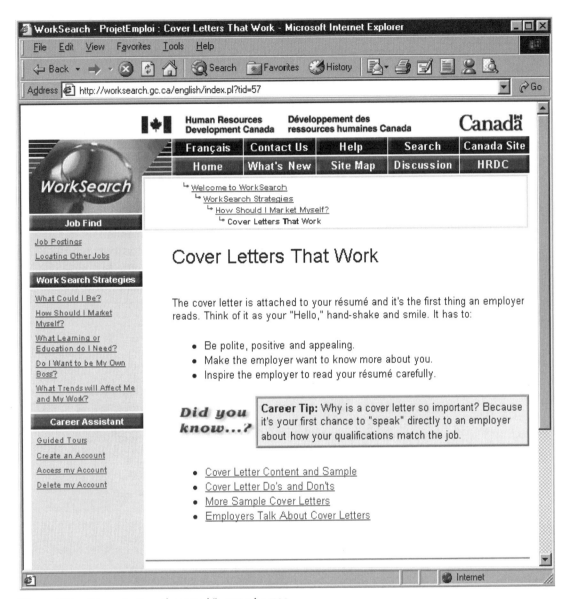

Figure 7.7   "Cover Letters that Work": 1024 by 768.

May 17, 2001 (www.worksearch.gc.ca/english/index.pl?tid=57) Human Resources Development Canada; reproduced with the permission of the Minister of Public Works and Government Services Canada, 2001.

is "No," because word count can vary considerably according to how much screen real estate is used for other types of information such as navigation bars and advertising banners. The following examples illustrate the word-count range.

A Screen with 37 Words

Appliances—Net Links
Brand & Manufacturer Central

The definitive About.com resource for appliance brand & manufacturer information, from your guide.

Clothes Dryer Venting Central

The definitive About.com resource for clothes dryer venting information, from your guide.

(About.com—April 27, 2001: www.homerepair.about.com/homegarden/
homerepair/cs/appliances/index.htm)

This text appeared on the first screen of the Web page and had to compete with four other elements whose text and visuals left little space for primary content. The screen included two navigation areas along the top of the page and down the left side, and two advertising areas—the top horizontal banner and the right-hand bar.

A Screen with 93 Words

DfE Strategy 4: Optimize Production Techniques

This strategy includes approaches to production that involve practices for "cleaner" production, i.e., the continuous use of industrial processes and products to increase efficiency, prevent pollution to all media (air, water and land), and to generally minimize risk to human health and the environment.

To accomplish cleaner production, you need to adopt a goal to make your processes as environmentally benign as possible.

Production techniques should:

- Minimize the use of ancillary materials and energy.
- Avoid hazardous compounds.
- Provide high efficiency production with low material…

(Design for Environment Guide—April 27, 2001:
www.nrc.ca/dfe/ehome/dfestra/dfestra4/dfestra4.html)

This content appeared on the first screen of the Web page. The real estate included two navigation areas—the top and left-hand navigation bars.

A Screen with 188 Words

…consequences of misbehaving. Any child with a spark of sass will find Peter's impish adventures remarkably familiar. Potter's warm, playful illustrations in soft colors invite children into the world of words and flights of fancy. Once there, she gently and humorously guides readers along the path of righteousness, leaving just enough room for children to wonder if that incorrigible Peter will be back in Mr. McGregor's garden tomorrow. This lovely boxed set—with locking mechanism and handle—contains Potter's first 12 original and authorized books: *The Tale of Peter Rabbit, The Tale of Squirrel Nutkin, The Tailor of Gloucester, The Tale of Benjamin Bunny, The Tale of Two Bad Mice, The Tale of Mrs. Tiggy-Winkle, The Tale of Mr. Jeremy Fisher, The Tale of TomKitten, The Tale of Jemima Puddle-Duck, The Tale of the Flopsy Bunnies, The Tale of Mrs. Tittlemouse, and The Tale of Timmy Tiptoes.* Each hardcover book, with original full-color illustrations, is small enough to fit inside a pocket—or a stocking! (Baby to Preschool)—*This text refers to an out of print or unavailable edition of this title.*

Was this content helpful to you?

(Amazon.com—April 27, 2001:www.amazon.com/exec/obidos/ ASIN/0723241120/o/qid=988396969/sr=2-2/107-6809188-8805316)

This content appeared on the fourth screen of the Web page. Earlier screens included three navigation bars at the top of the page and in the left- and right-hand margins. However, by the fourth screen, only the margin created by the left-hand navigation bar remained. The designer had allowed the text to expand into the right margin—a space originally taken up by the right-hand navigation bar.

A Screen with 282 Words

…as to prepare us to see this invisibility, to see without seeing, thus to think the body without body of this invisible visibility— the ghost is already taking shape—Marx declares that the thing in question, namely, the commodity, is not so simple (a warning that will elicit snickers from all the imbeciles, until the end of time, who never believe anything, of course, because they are so sure that they see what is seen, everything that is seen, only what is seen). The commodity is even very complicated; it is blurred, tangled, paralysing, aporetic, perhaps undecidable (*ein sehr vertracktes Ding*). It is so disconcerting, this commodity-thing, that one has to approach it …with "metaphysical" subtlety and "theological" niceties. Precisely in order to analyse the metaphysical and the theological that constructed the phenomenological good sense of the thing itself, of the immediately visible commodity, in flesh and blood: as what it is "at first sight" (*aufden ersten Blick*). This phenomenological good sense may perhaps be valid for use-value. It is perhaps even meant to be valid only for use-value, as if the correlation of these concepts answered to this function: phenomenology as the discourse of use-value so as not to think the market or in view of making oneself blind to exchange-value. Perhaps. And it is for this reason that phenomenological good sense or phenomenology of perception (also at work in Marx when he believes he can speak of a pure and simple use-value) can claim to foster Enlightenment since use-value has nothing at all "mysterious" about it (nicht Mysteriöses an ihr). If one keeps to use-value, the properties (Eigenschaften) of the thing (and it is going to be a question of...

(Contemporary Philosophy, Critical Theory and Postmodern Thought: From Spectres of Marx, by Jacques Derrida 1994 What is Ideology?—April 27, 2001: www.marxists. org/reference/subject/philosophy/works/fr/derrida2.htm)

This content appeared on the fifth screen of a Web page. As with many scholarly articles, the site has no navigation areas or margins, leaving all the real estate for text. Therefore, the word count is at the top end of the range for a monitor with a resolution of 800 x 600.

To Scroll or Not to Scroll

Scrolling rules
are in flux.

The Web page and Web screen are distinct entities that are connected by scrolling. The Web page is like a folded newspaper. The screen—the first thing the reader sees—is *above the fold*. To complete viewing the page, the reader has to scroll *below the fold*. One of the biggest debates in usability is that of the short page versus the long page. How much tolerance do users have for scrolling? When is a Web page too long? When is it too short? Almost every client we deal with believes that users hate to scroll, period. However, usability research suggests that the issue is complex, and users' willingness to scroll depends on a number of factors. For example, Neilsen (2000:115) says that users are more willing to scroll than in the past:

> I would still say that some users are reluctant to scroll navigation pages, but it is no longer as pronounced. My guess is that the prevalence of badly designed, long pages on the Web has inured most users to some amount of scrolling.
>
> Even if they would be willing to scroll many users will make their selection from whatever options are visible "above the fold" if they see one that looks promising. The two main conclusions from this finding are to make pages relatively short and to make sure that the most important links will be visible on most common monitors without scrolling.

Neilsen also distinguishes between scrolling on navigation and destination pages. With regard to navigation pages, he states:

Scrolling navigation pages are bad for users because they make it impossible to see all the available options at the same time. There will always be parts of a scrolling page that are invisible, so users will have to make their choice of their next action without being able to directly compare everything. Increasing the user's memory load is always bad for usability and increases the risk of errors.

However, destination pages are different because they are content-rich and have fewer navigation choices:

After a user has reached a destination page, studies show that he or she will scroll though a few screenfuls if the first screen seems promising. Users will almost never scroll through very long pages, though.

Usability researchers at User Interface Engineering (1998) had a similar, earlier finding on studies: "Users *say* they don't like to scroll. As a result, many designers try to keep their web pages short. But one of the most significant findings of our research on web-site usability is that users are perfectly willing to scroll. However, they'll only do it if the page gives them strong clues that scrolling will help them find what they're looking for."

You won't be able to find one guiding rule that works for scrollability, because the type of content on informational sites has so much variety. Unlike a news or e-zine site where the primary content is in article format, informational sites have content, possibly ranging from a brief paragraph to an archived document running many screens. Although some cases are obvious—for instance, one page per product and its specifications for an e-commerce site, organizing other types of information is generally far more ambiguous. You'll find that each Web page requires an independent judgment call as to whether you should keep content on one page or divide it among several pages. Each decision will have an *either-or* effect on users, that is, they will or will not have to:

> Page length is a judgment call.

- Drill down to reach content.

- Make several *print moves* instead of one single move to have a hard copy of the content. (Although recent print-friendly programming now enables developers to clump several Web pages into one downloadable document for printing, this tool is not yet in common use.)

One compromise to the above-and-below-the-fold controversy is to provide users with a summary of the text on the Web page's first screen. They can read the summary and decide if they wish to scroll and read the content. This type of format is fairly common on academic papers on the Web where the abstract for the paper comes first. However, it is not in frequent use elsewhere. Rather, content developers rely on the internally linked, scrollable page.

The Internally Linked, Scrollable Web Page

The internally linked, scrollable Web page is useful when you decide that content items are strongly related and should remain together, but the result will require users to scroll more than you and the client prefer. As Figure 7.8 demonstrates, the links in the first screen of this page act like a table of contents that allows users to navigate without having to use the scroll bar. The "Top of Page" icon/text allows users to know when they've finished a chunk of information. An important advantage of this type of page is that it allows users to print all the information with one print move rather than several.

Although the internally linked, scrollable Web page can help solve some issues of information structure, readability and printability, it can still present problems. If the text content of each clickable item is short and the "Top of Page" icon and/or text are clearly visible after only a short amount of scrolling, users will clearly understand they're on the same Web page. However, if the list of internal links at the top of the page is long, and the text chunks take up more than one screen, users often forget that they haven't left the original Web page. They lose their bearings and are likely to use the Back button, believing that they'll return to the original list. Instead, they'll end up on another page altogether. We think it would be useful for users if there were a Web convention, similar to "Top of the Page," that demonstrates to users, up-front, that they're on a scrollable page with internal links—perhaps a phrase at the top or bottom of the links such as "All on This Page" or an icon such as: ↕

Scrolling and Memory

As a writer/editor trying to make decisions with regard to the length of Web pages, you may find it useful to understand how

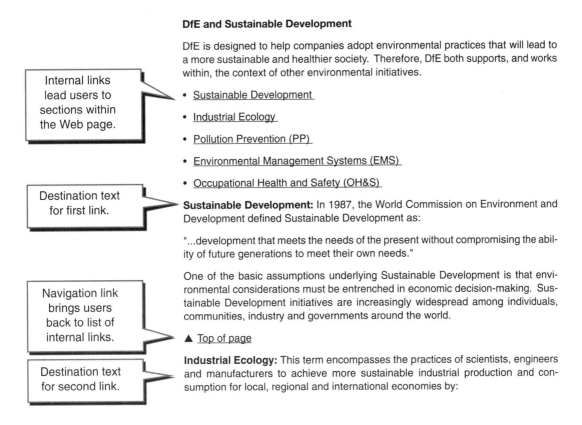

DfE and Sustainable Development

DfE is designed to help companies adopt environmental practices that will lead to a more sustainable and healthier society. Therefore, DfE both supports, and works within, the context of other environmental initiatives.

Internal links lead users to sections within the Web page.

- Sustainable Development
- Industrial Ecology
- Pollution Prevention (PP)
- Environmental Management Systems (EMS)
- Occupational Health and Safety (OH&S)

Destination text for first link.

Sustainable Development: In 1987, the World Commission on Environment and Development defined Sustainable Development as:

"...development that meets the needs of the present without compromising the ability of future generations to meet their own needs."

One of the basic assumptions underlying Sustainable Development is that environmental considerations must be entrenched in economic decision-making. Sustainable Development initiatives are increasingly widespread among individuals, communities, industry and governments around the world.

Navigation link brings users back to list of internal links.

▲ Top of page

Destination text for second link.

Industrial Ecology: This term encompasses the practices of scientists, engineers and manufacturers to achieve more sustainable industrial production and consumption for local, regional and international economies by:

Figure 7.8 A portion of an internally linked, scrollable page.
Design for Environment Guide—April 28, 2001 (www.nrc.ca/dfe/ehome/overview/sd/sd.html).

scrolling affects memory. The workings of human memory are complex and continually under study. However, computer-interface interaction specialist Christine Faulkner (1998:33) states that: "Human memory probably consists of a series of connected systems. There is not general agreement on the form it takes, but one of the most useful descriptions for the purpose of human-computer interaction consists of recognizing three types of memory."

- **Long term memory:** Where memories are stored.
- **Working memory:** Where conscious thought processes operate.
- **Sensory memory:** Copes with inputs from the senses.

In the past, psychologists used the term *short term memory* to describe a mental system that enabled us to hold limited information in our brains for a short time. The information in this system would decay fairly quickly if it wasn't constantly refreshed. They saw short term memory as a system operating separately from long term memory. Today, however, many psychologists use the term *working memory*, because, as Faulkner explains, they now envision both working memory and long term memory as "being aspects of the same organization but performing different functions and having different strengths and weaknesses. Both aspects are part of the same system."

Reading online is an activity that involves, primarily, our working memory. Faulkner (1998:37) states that: "…working memory has a considerable role to play in both language understanding and calculation. In both these cases, there is a need to hold ideas in your head while the process of interpretation of the words or the calculation is carried out. For example, to understand a sentence you need to remember the beginning while you read through, or listen to, the end. If you could not do that, you would be unable to recall the subject of the sentence."

> Reading Web text involves *working memory.*

How much can users remember when they're reading and scrolling at the same time? Consultant and writer Jef Raskin (2000:17) explains that users have a *locus of attention* which can be either an object in the physical world or an idea occupying their mind. He suggests that the human mind can only have one locus of attention at any one given time. For example, if you're learning to ride a bike, all of your attention will be on your physical interactions with the handlebars and pedals. You can't, at the moment, concentrate on navigating through a city or watching the clouds overhead. But, once you master bike riding and it becomes second nature, your attention can then move to other things.

However, one of the most important points about our ability to pay attention is that we can't completely control it. According to Raskin, we receive a great deal of visual and aural stimulation, much of which we unconsciously block out because our minds are not capable of handling all that information. Secondly, when we receive perceptions of things by making them our focus of attention (for example, by focusing on the hum of our computers) within seconds of shifting our attention to something else (for example, what we see on our screens) our memory of that hum will decay and chances are, we will not be able to recreate it in our minds. As Raskin (2000:18) notes: "Perceptions do not automatically become memories. Most perceptions are lost after they decay."

What does this mean for users who must scroll or use the PgDn button to move from screen to screen? According to Raskin (2000:21): "When you do two tasks simultaneously, neither of which is automatic, your performance on each task degrades—a phenomenon that psychologists, call *interference*—compared to your performance on each task alone, because the two tasks compete for your attention. The more predictable, automatic, and unconscious a task becomes, the less it will degrade or compete with other tasks."

> Scrolling affects our *focus of attention*.

When we connect Raskin's notion of locus of attention to that of working memory, we can see why it's so difficult to keep online text in our memories. Reading is an automatic task, but not when it's constantly interrupted by the need to stop and scroll. Scrolling forces users to shift attention from a cognitive task to a physical one involving small motor coordination. Although users may want to attend to both activities with equal attention, they can't. And, if as text scrolls upwards, the last line hasn't been held in users' working memory, it's unlikely that they'll be able to hold onto the meaning of the content at all.

A Call to Action: Improving Online Reading

The problems with online reading have to do with bad interface design and programming. You either have to click or scroll, both of which require cognitive attention. Some people get into the down-arrow habit where they just keep their finger on the key and let it scroll, but the text usually goes either too slow or too fast. Interfaces must be designed to accommodate our ability to pay conscious attention to only one object or situation at a time. There's no reason why the interface can't have a population-independent design that allows users to choose a scrolling rate that works just for them. Then when you press on the down-arrow key, you can read comfortably and don't have to pay attention to two activities at the same time.

Jef Raskin, Consultant and Writer
www.jefraskin.com

The Magical Number 7, Plus or Minus 2

In 1956, George Miller, a memory researcher, wrote a well-known article about the number seven and its connection to memory. What he noticed was that: "First, the span of absolute judgment and the span of immediate memory impose severe limitations on the amount of information that we are able to receive, process, and remember. By organizing the stimulus input simultaneously into several dimensions and successively into a sequence or chunks, we manage to break (or at least stretch) this infomation bottleneck."

> Limit the length of bulleted lists.

Miller (1956) describes research demonstrating that when the sequences or chunks are seven, give or take two, memory was improved: "The first point to note is that on patterns containing up to five or six dots the subjects simply did not make errors. The performance on these small numbers of dots was so different from the performance with more dots that it was given a special name. Below seven the subjects were said to *subitize*; above seven they were said to *estimate*."

Miller was hesitant to make a final judgment on the number seven because it can be difficult to assess what information is worth gauging as a number. Take, for example, the seven-digit North American phone number used for local dialing: 111-1111. We have no problem remembering these numbers, because they fall within the rule of seven, plus or minus two. What will happen in areas where people must now enter three-digit area codes as well? Now, they will have *ten* numbers to memorize, seemingly a challenge to our memory system. Alice Horning, a professor of rhetoric and linguistics, who studies how people remember what they read, suggests the additional three numbers will *not* overburden memory, because we will use the area code as one bit of information, rather than three bits. In other words, the 10-digit phone number will only be eight bits of information, still within the rule of seven, plus or minus two.

The more you study the impact of the number seven in our lives, the more intriguing Miller's hypothesis becomes. Miller himself saw it as mysterious:

> And finally, what about the magical number seven? What about the seven wonders of the world, the seven seas, the seven deadly sins, the seven daughters of Atlas in the Pleiades, the seven ages of man, the seven levels of hell, the seven primary colors, the seven notes of the musical scale, and the seven days of the week?

What about the seven-point rating scale, the seven categories for absolute judgment, the seven objects in the span of attention, and the seven digits in the span of immediate memory? For the present I propose to withhold judgment. Perhaps there is something deep and profound behind all these sevens, something just calling out for us to discover it.

Scrolling Considerations

When deciding if content should remain on one Web page, you should look carefully at how the content will scroll in the three different monitor resolutions. Your second consideration should be how your sentences and paragraphs will affect reading and memory. Technical communications researchers Carol Isakson and Jan Spyridakis (1999) studied how syntax affects memory. They found that people remember important information best in certain grammatical structures:

- A clause structure which always contains a tensed verb. For example, *he forgave the man* is more memorable than *by forgiving the man.*

- An independent clause rather than in a relative clause. For example, *She should say hello to the child is* more memorable than *They thought she should say hello to the child.*

- A relative clause at the end of a sentence. For example, if you wish to emphasize the formidable quality of a person, it's more memorable to write *Ms. X is a brown-haired woman who is formidable* rather than *Ms. X is a formidable woman with brown hair.*

Isakson and Spyridakis (1999:378) also recommend that a Web page's most important information should be in its first paragraph: "The fact that readers exhibit high recall for information in the first paragraph of a document should remind writers and editors of the importance of a good introduction. Readers get their bearings when they enter a document."

When judging the effects of scrolling, always keep in mind what is disappearing besides lines of text. Because information comes in so many varieties, we can't foresee all the possibilities you'll face. However, some common problems include:

- **Interactive quizzes and surveys**—users may have to click on buttons to answer such choices as "Yes," "No," or "Maybe." If the quiz or survey is long, they may scroll so far that the labels for these choices disappear. Consider repeating labels throughout so users don't forget their options.

- **Tables/Charts/Graphs**—allow users to see the titles and labels of the elements in tables/charts/graphs before they begin scrolling. Also put the same information at the bottom of the table/graph/chart for users who are scrolling upwards.

- **GUI interface**—on most Web pages, the visuals disappear as users scroll. In Chapter 6, we discussed the concept of Web intertextuality with regard to textual content. We said that every text leaves a mental imprint that affects the way we read the next text, and so on. The same concept applies to visual content. Try this experiment. Use the PgDn button on any given Web page and scroll screen-by-screen. Are you in a constantly shifting visual environment even though you haven't left the page? How does this affect your memory of what you've just seen?

Scrolling is a difficult issue because memory is a complex phenomenon and a Web page involves both textual and visual elements. Table 7.5 provides a summary of issues to consider and tips for writing/editing.

Writing/Editing Nuts and Bolts

Writing/editing content is about organizing information such as facts, opinions, ideas, concepts, and themes. However, other aspects of online writing/editing also require your close attention: consistency of style and copyediting/proofreading.

The Editorial Style Guide

Consistency refers to uniformity in a document with regard to such text elements as the spelling of unusual words, how references and sources are cited, and what is capitalized, italicized, and quoted. Every bit of text on a Web site requires your editorial scrutiny. This includes items that you may not consider content such as the text in navigation bars, every header and link, words in graphics and illustrations, copyright information, descriptions to help users register, and validation screens such as those that come up confirming a registration. You can't expect designers and

Table 7.5   Tips to Help Users Scroll Through Text

CONTENT/VISUAL ASPECTS	TIPS
Clause/Sentence/ Paragraph	■ Put the page's significant, thematic material in the first paragraph.
	■ Put the most important information in independent clauses.
	■ Remember that information in verbs with tenses such as *he finds* has more impact than those in gerunds, that is, *finding*, or in prepositional structures such as *for finding information*.
	■ Put important information at the beginnings and ends of sentences and paragraphs.
Lists	■ Always group items together that are related. The relationships help memory retention.
	■ Don't put too many items in one list of bullets or links. Keep in mind the rule of 7, plus or minus 2.
Other Content/ Visual Components	■ Repeat textual elements that identify user choices throughout a page.
	■ Consider repeating titles and label elements at the beginning and end of tables/charts/graphs.
	■ Advise your production team to continue one or more elements of the design, such as the background color of the left-hand navigation bar, to the bottom of the Web page in order to maintain visual unity.

programmers to make good text decisions for these Web elements because writing/editing is not their field of expertise—it's yours.

What Goes into an Editorial Style Guide

As the *Chicago Manual of Style* (1969/1982: 60) notes: "No style book will provide rules covering all matters of style encountered by the editor, and no editor worth the title will apply identical rules to every book manuscript." You should, therefore, use a variety of sources for building each Web site's editorial style guide. These can include:

Become a "Quality Controller"

It's very difficult to persuade people to understand that Web content needs editing, particularly the programming people. There's just a huge communications gap. Most techies have never worked in publishing, and they really don't understand what makes text readable. They think that when we hand over copy for programming that it should be the end of the process. They don't understand that when content goes online it needs proofreading. It's just like the print world. Until you see content in its final format, you can't be sure it's going to work right. I've found that if I call what I'm doing *quality control* as opposed to editing, I get a much better response.

Renee Hopkins, Web Content Editor
Edit-work.com
www.edit-work.com

- Your client's house style guide, if it exists.

- One or more style books.

- A general dictionary that applies to your national language. For example, if you're writing in English, you'll use American style for the United States, Canadian style for Canada, and British style for all countries whose educational system is based on language usage from the United Kingdom.

- One or more specialized dictionaries and/or lexicons for content with specialized terminology—for example, the types of terms found in scientific, medical, financial, and information technology texts.

Programmers Have Style, Too!

In Web development, the terms *style guide* or *style sheet* are always used to describe the system of HTML codes used by programmers to ensure that all design elements on Web pages are consistent. Anticipate confusion around the production table when you mention your own style guide/sheet. We suggest that you add the word *editorial* for clarification.

However, the most important thing to know about a style guide is that there are no hard-and-fast rules about what should be in it. There are two reasons for this.

> A style guide reflects *your* choices.

- **Different texts have different characteristics:** Every text is unique in its combination of terminology and text elements. For example, one Web site has medical information, while another provides investment advice. The former would contain specialized medical and biological terminology, as well as photographs, illustrations, and diagrams. The latter would have investment and monetary terminology and include tables and charts.

- **The style of a Web site depends on its audience:** How you handle various text elements depends on who will be reading the content. For example, if your Web content arrives from the subject matter experts filled with acronyms, this may be entirely suitable for an Intranet site where employees are familiar with organizational jargon. On the other hand, acronyms may not work on a public site where the audience is general. In this case, you'll have to determine if, when, and how to use these elements of the text.

Your style guide will reflect the editorial issues that you face regarding a Web site's content and how you've decided to handle them, thereby representing your personal editorial philosophy and decisions. Table 7.6 provides an overview of various issues and areas of Web editing with tips to aid consistency.

A Real-Life Style Guide

A Web style guide is a document that develops "on the fly" because you won't be able to anticipate all the style issues in your text until you meet them head on. You may also find that you change your mind en route, because a new situation arises in which a previous solution won't work. This will not cause a problem if the project schedule allows you to complete the entire text to final draft before it goes to the programmer. However, in our experience, this type of scheduling is rare.

For example, we edited the content for a scientific site. The client was in a hurry and wanted to get the programming, which was time-consuming, underway. He requested that we hand over the sections as they were edited. Figure 7.9 on page 240 is an excerpt from a style guide we developed during this process. It required three revisions to reflect two kinds of changes—new types of text

Table 7.6   Tips to Improving Textual Consistency

ISSUES/AREAS	TIPS TO CONSISTENCY
Vocabulary	■ Identify words with spellings that are not common usage and ensure that these words are spelled the same throughout the site. ■ Indicate how elements such as numbers, percentage signs, money, dates, and measurements will be expressed. ■ Determine the treatment of common compound words that are often treated differently—for example, *decisionmaking, decision-making,* or *decision making.*
Abbreviations and Acronyms	■ Identify which abbreviations/acronyms will be understood by the target audience and can be used throughout the site. ■ Determine whether abbreviations/acronyms that are not easily understood should always be spelled out, or can be abbreviated or made into an acronym after its first mention per Web page—for example, *human immunodeficiency virus (HIV).*
Italics, Bolds, Quotation Marks, and Parentheses	■ Determine words, phrases, and headers that should appear in italics or bold in the text. ■ Determine use of single and double quotation marks in the text, and whether punctuation will appear in or outside of quotes. (In English, the rules of usage are different in the United States and Britain.) ■ Determine text elements that may require parentheses—such as (e.g., apples and oranges).
Hyphens and Dashes	■ Note that many programmers do not know the codes of *en* and *em* dashes, resulting in inappropriate use of hyphens in many Web texts. Use the HTML special character list in the Appendix to provide the programming codes. ■ Use a style book to ensure consistency with regard to hyphen and dash usage. ■ Determine if specialized compound terms require hyphens.
Punctuation	■ Note that punctuation in text written specifically for the Web tends to be much simpler than that in print—for example, bulleted lists rarely have semi-colons at the end of each item, but may have periods, or if such items are short, no punctuation at all.

Table 7.6 (Continued)

ISSUES/AREAS	TIPS TO CONSISTENCY
Punctuation (continued)	▪ Identify specific uses of punctuation marks where usage varies considerably—for example, serial commas.
	▪ Determine whether standalone links will take periods or not have any punctuation at all.
	▪ Decide if link titles will take periods, colons, or dashes if they are followed by descriptions.
Capitalization	▪ Use a style book to ensure consistency of capitalization for terminology in areas such as science, religion, legal usage, and art as well as names applied to races, languages, peoples, government bodies, official titles, and so on.
	▪ Determine whether specialized terms require capitalization.
	▪ Determine whether the first letter after a bullet, colon, and em dash will be capitalized or not.
	▪ Determine the treatment of microcontent—for example, *Top* of *Page*, *Top* Of *Page*, *TOP OF PAGE*.
Text Shortening Methods	▪ Identify every possiblilty for shortening text—for example, "abbreviations/acronyms" rather than "abbreviations and acronyms."
	▪ Search similar Web sites for text-shortening methods that would be appropriate for your site.
	▪ Constantly balance the need to shorten text with the repercussions of going too far in breaking the rules of print. If your shortcuts are too drastic, they'll affect readability.
Graphic Design Issues	▪ Ensure readability through appropriate font types, for example, nonserif fonts are easier to read online than serif fonts.
	▪ Ask the designer/programmer to put spaces between paragraphs to ease eye fatigue.
	▪ If bulleted items are more than one line in length, ask designer to double-space between the bulleted items for easier readability.
	▪ Consider every aspect of text presentation with regard to readability and discuss issues with the designer and programmer. For example, is it easy for users to distinguish between the text color and the screen background color? (For more information on the interaction between text and visuals, see Chapter 5, "Is Seeing Believing? The Art of Visual Rhetoric.")

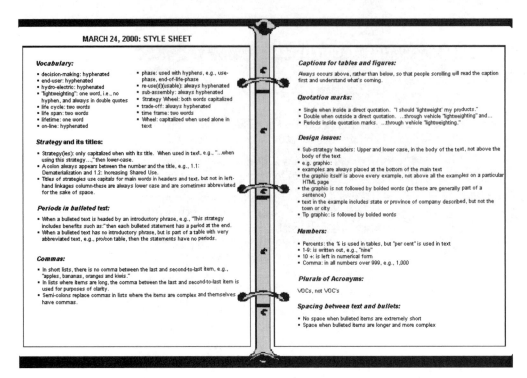

MARCH 24, 2000: STYLE SHEET

Vocabulary:

- decision-making: hyphenated
- end-user: hyphenated
- hydro-electric: hyphenated
- "lightweighting": one word, i.e., no hyphen, and always in double quotes
- life cycle: two words
- life span: two words
- lifetime: one word
- on-line: hyphenated

- phase: used with hyphens, e.g., use-phase, end-of-life-phase
- re-use(d)(usable): always hyphenated
- sub-assembly: always hyphenated
- Strategy Wheel: both words capitalized
- trade-off: always hyphenated
- time frame: two words
- Wheel: capitalized when used alone in text

Strategy and its titles:

- Strategy(ies): only capitalized when with its title. When used in text, e.g., "...when using this strategy...," then lower-case.
- A colon always appears between the number and the title, e.g., 1.1: Dematerialization and 1.2: Increasing Shared Use.
- Titles of strategies use capitals for main words in headers and text, but not in left-hand linkages column-these are always lower case and are sometimes abbreviated for the sake of space.

Periods in bulleted text:

- When a bulleted text is headed by an introductory phrase, e.g., "This strategy includes benefits such as:" then each bulleted statement has a period at the end.
- When a bulleted text has no introductory phrase, but is part of a table with very abbreviated text, e.g., pro/con table, then the statements have no periods.

Commas:

- In short lists, there is no comma between the last and second-to-last item, e.g., "apples, bananas, oranges and kiwis."
- In lists where items are long, the comma between the last and second-to-last item is used for purposes of clarity.
- Semi-colons replace commas in lists where the items are complex and themselves have commas.

Captions for tables and figures:

Always occurs above, rather than below, so that people scrolling will read the caption first and understand what's coming.

Quotation marks:

- Single when inside a direct quotation. "I should 'lightweight' my products."
- Double when outside a direct quotation. ...through vehicle "lightweighting" and...
- Periods inside quotation marks. ...through vehicle 'lightweighting."

Design issues:

- Sub-strategy headers: Upper and lower case, in the body of the text, not above the body of the text
- e.g. graphic:
- examples are always placed at the bottom of the main text
- the graphic itself is above every example, not above all the examples on a particular HTML page
- the graphic is not followed by bolded words (as these are generally part of a sentence)
- text in the example includes state or province of company described, but not the town or city
- Tip graphic: is followed by bolded words

Numbers:

- Percents: the % is used in tables, but "per cent" is used in text
- 1-9: is written out, e.g., "nine"
- 10 +: is left in numerical form
- Comma: in all numbers over 999, e.g., 1,000

Plurals of Acronyms:

VOCs, not VOC's

Spacing between text and bullets:

- No space when bulleted items are extremely short
- Space when bulleted items are longer and more complex

Figure 7.9 An excerpt from a style guide.

and re-visited editorial decisions. In order to keep the production team in the loop, we provided each new version of the guide to the client and programmer and identified each version by date.

However, this particular style guide was for one small Web project. If you work on a large Web site with thousands of pages and/or for a large organization with many contributors, you're likely to be dealing with much more complex editorial problems and solutions than we encountered in this project. Therefore, we recommend two online articles about editorial style guides and editing techniques from *Intercom*, the magazine for the Society for Technical Communication—Judy Peterson (2000): "Online Editing: Minimizing Your Turnaround Time," and Geoffrey Hart (2000): "The Style Guide is Dead, Long Live the Dynamic Style Guide." You'll find them at www.stc.org/search_pubs.html. Just type the titles into the Keyword Search.

> Don't forget about accessibility.

Your editorial style guide doesn't have to be limited to your text decisions. You can also expand it to include visual elements such as:

- The color and font type and size of headers.
- The color of visited links.

- Bolding, capitalization, and punctuation of text within graphic images.
- Corporate identity packages that include logos, fonts, and colors specific to the organization.

A Note About Proofreading

Quality text presentation requires time spent to proof text and correct errors. To do this, we strongly suggest that you use a hard copy of all Web pages, unless you're familiar with HTML and other programming languages and can edit on-screen. This means printing out the Web site, a time-consuming task in itself, particularly for a large site. Also, you may be familiar with proofreading marks, but you shouldn't expect anyone else on the production team to know what they mean. Although print graphic designers and printers learn proofreading marks as part of their training, many Web designers have no formal graphic arts training, and programmers none at all. Therefore, you'll need to use marks or terms that will be understandable to your team.

Although proofreading content on print-outs requires the same tasks as those for print documents, be aware of two issues particular to online content:

- **Database generated pages:** Remember to create and print out database-generated pages such as those that would occur after a user has finished a quiz or done a search on the site's search engine. These kinds of pages will not occur in a general printout of the site.
- **Text that doesn't print:** Check all text that does not appear in print-outs such as roll-overs and pull-down menus. Proofing this type of text means viewing the content online, identifying the Web page for the designers or programmers, and providing them with a typed correction.

Quality proofreading requires patience, an eye for detail, and the ability to read a document many times and still see it as fresh and new. This can be particularly difficult for you as the writer/editor, because your closeness to the material may blind you to errors. We strongly recommend having another person, who hasn't been involved in the writing process, proofread the material as a quality control measure. However, you may find that you're the only person on the team who can act as proofreader. Table 7.7 provides you with some tips to enhance your proofreading skills.

Keeping Track of Web Pages

Another challenge facing Web production teams is developing an efficient process for naming Web pages electronically. Because you'll be exchanging content documents with your client(s), designer(s), and programmer(s) by e-mail, your Web pages and their revisions (of which there can be many!) need to be easily identifiable to everyone on the team. It's a good idea to:

- Draw a schematic of each Web site section, a mini-information architecture, so that you know where the pages fit within that section. You may be adding or cutting content that will move pages up or down, and it's very useful to have the visual schematic for a reference.

- Give each site section its own folder on your directory. Within it, you can create subdirectories with different versions of the content as it undergoes revision.

- Give each Web page its own file. Resist the urge to clump pages together in one file; they may require separation at a later date.

File name conventions may already be in place if you enter production on an already existing Web site; however, if you're working on a new site, you may play a role in developing the conventions. Development teams have used many different types of conventions, depending on the size and scope of projects and/or software requirements—for example, numerically, alphabetically, using dates, and so forth. When developing the *Discover*CIBC site (see Chapter 6), we built file names in the following way:

- **Build**—the first component of each file name referred to its site section—in this case, *Building Your Career*.

- **BuildLevel2**—the next component of the file name indicated where the file fell in the information architecture of the section.

- **BuildLevel2attitude**—the third component was based on the Web page title—in this case, "Your Attitude is Key."

- **BuildLevel2attitude-j**—to indicate a corrected version from the client, we used the initial "j" for her first name.

- **BuildLevel2attitude-jc**—the rewrite added the initial of the writer's first name.

In some cases, teams must base their file name conventions on the old DOS-based formats of 8 dot 3, that is, eight characters, a

Table 7.7   Tips to Quality Proofreading

ASPECTS OF PROOFREADING	TIPS
Physical Environment	■ Proofread in a quiet environment that includes a comfortable chair and good lighting. ■ Consider using pencil rather than pen for corrections that you're not sure about. Too many crossed out items will make it difficult for programmers to read your notes.
Time and Concentration	■ Only proofread when you're rested. If you're tired, you won't be able to concentrate and you'll miss errors. ■ Proofread when you have adequate time. You can't rush the process. ■ Break up proofreading into time chunks that suit your ability to concentrate. When you feel yourself flagging, it's time to quit.
Textual Elements	■ After you've gone through the text once, read all headers separately. This is prominent information, and you want to ensure that it's correct. ■ Read the text again—this time, just looking at punctuation. ■ Read any text in all caps very carefully. It's harder to see errors in this kind of content. ■ Double check for correctness and consistency in text that occurs in graphic images. Usually designers have input this content, and text is not their strong suit. ■ Look for similar errors in similar types of text. For example, if you find quoted information with space problems between punctuation and quotation marks, there's a good chance the same problem will occur with other quotations on other Web pages.

period, and then three characters. This format is very limiting. For example, had this been the case for Discover*CIBC*, the file would likely have been *Bld2atti.j01* where we used the last three characters to keep track of revisions.

The important thing to remember is that no one method of creating file names is right. Our process for Discover*CIBC* worked well because the project was small and during the revisions, the files were passing only through the client's and writer's hands. Larger projects would likely require a more complex system.

Another important convention must be created to show the programmer(s) where links need to be placed and which text files they should use as links. In the following example of text from Dicover*CIBC*, which we were creating in a word-processing program, we underlined the words that we wished to appear as links on-screen, bracketed the names of the text files, and also highlighted the bracketed information in blue. Since the regular text was in black, the blue font made it easier for the programmers to identify linkages and appropriate text files.

> What is career management? A pro-active approach to planning your career steps through:
>
> - Knowing yourself.
>
> - Developing professionalism. [Link to Build2onthejob-j]
>
> - Building a positive attitude. [Link to Build2attitude-jc]
>
> - Seeking out opportunities.
>
> - Making a commitment to lifelong learning. [Link to Build2learn-j]

Keeping track of content is extremely difficult, if not impossible, on sites that have numerous sections and thousands of pages. The problem has become so pervasive that software companies are currently developing content management systems to help site owners. These systems not only manage site inventory and reduce duplication, they also enforce consistency on content. For example, you may find yourself writing within templates or to prescribed scripts. In this type of system, each text becomes an "object" that can be mixed and matched with other "objects" to create documents according to user needs. (For more information on these systems, see Chapter 9, "Keep CALM: Content and Logical Management.")

To Sum It Up

In Chapter 3, we discussed a project in which we attempted to live by the rule of thumb that users should reach content within three clicks. Although we found this impossible in reality, we suggest that it's an ideal worth adhering to as you make judgment calls on writing/editing *for* the Web page and *to* the Web screen. It is far too easy to keep adding material—"Oh, we'll just have them click down to…"—than it is to tighten content until it squeaks. Adhering to the ideal, however imperfectly, will assist you in creating good rhetorical Web pages that attract users' attention and keep their interest as well as reducing the number of screens per page. Our advice? Keep your red pen close, cut ruthlessly, and then, when you don't think you have a word to spare, cut again.

Resources for This Chapter

Books

The Humane Interface: New Directions for Designing Interactive Systems by Jef Raskin. A new approach to usability from the point of the user and common sense design. (Addison-Wesley: 2000)

The Web Style Guide: Basic Design Principles for Creating Web Sites by Patrick J. Lynch and Sarah Horton. Provides a thorough overview of Web site development from interface design to editorial style.

English Style Guides. These references provide general guidelines for grammar, punctuation, and usage.

- *Chicago Manual of Style* for American usage. (The University of Chicago Press: 1982)

- *The Canadian Style: A Guide to Writing and Editing* for Canadian usage. (Government of Canada: 1997)

- *Copy-Editing: Third Edition* by Judith Butcher for U.K. usage. (Cambridge University Press: 1992)

- *Write Edit Print: Style Manual for Aotearoa New Zealand* for New Zealand usage. (Daphne Brasell Associates Ltd.: 1997)

- *Style Manual for Australian usage.* (Australian Government Printing Service: 1996)

E-What: A Guide to the Quirks of New Media Style and Usage by the Editors of EEI Press. A supplement to traditional style guides with useful information on Web usage and terms as well as an annotated bibliography to further resources. Available at www.eeicommunications.com/press. (EEI Press: 2000)

English Syntax: A Grammar for English Language Professionals by Roderick A. Jacobs. This textbook provides a thorough discussion of the major constructions and intricacies of English. (Oxford University Press: 1995)

Web Sites

Edit-work.com (www.edit-work.com). Includes information on copyediting, proofreading, and style guides. Also has an editor's online forum.

refdesk.com (www.refdesk.com). A site that contains links to encyclopedias, maps and atlases, general and specialized dictionaries, and much more.

Wordsmyth: The Educational Dictionary-Thesaurus (www.wordsmyth.net). A searchable database for words that provides synonyms, related words, examples in sentences, parts of speech, and more.

The Dictionary of Difficult Words (www.lineone.net/dictionaryof/difficultwords/index.html). Definitions of approximately 14,000 unusual words.

Research and Documentation Online (www.bedfordstmartins.com/hacker/resdoc). Information sources and how to document them online from disciplines in the humanities, social sciences, history, and sciences.

Guide to Grammar and Writing (www.ccc.commnet.edu/grammar/quiz_list.stm). A comprehensive resource that includes quizzes and links.

The Authors Guide (www.pnl.gov/ag/agindex.html). A searchable reference to everything from acronyms, to editing marks, to bibliographic references, to commonly misused words and phrases.

Content + Technology: A Surprising Alliance

Hold your breath until the page loads.
If your face turns purple, the page is too big.

RICHARD CHANG'S RULE
(QUOTED IN R. DILLON, 2001a)

In Chapter 1, we told you about the challenges facing the team of Alex Soojung-Kim Pang who developed a CD-ROM version of the 1998 *Encyclopedia Britannica*. In his digital-age war story, technology seemed to create more problems than solutions. For many writers/editors who come from the print-based world, developing Web content sometimes feels like a technological battle. The skirmishes seem to be many. For example:

- Monitors have different resolutions and users won't see the same content.

- Different and older browsers can't support certain functionalities such as mouse roll-overs.

- A Web page title won't get hits on a search engine because the metatags haven't been written.

- Accessibility guidelines mean the project can't make use of the JavaScript programming language which allows for functionality such as pop-up menus.

- New technologies, such as Flash animations and audio/video playback, have bandwidth and hardware requirements that some users' equipment may not be able to meet.

The world of Web technologies is extensive and often highly technical. We don't intend, in this chapter, to bring you into the depths of that world. Rather, this chapter is designed to help you understand the basics of those Web technologies and meet the challenges of content delivery. At the same time, you'll learn some *tech talk* so that you can understand the language of other members of your production team, and be a more effective spokesperson for the role you want content to play on a Web site.

Make the Technology Transition

Chances are, you're accustomed to writing text and not having to worry about production. Also, you understand on an implicit level what works well in print-based media, and why. This isn't surprising because you grew up with books, newspapers, television, and films. Now, you're confronted with developing content in a new medium where text can be delivered in a variety of ways, and where words on a screen may not be the best mechanism for content delivery.

Adjust Your Mind-Set

In our experience, the writers/editors who have the best mind-set for developing Web content are those who've made a conscious decision to put print-based media behind them, focus on the advantages provided by Web technologies, and enjoy the possibilities. That's why when we get asked in writers' workshops: "How much technology do I need to know?" we answer: "You need to understand the potential of technology, not in-depth technical know-how."

> Focus on the advantages of Web technologies.

Another good reason for learning about Web technologies involves team dynamics. You want the members of your team to understand your concerns regarding high-quality text presentation. They, in turn, want you to comprehend their technological concerns involving content delivery. The more you know about *their world*, the better you will be at helping them achieve *your goals* for content. For example, you may want to deliver content in an interactive way that requires a special plug-in technology. Before you ask for that element, you need to have some idea of what it means in terms of usability and how it will affect the team in terms of additional work, scheduling, and budget.

Think Techno-Creative

When you begin to think about technology as an ally rather than an obstacle, you'll begin to find new possibilities for delivering navigation information and content to users. Take, for example, what's happened to the real estate on your screen, which is likely the most valuable space in your neighborhood. Web producers spend vast amounts of time and money figuring out ways to get as much information as possible on the first screen of a Web page so that users don't have to scroll.

However, navigation information is a space-gobbler. As sites have been getting bigger, navigation bars have grown in length and number, causing frustration for developers who need to design the space for optimum impact, writers/editors who need the space for text, and users who want to understand site structure at a glance and get at the content they require. An excellent alliance between content and technology has been the use of JavaScript (a programming language) and other software tools to create three different types of sub-menus or information capsules—pull-down menus, fly-out menus, and mouse roll-overs—that are hidden until activated by the users. These features are only visible when users either place their cursors over a navigation title or click on it. The hidden information may appear to slide out from underneath a link or fly out beside it. Links on the submenus allow users to move deeper into the site—a highly effective solution that meets users' needs and leaves more space onscreen for textual content.

Technology Basics

At its simplest level, the Web involves two major groups of people—the producers who create sites, and the users who interact with those sites. Each of these groups undertake separate activities and use separate technologies.

The Web Production Team

Web production for most informational sites is a process that usually involves a number of people with different skill sets who use a variety of software applications. Table 8.1 provides an overview of a Web team's activities and tools.

Here is an example of how a team works with different technologies to create an animation segment. Web animation is a term used to cover a variety of different products—for example, moving characters, logos, and symbols. Simple animations can

Let's Speak the Same Language

This chapter explains many specific technologies involved with Web production. The following are definitions of some general technical terms.

Functionality: The technology underlying those features of a site, other than links, that allow users to undertake an activity. For example, a site search engine's functionality allows users to search the site by its ability to sort through keywords and phrases using an underlying programming code structure. Other examples of functionality are download buttons for plug-ins/players, print buttons, and calculators on e-commerce sites.

Interactivity: The process by which users interact with content. Interactivity ranges from simple to highly complex. For example, when users click on forward and backward buttons, they are interacting with content in a simple way. A more complex form of interactivity is the completion of an online form. A highly complex interactivity involves users playing an Internet game, competing with players around the world.

Accessibility: Technology/design standards and guidelines that Web site owners put in place to ensure that people with different types of disabilities have easier access to Web content.

Proprietary: A piece of software code which is the intellectual property of a legal entity such as a database software manufacturer.

Table 8.1 Web Team Activities and Tools

TEAM MEMBER	PRIMARY ACTIVITIES	PRIMARY SOFTWARE TOOLS
Project Manager	■ Organizes and manages teams ■ Develops budget and schedule ■ Makes final decisions	■ Word processing ■ Financial management ■ Project management
Information Architect **Information Designer** **Content Strategist**	■ Designs site's hierarchy ■ Designs main navigation	■ Word processing ■ Flow chart/information design
Writer/Editor	■ Researches content ■ Writes/edits content ■ Copyedits/proofs content	■ Word processing software
Designer	■ Creates the GUI ■ Develops other visual elements	■ Design programs from manufacturers such as Macromedia, Adobe, and so on.
Programmer	■ Inputs all content ■ Programs navigation and interactive elements	■ Basic programming tools such as HTML and Web Editor ■ Specialized scripting languages such as XML, ASP, JavaScript, Java, and CGI/Perl.

be text sliding on the screen, changing images, and rotations of images. More complex animation involves 3-D imagery providing visual depth and richness. Currently, limited bandwidth restricts producers' ability to deliver 3-D images to users.

Animation can be costly. Therefore, the reasons for delivering content through animation have to be strong ones, particularly for informational sites *not* designed for children or youth. For example, many corporations use animation on "Splash" pages—introductory site pages that enhance branding. The development of an animation sequence involves all team members who have different roles and responsibilities.

- **Project manager:** Decides whether the type of Web site and its content, scheduling, and budget make the animation feasible.

- **Information architect/Information designer/Content strategist:** Decides if an animation sequence will enhance content delivery—for example, showing users how to use a piece of equipment through a step-by-step sequence. This team member also ensures accuracy and a logical flow of content.

- **Writer/editor:** Develops the concept for the animation based on the information it must convey. The writer/editor may work with the designer, subject matter specialist, and/or people working in information architecture to create a visual storyboard or Web board for the screen-by-screen sequences and provide descriptions of movements and transitions.

- **Designer:** Creates animation using specialized software such as Macromedia's Flash and Director as well as other tools.

- **Programmer:** Programs the functionality of the animation sequence using specialized software such as Macromedia's Flash and Director and other tools, and integrates the animation into the Web site.

User Technologies: From Browsers to Players

Users require a variety of software applications to be able to view and interact with a Web site. They usually have a suite of products, that is, a diverse collection of software applications chosen for their computer systems. They may customize these applications for their specific needs or simply leave them at default settings. (For more discussion about how users' choices affect viewing, see Chapter 7, "Writing/Editing *for* the Web Page; Writing/Editing *to* the Web Screen.")

Browsers: Windows to the Web

Without browsers, users couldn't view Web sites.

A browser encompasses the technology that allows users to view Web sites. The first Web browsers were text-based, had no graphics, and could not deliver anything more than basic content with links. Today's browsers are fully developed products that allow users to see graphics and text, listen to music, see a video, and interact with other users.

Today, there are more than 100 different browsers, not including the number of older browser versions that users still have on their systems or that are supported internally within organizations. These different browsers range from text-based to those that support multiple media. They're also designed for the various computer operating systems such as Windows 3X, Windows 9X, Windows NT, Windows ME, IBM OS2, Mac, DOS, Amiga, Unix, Linux, Solaris, Personal Digital Assistants (PDAs), and other wireless technologies. In addition, there are browsers for the visually impaired that convert text and visuals to voice.

As a site's writer/editor, you don't need to know all of the various browsers, but you do need to understand that even the two most commonly used browsers—Netscape and Internet Explorer—aren't identical products and may not deliver the same site to users in the same way. For example, different browsers may or may not:

- Support different types of functionality such as drop-down menus, mouse roll-overs, animations, and even text.

- Require users to take one or more steps to view site features such as a Flash animation.

- Allow users to customize their interfaces and functionality.

Plug-ins/Players

The basic technology for Web production is generally HTML code with embedded graphics created in a specific file format and possibly a small amount of JavaScript for a mouse roll-over or special effect. This allows developers to create Web pages with

Going Skin-Deep

New technologies now allow users to change the look-and-feel of their browsers and other Web elements such as the control panels that pop up when using a technology such as Winamp to access audio content. These new looks are called *skins* and can include changes in color and texture, buttons moved to different locations, and the use of customized graphic images. If you're curious about these alternative graphical interfaces, type *skins* into your search engine to get more information.

text and some graphics. Plug-ins/players are software used to provide additional functionality to a browser such as audio, video, animations, cross-platform document delivery, and interactivity. As major browsers are being upgraded, software manufacturers are integrating plug-ins such as Flash into new versions.

Although almost 250 plug-ins and players currently exist, the following six are in common use. If you wish to find out more about them, you can visit the manufacturers' Web sites.

> Plug-ins/
> players add
> functionality.

- Macromedia Flash for animations and interactivity.
- RealPlayer for audio and video broadcasting.
- Adobe Acrobat Reader for reviewing and printing .pdf documents.
- QuickTime and QuickTime VR for audio and video broadcasting as well as virtual reality tours.
- Windows Media Player for audio and video broadcast.
- Winamp for playing audio on the Web.

As the Web writer/editor, you may determine that a certain plug-in/player will help you enhance the delivery of Web content. How does this affect programming? Here are some scenarios:

- You want to deliver a CEO's message on a corporate Intranet through a Webcast. The site's programmer will have to ensure that the required plug-in/player is available on the organization's site so employees can view the Webcast. The Web video specialist will have to work with software tools such as Adobe Premiere to create the video for the site.

- You decide to provide a virtual tour of a residential home or commercial building on a real estate Web site. The programmer will need products such as Adobe Photoshop and Panoramix to create the virtual reality tour from photographs.

- You determine that a lengthy document with numerous pictures, tables, and charts should be in a portable document format (.pdf). The programmer or designer will use Adobe Acrobat to create the document.

Users need to know when a plug-in/player is required to access content. You can supply this information on the same page where the content is located and also provide links connecting users to the specific vendors or suppliers that provide downloads for the necessary plug-ins/players.

Making Audio/Video Decisions

Bandwidth is a major factor in determining whether you and your production team can deliver content through audio and/or video. Bandwidth is the amount of data in computerized form that can be sent from one computer to another in a given amount of time. The less data being sent, the faster it will move. For example, a file containing only text moves far more quickly than a video file that includes audio, animation, color, and so on. Other factors that will influence a team's decision regarding audio and/or video content include:

> Bandwidth can limit content delivery.

- **Source**—does the audio and/or video content come from an external source or does it have to be recorded especially for the Web site?

- **Broadcast quality**—does the audio/video clip have the quality required for the Web site?

- **Playing length**—is the length sufficient to deliver the appropriate content?

- **User play-back capabilities**—does the audio/video content require special plug-ins/players that all users will have or be able to access?

- **Streaming or downloading**—audio and video can be delivered in two ways. *Downloaded content* must arrive completely into the user's system before it will play, making playing length a major factor. *Streaming content* starts to play before all of the file reaches the user's computer, allowing the material to be delivered in a generally stable, continuous flow. The drawback to streaming is that users must have computer technology that is sufficiently advanced to handle the playback.

- **Type of play**—will the content be one-time play (it stops by itself), looping play (it repeats), or continuous play (it constantly plays new material and the user must stop it)?

- **Storage**—how will the content be stored so that users can access it again?

As your production team takes these factors into account and decides on the best way to deliver audio/video content, they'll also be making a choice to use a specific software tool, a specific file format, and/or a suggested plug-in/player. At this point, you're likely to hear tech talk about *.aif* or *.avi/.wav*—

terms that indicate file formats and are based on file extensions, that is, the three letters after the dot in the file formats. Table 8.2 provides a list of the most commonly used audio/video file formats, their purposes, and the plug-ins/players that users will need to access them. However, keep in mind that as bandwidth expands and audio/video delivery technologies constantly change, you and your production team must remain up to date on new formats that will be more efficient and more easily downloaded.

Although file formats have changed and bandwidths have increased significantly since human-computer interaction researcher Chris Johnson (1998:208-218) was writing about providing video over the Web, some principles from his research are still applicable:

- **Avoid video for video's sake:** "The first question to be asked...is: *why bother with video in the first place?*" If the answer can't be justified, then the inconvenience to users can also not be justified.

- **Edit the clip to maximize content and minimize file size:** "Unfortunately, the editing process cannot simply be based on artistic merit...the 'longer the film' then the 'bigger the file' and that the bigger the file then the longer it will take to download." Johnson's research demonstrates that only 2 out of 10 users wait 90 seconds for a download while the remaining 8 give up entirely.

- **Assess the impact of retrieval delays on overall task satisfaction:** Johnson notes that despite long download times, some users are satisfied and that "many other factors must be considered when assessing the costs and benefits of information retrieval." In other words, user input is extremely important when making video decisions.

- **Never take a designer's word for it:** In Johnson's research, designers created different graphical user interfaces (GUIs) with different tools (buttons, thumbnails, and so on) to access video content. Their predictions regarding which interface and access method would be the most successful were completely inaccurate. As Johnson notes: "The important point, however, is not that users preferred one layout over the others. Nor is it that designers cannot accurately predict user preferences. It is, rather that there is no substitute for direct user trials..."

Table 8.2 Audio/Video File Formats

FILE FORMAT	PURPOSE	PLUG-INS/PLAYERS REQUIRED
.au .aif .aiff .mid .mp3 .ra .snd .wav .cda	**Audio Delivery:** ■ Sources can be tape, CD, or computer-generated audio files such as midi. ■ These file formats can be delivered for both Mac and PC. ■ In some cases, the file formats are proprietary.	■ Microsoft–Windows Media Player ■ Real Networks ■ Winamp ■ MP3
.mov/.qt .mpg/.mpeg .ram	**Video Delivery:** ■ Sources are videotape, DVD, or CD-ROM. ■ These file formats can be delivered for both Mac and PC.	■ Microsoft–Windows Media Player ■ Real Networks ■ Adobe QuickTime

Different Ways to Deliver Content

Although the over-use of technological bells-and-whistles can hinder users' abilities to access meaningful content, many of these technologies can also be important allies in helping you deliver content effectively if they're used in a careful and judicious manner. Figure 8.1 demonstrates the various ways that users receive content.

Real-Time Delivery Tools

Real time refers to online events that are delivered live to users' desktops. Such events can be product launches, shareholder meetings, or interviews. Real-time delivery tools include:

> *Real time* is "live" events.

- Audio- or video-conferencing.

- Webcasting, that is, the computerized version of a TV show or interview.

- Some types of programs on Cyber TV. Although the convergence between computers and televisions is in its infancy,

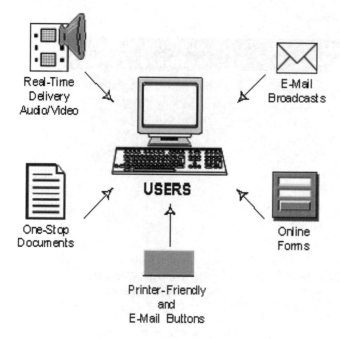

Figure 8.1 Users can receive content in a variety of ways.

this tool is already in existence and is likely to increase in usage. (For more information about future Web trends, see Chapter 11, "After Words and For Words.")

Audio- and video-conferencing technologies have been around for several years, but Webcasting is being used more frequently as bandwidths increase. If you and your client decide that a real-time Webcast is a good way to deliver content, you must consider the technological issues. For example:

- Webcasts require a specialized environment for recording and transmitting the event. Although you won't require a television studio, you'll need high-quality recording/broadcasting equipment.

- The technologies for delivering Webcasts to users don't support a great deal of camera movement. Too much motion breaks up the visual image, and users see jerkiness and disjointed pictures.

- Webcasts require a great deal of bandwidth. Users with dial-up Internet connections have a very difficult time seeing quality Webcasts because of limited bandwidths. Those with high-speed Internet connections and cable modems are able to receive much clearer Webcasts.

"Some people call animation 'dancing baloney' but..."

...using the right animation or multimedia element on your Web site can capture the attention of even the most jaded surfer. First, the image and its motion must be appropriate, or in context. A sunglass-wearing penguin doing the hula is a distraction unless your site is intended to entice vacationers away from a cold winter by offering them a tropical destination. Secondly, the animation must be professional. That means smooth action, at least 24 fps (frames per second). A Webcast or streamed video must also match TV-quality broadcast standards. A site aimed at attracting new graduates to employment at a major financial institution featured high quality streamed video of recent hires talking about their work experiences with the company. Because the video reflected quality production values, it presented a more credible view of the company. Finally, the multimedia element must communicate something that cannot be presented any other way. If you can say the same thing in text, then you only need the text and, besides, it's cheaper. But if what you want to convey can *only* be done with multimedia, then use the best example you can find.

**Beth Agnew, Writer and Technical Communicator
www.agnewcom.com**

Technologies involved with the delivery of video on the Web are expected to change dramatically in the next few years, allowing Webcasts to be viewed by a much larger audience.

Web Pages versus One-Stop Documents

You and your client have choices regarding the delivery of text documents on a Web site. As Figure 8.2 shows, you can either take content and divide it among several Web pages connected by links, or you can provide a one-stop document in two different ways.

- **Downloadable document:** A file created in a word-processing program such as Microsoft Word or Corel WordPerfect that allows the users to print out the document using their word-processing software.

- **Portable document format (.pdf):** This is a universal file format that allows documents to cross multiple operating systems. As Adobe Acrobat (2001) describes it: "Anyone can open your document across a broad range of hardware and software, and it will look exactly as you intended—with layout, fonts, links, and images intact." Scanned documents can be put into .pdf files, and documents from various word-processing programs can be converted into .pdf files.

We find that many clients don't even consider one-stop documents, particularly when converting their print materials such as manuals into an online format. They immediately jump to the conclusion that when putting material online it should become linked Web pages. The questions that you and your client should ask are: What makes the most sense for the user? What is the purpose of providing interactivity and linking for this particular document? Would a one-stop document be more efficient, useful, and cost-effective?[1] Table 8.3 provides pros and cons of both types of formats.

Online Forms

Online forms serve many purposes, such as delivering content to users or capturing information. For example, an online

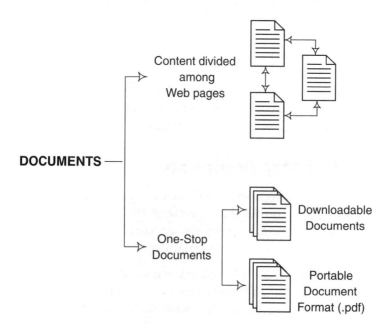

Figure 8.2   Text document choices on the Web.

Table 8.3 Pros and Cons of Linked Web Pages versus One-Stop Documents

YOUR CHOICES	PROS	CONS
Linked Web pages	Breaks up the content, adds interactivity, allows users to link through the content in ways that best suit their learning styles. (For more information, see Chapter 6, "Links, Logic, and the Layered Reader.")	The document loses its linear logic, and users aren't able to obtain an easy print-out of the material, because they must link around the site to gain the information they require.
One-Stop Document	Keeps the document in its complete, linear format and only requires users to make one "print move" to have a hard copy.	*Downloadable document:* Users who don't have the software, or an updated version of the software, may not be able to access the file. *.pdf document:* Such files are often large, are hard to read on the screen, and can take a long time to download and print. As well, users need the Adobe Acrobat Reader plug-in.

résumé-builder is a form that assists users in creating their own personalized résumé. Web site owners use forms to gather information for databases. Some examples of the latter are:

- Survey forms.
- Order forms.
- Information request forms.
- E-mail forms that allow users to link to Webmasters or other individuals in an organization.
- E-commerce shopping carts.

Creating online forms requires specialized software such as a Web editing program, Microsoft FrontPage, and Macromedia Dreamweaver, or they can be created using other programming languages.

E-Mail Broadcasts

E-mail can be a major communications tool for delivering content. The E-mail broadcast is a new technique used by organizations to deliver material such as special announcements and membership newsletters. Such mailers are inexpensive, timely, and can reach large number of individuals. They can be self-contained or may have abstracts with links to Web sites that carry the full content. E-mail broadcasts can be provided by application service providers (ASPs), an emerging industry that provides business services over the Web.

Print-Out and E-Mail Buttons

Content delivery includes print-outs and means by which users can send each other information. Although some of these mechanisms require additional programming (and therefore, time and costs), they can enhance the content of your site for users and result in additional site traffic and visibility.

- **Print-out Buttons:** Many users want print-outs of content. However, some users don't have printers with enough memory to handle the graphics on Web pages, while others don't want or need the graphics. Increasingly, informational sites provide buttons labeled as "Printer-Friendly Format" or "Printer-Ready" that are links to graphic-free Web pages that contain only the textual content.

- **E-Mail Buttons:** One way to increase your site's visibility is to provide users with a way to e-mail content directly to colleagues and friends. This feature is particularly useful for specific types of content. For example, *The New York Times* (www.nytimes.com) provides an "E-mail This Article" button for users, while Epicurious, a gourmet food site (www.epicurious.com), has an "E-mail this recipe to a friend" button. E-mail buttons enable users to send information without having to download it to their systems and then resend it.

Build Up Your Tech Vocabulary

Learn *tech* to enhance teamwork skills.

Designers and programmers tend to use acronyms, abbreviated forms of language, and their own terminology to talk about technologies, file formats, and scripting languages. The more extensive your tech vocabulary, the better able you'll be to understand and participate in the talk around the production team's table.

Avoid the Culture Clash

I find there's a huge difference in language between the technical people and content people. For example, the technical types will use a different name such as *permission level* for a familiar term such as *password*. It's really a cultural difference. The techies are very process-oriented and focused on their priorities. They think in a much more linear way than writers and editors do. Since you can't avoid discussing technology on a Web project, my strategy is to identify someone on the tech team who can bridge that cultural difference and translate terms for me in a way that I can understand.

Charles Barthold, Web Content Strategist
members.home.net/c.barthold/resume/cbpage/
index.htm

More File Formats

Earlier in the chapter (Table 8.2), you learned about different audio/video file formats such as .aifs and .wavs. Table 8.4 provides you with other commonly used file formats that you're likely to hear about in team discussions.

Scripting and Programming Languages

Every site needs to be programmed using one or more computer languages. Programmers are either trained in the language or in a software program that has the language built into it. The selection of a specific language is based on the type of functionality required by the site. Table 8.5 on page 266 provides you with the names and extensions of some commonly used scripting and programming languages.

Making Sites Visible: Web Searching

Increasingly clients are working on techniques to ensure that their sites are picked up by search engines and directories. As a Web writer/editor, you may be involved in the creation of the keywords or phrases, known as *metatags* and *meta descriptions*, that optimize a site's ability to capture search engine traffic.

Table 8.4 More File Formats

GRAPHICS EXTENSIONS	SOFTWARE/PURPOSE
.bmp	■ Bitmap format ■ Used for creating graphics ■ Common to many applications
.cdr	■ CorelDraw ■ Used for creating graphics
.gif	■ Graphics Interchange Format ■ Supports animation.
.jpg/jpeg	■ Graphics file format ■ Used specifically for the Web
.tiff	■ Tag Image File Format ■ Used for creating graphics. ■ Common to many applications
.png	■ Portable Network Graphics ■ Universal file format that can cross all platforms ■ May replace .gif
ANIMATION EXTENSIONS	**SOFTWARE/PURPOSE**
.dir	■ Macromedia Director file ■ Provides animation and interactivity ■ Requires Shockwave plug-in
.fla	■ Macromedia Flash ■ Provides animation and interactivity ■ Requires Shockwave plug-in
OTHER EXTENSIONS	**SOFTWARE/PURPOSE**
.mpp	■ Microsoft Project file ■ Used for project management files
.ppt	■ Microsoft PowerPoint file ■ Used for creating slide and overhead presentations
.rtf	■ Rich Text Format ■ Retains document formatting in word-processing programs

Table 8.4 (Continued)

OTHER EXTENSIONS	SOFTWARE/PURPOSE
.wsz	■ Winamp skin ■ Visual skin for the Winamp control board (audio)
.xls	■ Microsoft Excel Spreadsheet ■ Used for spreadsheet applications
.zip	■ WinZip ■ Compresses files for transmission ■ Requires WinZip software to extract files from zipped format

Web Search Engines and Directories

Users have two ways to search for information on the Web—through various types of search engines such as Google or directories such as Yahoo!

There are 3,600+ search engines/directories.

Web Search Engines

Web search engines, that is, those that are external to Web sites, use an automated software program known as a *spider* (also known as a *crawler* or *bot*) that searches the Internet based on keyword(s) input by a user. Some search engines have a broad reach, searching through millions of Web pages on the Internet. Others provide more narrow searches based on factors such as language, geography, or topics. *Meta-search engines* such as Copernicus only search other search engines. However, the rapid growth of the Internet makes it impossible for any search engine to cover its intended territory. Internet researcher F. Saunders (2000:31) notes that: "Experts estimate that the amount of information on the Net is expanding by 2 million pages a day and that the best search engines cover no more than 16 percent of those pages...Spiders take months to finish one incomplete sweep of the Web, during which time tens of millions of pages have appeared, changed, or disappeared."

After a search engine has gathered pages off the Web, it indexes the pages to determine content, and then builds a search page based on the results. As Figure 8.3 on page 267 shows, this search page is then stored in a database where it can be retrieved by a user through the appropriate keyword search. Web design specialist

Table 8.5 Scripting and Programming Languages

LANGUAGE	EXTENSION	PURPOSE
Microsoft Active Server Pages	.asp	Used to code Web pages that connect to databases.
Hyper Text Markup Language	.htm/.html	Most commonly used language for building Web sites.
Extensible Markup Language	.xml	A new language for creating vector graphics for use on Web sites, cell phones, and PDAs.
Java	.jav	A powerful cross-platform language used to create full-featured programs, complex interactive forms, and special effects.
JavaScript	.js	Not to be confused with Java, this language is local, that is, part of a Web page and integrated with HTML. It's used for interactive elements such as mouse rollovers and pop-up windows.
Common Gateway Interface (CGI)	.cgi	A language used to create and connect forms in order to post information to, or get information from, a server. Often used with PERL.
PERL	.pl	A language used to create and connect forms in order to post information to, or get information from, a server. Often used with CGI.

Thomas Powell (2000:241) describes the process this way: "The best analogy...is that the search engine builds as big a haystack as possible, then tries to organize the haystack somehow, and finally lets the user try to find the proverbial needle in the resulting haystack of information by entering a query on a search page."

As noted above, no one search engine is capable of searching the entire Web, given its millions of sites and billions of pages. How can you find out the scope and reach of different search engines? Search Engine Watch (www.searchenginewatch.com) provides a regular report on the number of indexed pages by commonly used search engines. Table 8.6 shows the results for April 6, 2001; however, it's important to remember that these numbers are self-reported and unaudited.

Web Directories

Directories are built by a company that uses human editors to hand-pick sites and put them into specific categories such as

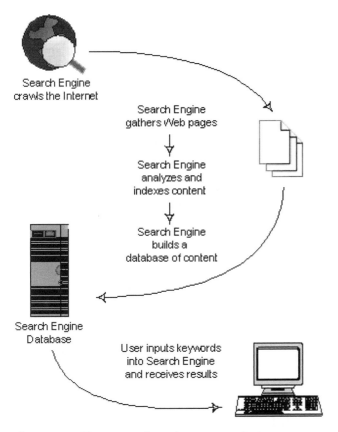

Figure 8.3   How a search engine gets results to a user.

travel, health, business, education, and so on. When the user inputs a keyword or keywords, the directory only searches among its chosen sites. As new technology writer Michael Miller (1999:11) explains: "A directory doesn't search the Web—

Table 8.6   Indexed Web Pages per Search Engine

WEB SEARCH ENGINE	NUMBER OF INDEXED WEB PAGES
Google	1,347,000,000
FAST	575,000,000
AltaVista	550,000,000
Inktomi	500,000,000
WebTop.com	500,000,000
Northern Light	350,000,000
Excite	250,000,000

Source: April 6, 2001 (searchenginewatch.com/reports/sizes.html).

in fact, a directory only catalogs a very small part of the Web…in many ways, these Web directories look and work like traditional print Yellow Pages."

Web design specialist Powell (2000:239) notes that the distinctions between directories and search engines are beginning to blur:

> Yahoo is probably the most famous directory around, but it now provides search-engine features as well. In fact, most of the search engines have begun to offer directory links as well as searching. Some popular directories like www.about.com or www.dmoz.org are organized by individuals who are responsible for a particular type of content. The benefit of a directory is that it limits links to the "good sites" and may even provide reviews of sites.

Titles, Links, Metatags, and Meta Descriptions

Be prepared to write/edit for searching.

A search engine/directory looks for clues on a site to find out what it's about and how to rank it as relevant to a user's keyword search. A Web page has four important elements: its title and links—content that is visible to the user, and its metatags and meta descriptions—content that can't be seen by the user. (To view invisible content, place your cursor on the page, click your right mouse button, and then click "View Source" in the dialog box.)

- **Title:** The title appears as the clickable link on the hit-list of the search engine/directory.

- **Links:** Most search engines look for landmark pages, that is, pages with many external links as well as other pages that link to them. Because most "Home Pages" have numerous links, these tend to rank higher for a search than pages deeper on a site.

- **Metatag:** A keyword or a group of keywords programmed into the Web page that triggers search engine traffic. Without metatags, a site may not be found by search engines. Metatags need to reflect a site's content because the keyword(s) will be part of the hit description. Therefore, they must be carefully chosen to attract the site's target audience. Some search engines will rank a site based on its findings in the metatags.

- **Meta description:** A sentence programmed into the Web page written specifically for a search engine. These chunks of information are very important for the marketing of a site because they appear as the site's description on the search engine's results.

How do these elements work together to get a top hit on a search engine/directory? On May 29, 2001, we typed in the keyword *women* into the Google search engine. Here is the first hit—a site called Women.com (www.women.com).

```
Welcome to Women.com: Where women are going
Search: [enter a keyword] | full search and help. Channels
| Magazines & Sites | Community | Join Women.com FREE! ...
For women of the world, Marie Claire. ...
Description: Where women go for daily information and
inspiration on health, career, relationships, entertain-
ment,...
Category: Society > People > Women > Indices
www.women.com/ - 50k - Cached - Similar pages - Stock
quotes: WOMN
```

Figure 8.4 shows the title, metatags, and meta descriptions coded into the "Home Page" of this site. Notice how the search engine picked up the "Home Page" title and a version of the meta description.

```
<title>Welcome to Women.com: Where women are going</title>

<meta name="description" content="Women.com is where women are going
for information and inspiration.  Every day more than 6 million women
visit for horoscopes, magazine features, tools, shopping, games,
expert advice, and community.">

<meta name="keywords" content="women.com, web sites for women,
magazines, women's community, female, jobs, careers, workplace,
fashion, wardrobe, relationships, dating, marriage, weight loss, lose
weight, fitness, diet, investing, finance, careers, beauty, recipes,
free stuff, horoscope, astrology, celebrities, money, news, sex,
health, travel, style, games, bingo, woman, girl, home decorating,
family, babies, pregnancy, baby, parenting, moms, mothers, children,
work, employment, advice, small business, work from home, advice,
shopping, shop, prevention, healthy ideas, women's wire, Magazine,
Cosmopolitan, Country Living, Country Living Gardener, Good
Housekeeping, House Beautiful, Marie Claire, Redbook, Town & Country
Weddings, Victoria, Astronet, B. Smith With Style, Bingo Online,
eHarlequin, Harlequin, Satellite Sisters">
```

Figure 8.4 The title, meta descriptions, and metatags used on the Women.com site.
May 29, 2001 (www.women.com).

The choice of metatags and meta descriptions are sometimes made by a site's programmer—rarely an optimal situation because most programmers are not familiar with content. As the Web writer/editor, you'll be writing Web page titles and may be asked to help with metatags and meta descriptions. Table 8.7 provides you with tips to enhance your site's ability to gain search engine/ directory traffic.

Table 8.7   Tips to Writing Titles, Metatags, and Meta Descriptions

WHEN WRITING...	YOU SHOULD...
Page Titles	■ Be concise.
	■ Ensure that the title is descriptive of the site.
	■ Make the title appealing to your target audience.
	■ Remember that titles are also used for bookmarking.
Metatags	■ Develop a number of keywords that reflect the content.
	■ Consider also including keywords within the content of the page because many search engines search through text, particularly near the top of a page.
	■ Perform sample searches for similar sites to see rankings. Check out the metatags on sites that make it high up on hit-lists.
	■ Avoid keywords that are in such common use that your site will be competing with millions of other sites.
	■ If you need some help in determining keywords, visit www.searchengineguide.com which has a link to Wordtracker—a listing of the top 500 keywords searched on the Internet on a weekly basis.
Meta Descriptions	■ Ensure that your description has 200 characters or less.
	■ Use keywords from the site.
	■ Don't repeat words.
	■ Consider using words from the title.
	■ Consider having the description as the first sentence of the "Home Page."

To Sum It Up

This chapter was designed to provide you with an overview of Web technologies. Some writers/editors we interviewed for this book found that having technical know-how, particularly aspects of HTML programming and writing metatags and meta descriptions, was important in gaining work. Others found that they weren't expected to be involved in this aspect of production at all. If you decide to deepen your knowledge about Web technology, you'll find many resource books on technology from both introductory and advanced perspectives. As well, we suggest going to magazines and Web sites for information. With Web technologies changing so dramatically and rapidly, you'll find that these resources often have the most up-to-date information.

Resources for This Chapter

Books/Magazines

Smart Computing in Plain English. A magazine series with easy-to-understand articles about today's technologies, trends, and future possibilities. Available at www.smartcomputing.com.

Web Design: The Complete Reference by Thomas A. Powell. An in-depth treatment of the theory, tools, and technologies for the Web, including basic information on search engines and directories. (Osborne/McGraw Hill: 2000)

How Networks Work by Frank Derfler and Les Freed. Covers the basics of integrated systems and networks in a colorful and graphical fashion. (Que: 1998)

How Intranets Work and *How the Internet Works* by Preston Gralla. Two useful and easy-to-understand books that cover the technology fundamentals. (ZD Press: 1996)

Essential Design for Web Professionals by Charles Lyons. Illustrates the entire design process and technologies through case studies. Includes design requirements for disabled users. (Prentice Hall: 2001)

Guide to Maintaining and Updating Dynamic Web Sites by Jeannie Novak and Pete Markiewicz. A case study approach to illustrate long-term planning requirements for all sites, large and small, from both technical and non-technical perspectives. (John Wiley & Sons: 1998)

Designing Web Graphics by Linda Weinman. Demystifies graphic design and includes a strong technical point of view. (New Riders: 1998)

Web Sites

TechTutorials.com (www.techtutorials.com/fileformats.shtml). Provides an alphabetical list of different file formats by extension and then full titles.

Web Tools (scout.cs.wisc.edu/addserv/toolkit/webtools/plugins.html). Provides a list of the most commonly used plug-ins and links to manufacturers' sites.

NetMechanic (www.netmechanic.com). This commercial site provides free examples of site problems and has a free newsletter.

TechEncyclopedia (www.techweb.com/encyclopedia). Provides definitions for information technology terms.

Search Engine Watch (searchenginewatch.com/firsttime.html). Comprehensive information about search engines and searching, including resources, listings, and reviews.

Search IQ (www.zdnet.com/searchiq). Articles and information on search engines, including a rating of meta search engines according to their specialized features.

Search Engine Colossus (www.searchenginecolossus.com). Provides links to search engines in 149 countries.

Beaucoup (www.beaucoup.com). A site that lists specialized search engines, including those that link to computer and software resources.

Cast Bobby (www.cast.org/bobby). A free service for Web site owners that helps them identify and repair barriers to accessibility.

The Web Accessibility "How To" Site
(www.webaim.org). Information on how to use technology to make sites accessible. Includes an "Accessibility Makeovers" section that provides "before" and "after" screens.

Texas School for the Blind and the Visually Impaired: Links to Adaptive Technology (www.tsbvi.edu/technology/index .htm). Provides information about technologies that can make Web sites more accessible.

Endnotes

1. The usefulness of hypertext versus nonhypertext is an issue that hasn't yet been solved by human-computer interaction researchers, cognitive scientists, and writing theorists. As hypertext researchers Jean-François Rouet, Jarmo Levenon, Andrew Dillon, and Rand Spiro (1996:6-7) note: "The analysis of tasks and activities for which hypertext may be relevant and useful has to date been surprisingly shallow...Assuming the proper situational context..., would any regular reader benefit from using a hypertext system? Anyone who has ever observed students interacting with a computer application may guess that the answer is negative, for several reasons. One reason is that there are huge individual differences in the way people interact with information systems. Confronted with an information search task, for instance, it is rare that two readers or searchers will display the exact same pattern of selections."

CHAPTER 9

Keep CALM: Content and Logical Management

What's Inside:

- Defining content management
- Issues of quality information
- Content management process and strategies
- Issues of large Web sites
- The whys and hows of localization
- Tips to translating online content

A carelessly planned project takes three times longer to complete than expected; a carefully planned project takes only twice as long.

Anytime things appear to be going well, you have overlooked something.

If a test installation functions perfectly, all subsequent systems will malfunction.

It is impossible to make any program foolproof because fools are so ingenious.

No matter how much you do, you'll never do enough.

FROM "MURPHY'S LAWS FOR PROGRAMMERS"
LAUGHNET. 1997

In the early days of the Web, the term *content management*, as we understand it today, didn't exist. Organizations building informational sites took documents, often from different in-house contributors, and dumped them online. In general, no one worried about consistency, what would happen when content required updating, or if content put on the site post-launch was actually accessible to users. Most clients were far more interested in bells-and-whistles that they thought would attract users.

As the Web approaches its 10th birthday, people are beginning to understand that it's a new medium with different demands, not all of which are yet understood. However, one aspect that is clearly coming to the forefront of client/employer concerns is that Web content is not a static entity that they can post and then ignore. Rather, content is dynamic, requiring constant management not only post-launch but from the very beginning of a Web site's development. There are several reasons for this, including:

> Content
> is dynamic.

- In the Information Age, data and information are increasingly valuable commodities, and valuable commodities require quality care.

- Societies are undergoing constant change, and no organization can afford to stand still and expect to remain relevant. Therefore, as in-house policies, products, goals, and staff inevitably alter over time, new content is developed that displaces earlier material.

- Constant growth of the Web means that new users are coming online who have different information needs that must be understood and met.

- Web sites must be dynamic, constantly providing new content in order to attract users.

- Technological change offers organizations new, more efficient, and more effective methods of delivering information to users. (For more information, see Chapter 8, "Content + Technology: A Surprising Alliance.")

Content management has become so important, particularly for large organizations whose Internet, Intranet, and/or Extranet sites may have thousands of pages, that new occupations have emerged in Web production such as content manager and content librarian/archivist. Because Web writers/editors are often the people most familiar with a site's content, they may find themselves moving into these occupations or assisting clients in these positions.

The Many Faces of Content Management

What exactly does a content manager do? Here's one definition from the Macromedia Web site (2001): "Provides a consistent style and tone. Works closely with client to gather all information and materials for the Web site. Understands fundamentals of Web ready copy, and has a clear understanding of the overall goals and communication objectives of the site. Works with the information architect to implement content in an efficient manner." However, as we've noted throughout this book, the Web is so affected by fads and buzzwords that its terminology is in constant flux. For example, other positions with responsibilities for content management include the traditional *Webmaster* and newer titles such as *knowledge manager, document manager,* and *information manager.*

> Content management has no fixed definition.

Do these occupations actually differ in terms of duties and responsibilities? The frustrating answer is, "It depends." As knowledge management researcher Corey Wick (2000:515) notes, definitions in the area of knowledge and information are very hard to pin down and are *local* to the people and organizations involved.

> Thus, it is only logical that people with accounting or finance backgrounds think of knowledge management in terms of "intellectual capital," focusing on aims of maximizing a company's revenues by fully leveraging the collective know-how ...of its people. Similarly, technical communicators will likely think of knowledge management as extracting and synthesizing knowledge from people with specialized knowledge (usually subject matter experts) and developing it into an easily understandable form (print or Web documents, multimedia applications, help files) for people who lack that knowledge. Furthermore, technologists (programmers, developers, corporate chief information officers) might think of knowledge management as developing knowledge management applications, implementing pre-packaged applications, and maintaining the information technology infrastructure needed to support these applications.

In other words, we can't predict precisely what you might do if you became involved in content management, because it will depend entirely on your client/employer, his or her organization, and your own skills and interests. Therefore, we suggest that one of the best ways to explore this new area of Web work is to learn about quality information and the content management process.

Writing Your Job Description

In my experience, the role of a content manager varies as much as each individual company's business does. Typically, this position does *not* involve writing, but may well include working closely with a writer and editor, or a team of writers and editors, to help ensure the appropriateness and quality of the content. And content includes images, color swatches, prices, video- and audio-clips, and any other element of page design. So the position also typically includes working with either a content management tool or a team of developers who publish the content.

Other aspects of the role may include establishing workflow procedures—making sure the content goes through the necessary approval and copyediting/proofing channels before it goes live, helping designers and/or developers create page templates, and training content developers on the use of the templates, the style guide, and general publishing procedures including whatever content management tool is being used.

My advice would be to ask a lot of questions about the systems the company has in place now. Find out who creates the content, who schedules it, who approves it, who publishes it, and then as much as you can about style guidelines, templates, etc. This field is so new that much of the time you can write your own job description, depending on what the company does now and your creativity in making it all work better.

Rachel E. Radway, Writer, Editor, Content Consultant
www.drizzle.com/~reradway

Managing for Users

No matter what aspect of content management you're involved in, your focus on the usability of your site must never waver. As we've noted throughout this book, clients often forget users as they struggle with the many issues involved in getting a site up and running. Two areas that content managers must monitor very closely are the quality of the information that goes online and the usability of the interface design.

Extending Our Human-to-Human Reach

I work on a government Web site that pulls together information from many different departments and agencies. One of our biggest challenges is to determine what should be included and what should be left out. Many of my partners want to add information because they think it's interesting. Often, it *is* interesting, but that isn't sufficient. Too often we forget the purpose of the information, and how and why people will use it. I have to constantly bring the user back into the mix, but my focus is not on who they are—that way we write to some mythical individual who doesn't exist—but why they come to our site. I believe users want information that's concrete, detailed, and actionable. I believe people don't browse but come to our site for a purpose—to find out what we offer them that relates to what they are trying to do. I think of the Web, not as a technological means for getting needed information to people, but as a way of extending our human-to-human reach.

Isabel Alexander, Web Content Manager

What Is Information Quality?

How can you decide if an item of information for your organization is worth putting on the Web site? In some cases, the situation is clear—for example, a new product or service needs to be showcased for consumers. But in many other cases, the decision may not be so easy. For example, your organization has press releases dating back five years. Do you delete the information, or do you store it in such a way that users can access it through the site search engine? Unlike paper documents whose storage requires physical space which must be maintained, digital files can be stored with almost no expense. The issue, therefore, is the quality and value of the information.

Intellectual capital researchers Kuan-Tsae Huang, Yang W. Lee, and Richard Y. Wang (1999:43-44) examine information quality (IQ) based on a consumer perspective: "In this view, *IQ* should not be defined by providers or custodians of information, such as IT departments, but instead, by information consumers…[thus] *IQ* is defined as *information that is fit for use by information con-*

Users determine information quality.

sumers." In Table 9.1, we've adapted their framework for information quality specifically in the context of Web site consumers.

One of the most important things to remember about information quality is that it has *nothing* to do with technology. Knowledge management specialists Thomas H. Davenport and Laurence Prusak (1998:173) note that: "You can buy as many Notes or Netscape licenses as you want; you can create a very attractive Web page; you can even put some Java-based interactive applications on your system—but it doesn't mean anyone will use or get value out of your investments in technology and sophisticated programming." Content based on user needs must always be in the driver's seat, "steering" the decisions about design, architecture, navigation, databases, and/or search engines.

User Interface Economics

Every step in building a Web site—from the development of the information architecture, to the navigation design, to the graphical user interface (GUI)—must meet users' needs. Human-computer interaction researcher Richard Dillon says that "before we design products, we must assess users' needs and, as we develop the product, we must continue to test usability." However, many product producers don't take these important steps. Why? Dillon (2001b:20-21) points to 10 common myths about user interface (UI) design that result in poor quality:

Table 9.1   Information Quality (IQ) Categories and Dimensions

IQ CATEGORY	IQ DIMENSIONS
Intrinsic IQ: Information that has quality for the user in its own right.	■ Accuracy ■ Objectivity ■ Believability ■ Reputation
Contextual IQ: Information that must be considered within the context of the user tasks.	■ Relevancy ■ Value-added ■ Timeliness ■ Completeness ■ Amount of information
Representational IQ: User issues surrounding systems that provide information such as databases.	■ Interpretability ■ Ease of understanding ■ Concise representation ■ Consistent representation
Accessibility IQ: User issues surrounding the provision of information.	■ Access ■ Security

1. The quality of the user interface doesn't matter.

2. If the functionality in your software is good, users will buy it despite poor user interface.

3. Designers can design good interfaces by relying on interface guidelines and principles.

4. Programmers and engineers (or graphic artists) without UI training can design good user interfaces.

5. All you need to design good UI is a good UI toolkit (or GUI HTML editor).

6. You can design good interfaces without contact with users.

7. As far as Web navigation goes, just provide the links.

8. UI design can be added on after the rest of the product is designed.

9. Usability is subjective and cannot be measured or "engineered."

10. UI design can be done right the first time.

And what happens when a user interface doesn't meet user needs? Dillon provides some illuminating examples (see Table 9.2) of what he calls "User Interface Economics," that is, the connection between truly usable products and the ways that they can save an organization money.

Needed: A Community of Expertise

Web sites require people who are content providers, graphic artists, writers, usability designers, database designers, programmers, and marketing specialists. If you fail to have any one of these areas of expertise on the team, your site is likely to fail. If any one of these experts dominates the discussions, again your site is likely to fail. And if any one of these experts ignores the needs of the other members of the team, failure again. For example, database people don't care about usability, while writers and editors don't want to know about programming problems. Web teams have inevitable conflicts and cultural clashes. Constant attention to usability and usability testing can avoid issues that involve "my opinion versus your opinion."

Dr. Richard Dillon, Professor of Psychology
Carleton University, Ottawa, Ontario
www.carleton.ca/cure

Table 9.2 User Interface Economics

AREAS OF IMPROVEMENT	EMPLOYEE ACTIONS	IMPROVEMENTS	RESULTS
Increased Productivity	2,500 employees making 10 transactions per day.	Able to save one minute per transaction over a period of 10 years.	550 person-years of savings. At a $30,000 salary per employee, this equals a savings of $16,500,000.
Reduced Training Costs	2,500 employees having training days.	Avoid two days of training per year over a period of 10 years.	160 person-years of savings. At a $30,000 salary per employee, this equals a savings of $4,800,000.
Preventable User Errors	2,500 employees interacting with a product.	Avoid 200 errors per year at 10 minutes per error over a period of 10 years.	5 million preventable errors or a savings of 434 person-years. At a $30,000 salary per employee, this equals a savings of $13,020,000.

Source: , "Integrating User-Interface Design into the Software Development Process" by Richard F. Dillon (2001b).

The Content Management Process

Content requires constant care.

Organizations are learning many lessons as they attempt to rebuild their sites to better manage content and make use of more up-to-date technologies. In our experience, clients often wish they'd had 20/20 hindsight when building their first Web sites. They wish they'd better understood the commitment required by a Web site, particularly as Internet growth exploded. E-commerce journalist June Gross (2001) describes the problem this way:

> Businesses and organizations often learn the hard way about how to operate a Web site that is clean, responsive, easy to use, safe, secure and effective. Following an all too common scenario,

someone in-house has the idea and soon a page is launched. Other ideas percolate and another page is attached, then 10 or 20 more. Soon a developer is hired who, all in a rush and without a real plan, adds other features. Later, undocumented patches and other quick fixes manage to keep the thing online.

At some point, people in the organization begin hearing complaints. Or they start worrying about who might be able to tap into the site and contact its visitors. Or the site crashes, once, twice or many times. Perhaps it is all but forgotten and grows stale, or needs to be migrated—which is difficult at best, because the site is so entangled with undocumented programs.

And many clients tell us that, although they thought they knew what users wanted, they now realize that meeting user needs is a far more complex issue than they'd ever bargained for. High technology executive Hank Barnes (2001:34) is writing for e-business site owners, but what he has to say applies to all informational sites:

> …according to a recent Forrester Research study, most e-business sites have abysmal conversion rates of only 2 percent because usability is so poor. And, it's not just technical functionality that's to blame. Much of the time, users simply can't find what they're looking for, even if it's just information, which, by the way, is still what most users are seeking online. Most of us know that our sites are not meeting our customers' needs as well as they could or should, so this isn't a new story. This is the real problem that content management should help us solve.

Content, then, is a product that requires constant vigilance and maintenance. Although the management of content begins after a site is launched, the planning for it should begin at the initial stage of a new Web site's development or a redesign when site owners and other team members establish the goals of the site, its target audience, and what and how content should be presented.

Building the Team

Content management has two different aspects—content and technology. *Managing content* requires management of the people who develop and maintain content. *Managing technology* involves choosing the software that helps to organize and store site information and overseeing the people involved in running the software and hardware. Table 9.3 identifies the members of a content management team and their roles and tasks.

Content managers are also people managers.

Developing a Strategy

If you're involved with content management from the very start of a new Web site or the redesign of an old one, you'll be involved in helping design an information strategy. Table 9.4 outlines the key management questions that need to be asked at this stage in the content management process.

Table 9.3 The Content Management Team and their Roles and Tasks

POSITION	ROLE	TASKS
Web Manager	Understands overall Web site from both content and technical perspectives.	Develops the overall Web site development plan.
Content/ Knowledge/ Information/ Document Manager	Understands the collective knowledge within an organization. Knows the amount and type of knowledge that needs to be collected and distributed among employees and clients.	Evaluates information that already exists and how it has been used. Determines new information needs and where new information can be found within an organization.
Content/Subject Matter Expert	Has the subject expertise and may be the content creator for the site.	Creates the technical documentation required, based on the archival information, or develops new content based on client requests.
Writer/Editor	Ensures that content is written in a manner that meets users' needs.	May create content or edit existing content created by the content/subject matter specialists.
Web Production Team	Ensures that the look-and-feel of the Web site meets users' needs.	Supports the architecture and navigation design, creates the graphical user interface (GUI), and programs the Web site. (For more information on the building of a Web site, see Chapter 3: "Organizing a Web Site, 'Elementary, My Dear Watson.'")

Table 9.4 Key Content Management Strategy Questions

KEY QUESTIONS	SUBQUESTIONS
Who are the members of our target audience? What information do they need and how should it be presented?	■ What information in our organization needs to be disseminated or distributed? ■ Does our site have a global audience and, if so, will we have to make localization decisions, that is, write different content for different nationalities/cultures? ■ If we have a global audience, what will be the translation process? ■ Do we have users with accessibility problems and how will we address them?
Where is the knowledge/content located in our organization?	■ Does it already exist or does it need to be created? ■ If content already exists, who will research and collect it? If it requires revising, who will do that work? ■ If the content doesn't exist, who will create it? ■ Do Web site contributors require training to help them revise and/or create content?
Who needs to be involved in the content review cycle?	■ If the site is a redesign, who created the original content—an individual or members of a business unit? ■ How will future content be created and who will participate in its creation? ■ Who will handle user complaints about content once the site has been launched/redesigned? ■ Who will decide if and when content is no longer useful? ■ Who will determine if older content has sufficient value to be archived on the site and retain the legacy of the organization? ■ Who will be the ultimate "sign-off" authority for all content?

continues

Table 9.4 Key Content Management Strategy Questions (Continued)

KEY QUESTIONS	SUBQUESTIONS
What technical requirements exist? (For example, will the site be built solely through HTML-coded Web pages or will it also require a sophisticated database with a search engine function?)	■ What software and hardware are required to ensure that we have future capacity for good content management?
How will we measure outcomes?	■ Should we conduct user focus-testing before and after the site is launched? ■ If we examine visitor statistics, what will we consider successful? ■ If the site is a redesign, what do we expect in increased traffic and/or sales?

Making Plans

Good planning is essential.

The answers to these questions will help you and your team initiate content management by setting up two types of plans for developing and managing content: decision-making plans and workflow plans.

Decision-Making Plans

A decision-making plan outlines the tasks that need to be done and the person(s) involved in making the particular decisions regarding those tasks. Table 9.5 on page 288 provides you with a generic step-by-step decision-making plan.

Workflow Plans

A workflow plan differs from a decision-making plan as it as outlines the work involved in completing specific work within a larger process. This type of plan identifies:

■ The key steps of this specific work.

■ The work's deliverables.

■ The sequential order that tasks must be undertaken and completed.

- Tasks whose deliverables must be completed at the same time.

- The interrelationship among the work teams, the deliverables, and the timelines.

Content manager Mignon Fogarty works on Web sites involving many different content contributors. She says that you need a clear process for creating content. "Who gets to review each piece, and when? When do you commission art work? When do you copyedit? When do you send out for external review? I like to have a flow chart above my desk so everyone can see the process." She suggests several strategies:

- **Helpful file names:** "You need file names that instantly identify the file and its author. Including the date can be helpful as well as an extension with the author's initials. It's also a good idea to give your word-processing and HTML files the same name. It makes things a lot simpler down the road when you want to find that old version of something you now have online." (For more information, see Chapter 7, "Writing/Editing *for* the Web Page; Writing/Editing *to* the Web Screen.)

- **Version control:** "It's almost guaranteed that you'll need to go back to old versions of both your word-processing and HTML files. If you don't have a content management tool that takes care of version control, keep old versions somewhere."

- **File control:** "You never want two people working on the same content at the same time. It might seem like a way to speed up the process, but it will really be a headache to try to resolve the two files. If you have version control software, it can take care of this for you, but there are always ways around the software, so you have to make it very clear to everyone who can access files that only one person touches a file at a time."

- **Sorting:** "If you do have the luxury of a content management system, you'll probably have to do some configuring. Some things I find useful to sort include author, assigning editor, date due from author, date due to production, date posted, copyeditor, site section, and reviewer."

Organizational Buy-In

As these plans demonstrate, good content management doesn't exist in isolation from the rest of the organization, and will cre-

Table 9.5 A Content Manager's Generic Decision-Making Plan

STEPS	TASKS	PEOPLE INVOLVED
New Site: Identify what has to be created **Redesign:** Identify what revisions are required	■ Identify audience and its needs. ■ Develop architecture, navigation, and graphical user interface (GUI). ■ Revise or create content.	Senior management, usability specialists, Web production team, subject matter specialists, writer(s)/editor(s), localization specialists/translators
Identify Key Players	■ Seek management buy-in. ■ Identify knowledge-holders. ■ Bring technology people aboard.	Senior management, business unit managers/personnel, Information Technology (IT) department
Create Review Process	■ Identify who must review content before and after it arrives. ■ Set up a method of labeling content as it arrives. ■ Identify who must review content if it requires revision by writers/editors.	Senior management, business unit managers/personnel
Identify Timelines/ Benchmarks	■ Identify key items required for successful completion. ■ Identify length of time for delivery including approval steps. ■ Identify who is required for those approvals.	Content management team, senior management, business unit managers
Create/Revise Content	■ Set up research plan to find information and identify gaps. ■ Assign writing/editing tasks	Subject matter experts, writer(s)/editor(s)
Test Product	■ Set user testing schedules. ■ Analyze and evaluate feedback. ■ Get approval for revisions. ■ Implement revisions.	Usability specialists, senior management, business unit managers, Web production team, content management team

continues

Table 9.5 (Continued)

STEPS	TASKS	PEOPLE INVOLVED
Put Final Content on Site	■ Have all completed documents and other types of content. ■ Ensure documents are ready for Web publishing.	Content management team, IT department
Evaluate Impact	■ Evaluate user queries and requests. ■ Determine revisions.	Senior management, business unit managers, content management team
Revise as Needed	■ Complete rewrites. ■ Get approvals. ■ Relaunch content.	Senior management, business unit managers, content management team, IT department

ate demands and challenges for many individuals who may not have anticipated the extra work involved. Therefore, content management requires corporate leadership, management support, and employee buy-in.

> You'll need support at all levels.

Good Policies from the Get-Go

During the development of a Web site, clients will set policies that affect content *development* that will later affect content *management*. These policies include site design standards such as the site's look-and-feel and site assets that can be electronic forms, illustrations, audio, and/or video. The more thought and care that go into these policies, the smoother the transition will be to managing the content after the site's launch. Table 9.6 on page 291 illustrates some of the policies that will help an organization manage a site.

Accessibility Policies

The power of the Web is in its universality. Access by everyone regardless of disability is an essential aspect.

TIM BERNERS-LEE, W3C DIRECTOR

2001

The Need for Corporate Cooperation

In a previous position, I was working on a client project for a company created out of three separate companies in a merger. We'd been given the Marketing Manager as our main point of contact but also needed to work with the three business area heads. What we didn't understand until some way into the process was that there was a clash between what the Marketing Manager wanted, as a representative from the whole business, and what the other managers were expecting for their areas' needs. The issues were the lack of cohesive structure in the company and the lack of communication within. While we obviously wanted to accommodate everyone as best we could, we realized that the "one point of contact" issue was very relevant as we were spending a lot of time running from person to person and not achieving the consistency we needed to move forward. What the company really needed was some business strategy to fully integrate them as a single company, to pull down the barriers that were still in place from throwing them together years ago, and to move towards a clear company vision.

Elizabeth Varley, Consultant in Content Strategy and Managing Editor, DigitalEve UK magazine

A growing trend is increased accessibility.

One of the growing forces in today's Web development is the idea that sites should be accessible to people with visual, hearing, and motor disabilities. The World Wide Web Consortium (W3C) developed a set of accessibility guidelines that is now being implemented by governments and organizations worldwide. These guidelines involve design accessibility issues such as:

- Presentation of text and graphics.
- Use of color.
- Design of tables, charts, and forms.
- Use of frames, applets, and scripts.

You'll find the complete accessibility guidelines with design issues organized by priority at www.w3.org/TR/WCAG10/full-checklist.html. In addition to the guidelines, some organizations have begun to use evaluation tools to help them analyze and redesign their sites in order to reach a broader audience. You'll find a list of these tools at www.w3.org/TR/WCAG.

Table 9.6 Some Content Management Policies and Organizational Requirements

POLICY	ORGANIZATIONAL REQUIREMENTS
Web Manager has the final authority to approve content location on the site and/or in the database.	Information architect and content developer must provide very clear definitions as to the type of content by Web section and page.
Subject matter experts can publish content to the Web site.	Organization should provide training in writing, site design development, and the use of the appropriate software tools as well as an in-house editorial style guide. (For more information, see Chapter 7, "Writing/Editing *for* the Web Page; Writing/Editing *to* the Web Screen.")
Web site production team is responsible for the site's look-and-feel including colors, fonts, icons, and localization design.	Organization must provide a clear design style guide and provide team with requirements regarding the international audience.
Web Manager and IT department control the development of data collection structures that require programming.	Organization must set up appropriate database design and software to capture information and allow for ways the information could be presented such as by topic, date, index, and/or internal site search engine.
Web site production team must meet specific technical requirements regarding assets such as photos, audio/video, Webcasting, and so on. Although some of these assets may be identified in the organizational design style guide, fast-changing technologies may mean that the guide is out-dated.	Organization has to define those site assets requiring technical assistance and acceptance. For example, an organization may not allow video due to bandwidth restrictions or use of Flash due to browser restrictions and lack of IT support.

Copyright and Trademark Issues

A common misconception is that content on the Internet is in the public domain. However, that applies only to situations in which the copyright has expired or the owner has put it into the public domain. Illegal use of intellectual property is on the rise. A recent survey by Net Protection found that, in Europe and the United States between 1998 and 2000, copyright infringement was up 105 percent. A similar situation applies to trademarks. Trademark infringement is not just use of logos visually on a site but also at the metatag level to attract visitors. The same Net Protection survey found that metatag infringements were up 1,280 percent.

As the content manager, you should have policies in place regarding two aspects of copyright and trademarks—protecting your own site's assets, and making use of the assets of other intellectual property right owners. Assets include not only text, but also illustrations, photographs, and audio- and video-clips. To establish good policies and practices, you should:

- Know the copyright and trademark legislation in your country, especially as it applies to the Internet.

- Explore software tools that exist to protect digital assets, but be aware that hackers are usually able to break the codes.

- Have your site's copyright notice visible on every Web page.

- Give credit where credit is due on your site by obtaining permissions and citing copyright owners.

The Long-Term View: Rebuilding and Maintaining

About three years ago, we began to encounter managers who needed direction on how to go about managing and maintaining their Web sites. They were starting to understand the value of their sites, but realized their material was outdated, or had received user complaints that they wanted to address. Some didn't have a site management plan and no management processes in place. Others had plans, but they weren't followed. When we introduce clients to the issues involved in fixing these sites, many feel that they're building a site from scratch. In fact, the process is similar to creating a new site because existing sites often have problems whose solutions often require major site overhauls. These problems include:

> Some sites require complete overhauls.

- **Design**—the look-and-feel no longer matches the organizational image.

- **Size**—the site has grown too big for the underlying site infrastructure.

- **New features**—although added to increase functionality/interactivity, these news features don't actually add value to the content.

- **Lost information**—certain content can no longer be found on the site.

- **Information flow**—it's become far too cumbersome.

- **Navigation**—users find it awkward to get around the site.

- **Web page programming**—the pages were created manually using HTML and then edited using a Web editor, causing difficulties and time-consuming corrections.

- **Broken links and dead e-mail contacts**—no process is in place for checking and maintaining linkages.

We recommend, at the outset, that clients put a site management plan in place before they begin to rectify individual problems. This plan requires full team involvement and will set a process in place where the right questions are asked and good answers are found, resulting in major development steps, resource planning, identification of key players, timelines, and deliverables. Table 9.7 provides some items that should be considered when redeveloping an existing site.

Big Site Basics

Many organizations have Intranets, Extranets, and/or Web sites with thousands of pages. Such sites can include online technical documentation, human resource policy manuals, online learning modules, product catalogues, customer service information files, and/or workgroup files for research and production. This material forms a site's *knowledge base*.

The Evolution of Knowledge Bases

The term *knowledge base* can be defined as the storage of information relating to customer inquiries, employees in need of product knowledge, technical documentation, and product solutions. Generally, this type of information is generated by a subject matter expert who added it to an online database. Organizations that develop such knowledge bases have, in the past, turned to mass publishing tools or customized solutions. However, these knowledge bases have generally received contributions from many in-house publishers without any standards being in place. Therefore, their development has been haphazard and error prone. Information becomes buried, resulting in financial losses if employees can't find the information they need. This has become a particularly difficult situation for organizations that rely on their Intranets as a replacement for paper documentation.

> A knowledge base needs standards.

Table 9.7   Site Management Planning Considerations

MANAGEMENT ITEM	DETAIL	RESPONSIBILITY
Page Performance	Do the site/pages download quickly or slowly? Are there broken links to pages that no longer exist?	Web manager
External Links	Are the links to external locations being checked, updated, and corrected?	Web manager, subject matter expert
Navigation	Is the navigation still appropriate to the overall site? Are the links working on all navigation bars?	Web manager, content manager
E-Mail/Alias Addresses	Are all E-mail addresses on the site correct, and are the correct individuals attached to the correct pages?	Web manager, communications manager, human resources manager
Legal Information	Are the copyright clauses, privacy notices, and other legal statements current and accurate, and located on the correct pages?	Web manager, legal counsel
Site Structure	Is the site structure at the programming level correct? Who is responsible for managing the servers and the file structures? Who is responsible for archiving or deleting content?	IT department, Web manager, content manager
Browser Compatibility	Is the site being delivered for a specific browser? Are browser compatibility checks being done to ensure correct viewing?	Web manager, designer, programmer
Search Engines	Has the site been registered on search engines and have the listings been maintained? Are the metatags appropriate?	Web manager, content manager, programmer
Error Messages	Are the error messages logged and corrected?	Web manager, programmer

Time for More Technology?

It's only been in the past couple of years that many organizations have started to recognize that they've created vast amounts of information that is labor intensive to create and maintain. As they've continued to create content, more people become involved, resulting in more approval stages and constantly changing policies. To help with content management, many organizations with large sites are turning to customized site management tools.

Using A Content Management System (CMS)

If you're dealing with thousands of pages of data and content as well as numerous people contributing material to your site, you may want to investigate different content management systems. Teresa Elms, a Los Angeles freelance Web content consultant, has worked for organizations with these systems and believes that, although the technology is primitive at the moment, it's the wave of the future: "Some sort of tool is needed to overcome the sheer *volume* of routine grunt work that goes into all aspects of content development in business, academia, and government. I'm convinced that nearly every organization of any size will soon be forced to make a decision about managing internally generated content at the source." She notes that a CMS has five objectives:

- **Inventory control of content assets**—to figure out what's on hand and where, so you can find it again and reuse it.

- **Eliminate content redundancy**—to detect duplicate items automatically, detect all links pointing to each copy of the item, then rationalize links; and consolidate duplicates to save space.

- **Version control**—to track all versions of assets and link multiple assets that belong together.

- **Content usage analysis**—to track volume of usage and sources of access by object for statistical analysis.

- **Dynamic content serving**—at minimum, this means assembling content using server-side scripts, e.g., inserting a standard header and footer and rotating home page main content or advertising. More advanced systems take an object-oriented approach. The idea is to maximize the internal cohesion within an object while minimizing its coupling with external objects. Multiple frameworks or templates then assemble these objects in different contexts to tell different stories.

- **Consistent style and navigation enforcement**—to provide consistent brand identity although, ideally, each division or department has flexibility to establish their own look.

Making the CMS Decision

Your site may be so large and cumbersome that it's an obvious candidate for a CMS. But, perhaps, your site is not that big and you're uncertain whether the time and costs of implementing a new system are worthwhile. Table 9.8 sets out the questions you should be asking and can help you determine if your organization needs to put such a tool into place.

Writers/Editors Will Have to Get On-Board

A CMS won't cure any of the people problems involved in content development or automatically create content out of garbage, but it can help stop content value erosion caused by obsolescence, inaccuracy, inconsistency, inaccessibility, incomprehensibility, and loss, among other things. If you plan to be in the online content business for the long haul, this is not optional stuff. This is a hot technology. You've got to learn to think about content in an object-oriented way that can be incorporated into a content delivery system. It takes practice. It feels like an unnatural act. But once you get a decent object library built (and you'll throw away your first couple of attempts), from that point on reusability of content and dynamic content generation will greatly speed content production and lower costs. If you can't do that in the next year or two, you'll be forever unable to compete. Don't think "literature." Think "applied epistemology." Or go back to straight writing, then team up with a Web content developer who can make the conversions for you. The writing role and the Web content development role are separating even as we speak.

Teresa Elms, Web Content Consultant

Table 9.8 Does Your Organization Need a Content Management System?

QUESTION	RATIONALE
Is a database required?	The larger the site, the more likely the need.
Is a customized solution required?	This depends on the information requirements. The more complex your content is, the more appropriate a customized solution may be.
Is a database information architect required?	In general, large sites require people experienced in database development.
Can the tool be used with little or no training?	This depends on whether it's a management tool or mass publishing tool. When the latter is involved, non-technical staff will usually require training.
How expensive will the tool be?	Software solutions usually have many related costs such as a purchasing or licensing plan, specific costs for site server and development, and annual subscription costs for maintenance and server-side software renewals.
Can changes to the knowledge base be completed in-house or must we go back to the specific software developer?	Generally, well-designed structures with careful thought given to the handling of information tend to have a longer life. As well, if the proper design has already been implemented, some tools will be easy to adapt in-house. However, organizations that do not have in-house capacity may require additional help.
Will the tool allow for growth to the database?	Some software products are not designed for large sites, and the tool will not allow for growth.
Are you looking for a site management tool versus a document management tool?	Some software tools use the terminology interchangeably—be aware of the specific needs of your site, and analyze and purchase accordingly.

Think Global; Act Local

The Web is a communications medium accessed increasingly by international users. CyberAtlas (2001), a site that collects Web facts and statistics from researchers around the world, notes that:

> The United States still has more people online in the world, but its share of global users continues to shrink…For example, the U.S.

share of the world's Internet users fell from 40 percent to 36 percent over the last year [from 1999 to 2000]…Western Europe (22 percent) plus the remainder of the English-speaking world (12 percent represented by Australia, Canada, urban South Africa and Britain) now form a bloc that rivals the American share of Internet users.

The Role of the Solutions Architect

Many previous software development efforts consisted of gathering requirements, prototyping, and rushing to production—the fabled "think, thrash, and throw" project approach. The results were cost overruns and dysfunctional systems. Good solutions architecture means focusing on the solution to be delivered to the user, not the technology used, and establishing good planning right at the start. In our company, the process has four steps. 1. During inception, the business analyst sits with the client to find out what they want. The analyst doesn't get into the "technology wars," and I only play a supporting role at this point. 2. Once we know what the system is supposed to do, the next step—architecture evaluation and elaboration—is critical. We evaluate different software and hardware approaches before coding begins, and consult the client on which solution makes the most sense. 3. Next is the actual construction of the code and its components with testing integrated into the process from the very start. 4. The final step is transition, when we pass the system over to the client. Quite often, several different phases are underway on different iterations of the overall site.

Throughout this process, I use different types of architects with highly specialized skills. For example, the database architect looks at the data, normalizes patterns amongst the data, builds logical structures, and works with the development team on integrating that data into the application. The systems architect works on how all the components fit together; the software architect works within the software to ensure that the system will run efficiently; and the network architect figures out how all the information gets piped together and exposed to the Internet.

Sean O'Neill
Director of Architecture, E-Solutions
EYT Inc.

In other words, if your organization wants its products and services to attract the growing international market of Internet users, then your content management strategy must include consideration of globalization issues and a *localization* policy.

What Is Localization?

Web designers and analysts Aaron Marcus, John Armitage, Volker Frank, and Edward Guttman (1999) provide useful definitions that can help you better understand the concept of thinking globally, but acting locally:

> Adapt content to the culture of the target audience.

- **Globalization** is "…the worldwide product and consumption of products…[and] includes issues at international, intercultural, and local scales."

- **Internationalization issues** are "…the geographic (location), political, and linguistic/typographic issues of nations or groups of nations." Internationalization generally refers to setting formal standards for manufacturers and other producers of products and services.

- **Intercultural issues** are "…the religious, historical, linguistic, aesthetic, and other more humanistic issues of particular groups or peoples, sometimes crossing national boundaries."

- **Localization** is "…the issues of specific small-scale communities, often with unified language and culture, and usually at a scale smaller than countries or significant cross-national ethnic 'regions.' Examples include affinity groups (e.g., French 'twenty-somethings' or USA Saturn automobile owners), business or social organizations,… and specific intra-national groups (e.g., India's untouchables or Japanese housewives)."

Localization is creating or adapting Web content for very specific target audiences. However, you must be aware that Web use around the world varies widely. Literacy researchers Aliki Dragona and Carolyn Handa (2000:56-60) studied Web use and accessibility in Greece for people "who are middle or upper class, bilingual, well educated: their financial status can afford them personal computers, the latest software, and Internet access." In doing so, they discovered that North Americans hold general assumptions about the Web that don't necessarily apply to those in other countries and cultures.

- **Equipment:** "Many of us assume that people own computers that can access the Web in color and sound. We also assume that people can purchase and continually update technological equipment."

- **Cost:** "Many of us assume that dial-in charges and phone bills are similar everywhere to the relatively inexpensive rates common in the U.S."

- **Content:** "Many of us assume that today practically any kind of information we want might be found on the Web."

- **Web value:** "Many of us assume that people see the Web in a positive light, as something good and useful....We also assume that the commercial aspects of the Web are more or less culturally neutral and that the ideology imparted by advertising and mass consumerism can be easily ignored."

- **Web use:** "Those of us who are familiar with the Web assume that people will go to a machine for information and entertainment instead of to other people, or other means of information and entertainment."

Globalization is not Americanization

It's very important for us to understand that, although a great deal of Web content is in English, the spread of information is not about spreading American culture and values throughout the globe. Nor should we expect people from other countries and cultures to understand or want to buy in to our ideas and values. Localization means adapting information for a particular customer, language group, region, or country. This includes technology which is not culturally neutral. Something as seemingly simple as the date and time format differs from country to country. And graphics, for example, can be misleading because visuals are learned in a social context and are loaded with different histories. Organizations have to re-engineer their Web sites to reflect these differences. To do this well, an organization must do research, not just about a country, but about groups within that country—sub-cultures that have their own particular ways of thinking and doing things.

Nancy Hoft, International Communications Consultant
www.world-ready.com

If your organization wishes to achieve localization on its site, it must set in-house standards regarding intercultural issues and preferences, and all members of the Web production team must develop a sensitivity for the needs of your intended target audience.

When Going Global

Your organization may already know that it wishes to attract global users. However, many owners of informational sites may not be aware of their international audience. How can you find out who is coming to your site? A good starting point is tracking site visitors and sorting through site logs to identify main users and their countries of origin. If you find large groupings from geographic areas outside your own country, then you might consider localization. As Table 9.9 demonstrates, this strategy requires decision-making in a variety of areas. Essentially each organization must examine its own plans and resources before determining what approach it should take.

International English or "What's in a Word?"

Millions of people outside of North America and Britain speak English as either a native language, a second language, or a foreign language. Sociolinguist Rodica Albu, author of *An A-Z Introduction to the Study of Varieties of Present-Day English*, (1998), says:

> There are around 40 geographic varieties of present-day English. In countries where English is a first language, it exists as a subvariety of either American or British English as in Wales, Scotland, Ireland, South Africa, Australia, and New Zealand. However, English speakers in India, the Caribbean, and Africa tend to form standards of their own. Speakers of all these varieties generally understand each other very well, but the spread of English through mass media and migration doesn't necessarily standardize the vocabulary, grammar, pronunciation, and speech habits of all these users.

As a result, you can never be certain that, just because your site uses English, its messages will be well understood by this huge variety of users. Sociolinguist James P. Gee (1999:52) explains that the meanings of words are socially and culturally determined:

> Your English has "hidden" assumptions.

> I [take] the view, which is becoming progressively more common in work in cognitive science and the philosophy of mind, that the human is, at root, a pattern recognizer and builder. However, since the world is infinitely full of potentially meaningful pat-

Table 9.9   Key Considerations for a Localization Plan

ITEM	CONSIDERATIONS
Users	Your visitor numbers indicate a large international audience. ■ Can your organization do the research necessary to identify the demographics of your visitors? ■ Do you understand how and why these visitors are using your site? ■ How can you improve the site for international visitors?
Sales Issues	The sales of your business are focused on, or growing in, other countries. ■ What are your customer needs and how can your organization best meet them? ■ Are you knowledgeable about the currencies and tax systems in other countries? ■ Does your organization have an international distribution system in place? ■ Are there country-specific trading regulations to consider? ■ Are marketing, product information, and warranty information packages available in the appropriate languages? ■ Is product service readily available in that country?
One Web Site versus Several Web Sites	Your organization needs to localize information. Should you have: ■ One Web site whose design and language are culturally neutral? ■ Different Web sites localized for different countries, cultures, or audiences? ■ One Web site that localizes particular product information areas and then provides country-specific sections within the site? This is often the solution when a site is very large and the organization can't afford to localize all its components.
Staffing Issues	Localization usually requires staff training and may require additional specialists who understand the social, political, cultural, language, literacy, and technical issues involved in presenting localized Web content. These may include: ■ Translators who provide translation and language adaptation. ■ Cultural specialists who ensure that content respects a specific culture's values and taboos. ■ Marketing specialists who ensure that marketing plans won't adversely affect the organization's message to a specific culture. ■ Business specialists who ensure that distribution channels and business activities do not conflict with another country's regulations and cultural business practices.

terns and sub-patterns in any domain, something must guide the learner in selecting which patterns and sub-patterns to focus on. And this something resides in the cultural models of the learner's sociocultural groups and the social practices and settings in which they are rooted.

Because all of us recognize patterns based on our cultural upbringing, we build up cultural models that we generally accept without question. Gee provides the word *bachelor*—a deceptively simple word that's loaded with cultural implications. What exactly is a bachelor? "An unmarried man," you might say. But Gee (1999:58) asks if these men are bachelors:

- The Pope?

- A man who's been divorced three times?

- A gay man?

- An elderly senile man who's never been married?

The answers are "No," because, although all these men are unmarried, our idea of a bachelor is based on a cultural model of a man who has never been married, but is eligible or wants to be eligible for a heterosexual relationship that leads to marriage. These interpretations of *bachelor* are based on Western culture. How might *bachelor* be interpreted in Asian, Indian, or African cultures? Likely in very different ways.

If your Web site is attracting English speakers from a wide variety of cultures, you'll have to rethink many of the assumptions "hidden" in your language. Table 9.10 provides some additional tips to using English in an international context.

Culturally Correct Design

Throughout this book, we've been offering you text and design advice that's been suitable for North American and some European countries. If you're going to be writing/designing for international audiences, you may have to rethink your text presentation. Technical communicator David Gillette (1999:16), writing about international design, notes that many sites created in North America are too complex for users in other countries:

> Are your Web pages too American?

> What upsets most of them [users] is what they call your "typically American Web design." They say that you assume one-user/one-computer access to the Internet, and this assumption has led you to design a site suited only to the technological and

social context of an American office…You've broken your information into small chunks clustered on pages through your site…Your Web hierarchy is complex and multilayered to allow for a great deal of subdivision, classification, repetition, and information "chunking." This is appropriate design for American workers, who often have nearly unlimited, continual access to the Internet on individual computers. But for international employees who share computer resources with other employees and print out information for later use, your site takes too long to view and is unnecessarily complex.

Good design for international audiences also includes careful understanding of the graphic user interface (GUI) and other visuals, and how they might affect or be interpreted by different cultural groups. Information architect Olin Lagon (2000) describes a

Table 9.10   Tips to Writing English for an International Audience

ISSUES	YOU SHOULD…
Standardization	■ Use standard spellings.
	■ Avoid slang and jargon that could be misunderstood by both native and non-native English speakers.
	■ Don't use idioms and clichés. For example, speakers of English as a Second Language (ESL) might have trouble understanding that an *eager beaver* is a person with a lot of energy who's always willing to help out and get things done.
Clarity	■ Don't use the passive voice—it creates ambiguity.
	■ Make sure pronouns have clear antecedents. English pronouns can be very difficult for ESL speakers.
	■ Define any term that users might not understand.
Simplification	■ Keep it simple—avoid long sentences with complex grammar.
	■ Avoid verbs that require multiple words—for example, instead of writing the phrase *pulling in*, use the word *attracting*.
	■ Avoid phrases such as *priced-right, long-lasting light bulbs* that string together adjectives and nouns. Create more easily understandable phrases such as *Light bulbs that are low in cost and will last for a long time.*

situation where an American Web manager's cultural sensitivity didn't go far enough:

> A globalization manager with a very large business said his company thought it had the right approach: He translated the American-targeted copy into the local language and changed the photograph, switching to models of the targeted ethnicity. The photograph pictured a man and woman of the correct ethnicity, with the woman demonstrating to the man how to use the company's product. This was an unacceptable breach of accepted gender roles in the target country. Furthermore, even though the models were of the correct ethnicity, they had an American look. It also didn't help that the man in the picture wore a green shirt, something associated with people from a neighboring country with whom the target market had less than friendly relations. The globalization manager quickly learned that his team had made mistakes, as his foreign customer was shocked with the results. With one seemingly innocent picture, his group had committed multiple cultural offenses.

Table 9.11 provides topics of consideration when viewing the GUI through a localization perspective.

Translation Techniques

Your organization may decide to translate content using in-house translators, a translation company, or freelance translators. No matter how it gets done, translation involves two important issues: *adaptation* and *ambiguity*.

Considering A Machine Translator?

Although it's unlikely that any machine can take the place of a human translator, machine translation systems can be functional for organizations that require rough translations or want to supplement and/or aid their translators. If you're interested in using machine translation in your organization, you'll need to research the different types of systems, from fully automatic translation systems to computer-based translation tools. According to the European Association for Machine Translation (2000): "There is long experience with various human-assisted MT implementations in large organizations, e.g. involving input control, terminology management, revision of MT output, integration with authoring and publishing systems, etc., and there is rapidly increasing experience with computer-aided translation systems (e.g. translator workstations, translation memories, localization support systems, etc.)."

Table 9.11 Design Element Considerations

DESIGN ELEMENTS	CONSIDERATIONS
Color	Some colors may create certain responses or have specific interpretations. Review each color and confirm for individual and combined use in design.
Visuals	Many countries and cultures have culture-dependent symbols that will affect users' interpretation of the visuals on your site. You should be aware of visuals that are often culturally determined such as: ■ Religious symbols ■ Animals ■ Numbers ■ Body parts, language, and gestures Research cultural imagery to ensure graphics won't cause misinterpretations or offense.
Icons	Not all icons mean the same things in different cultures. Use neutral graphics with localized labels, captions, and legends.
Textual Directionality	Not all languages have text that runs in the same direction. Some languages are: ■ Left to right ■ Right to left ■ Vertical Consider how such differences will affect functionality such as surveys, online forms, and so on.
Alphabetical/ Ideographic Languages	Some languages have ideographs that can't be ordered by traditional English alphabetic sorting order. These languages include: ■ Chinese ■ Japanese ■ Korean Consider how such differences will affect functionality such as surveys, online forms, and so on.

Using Adaptation

Adapting goes beyond translating.

Translation generally refers to an accurate and precise rendering in one language (the target language) text from another language (the source language). Adaptation is a step beyond this process. A translator/adaptor changes the content and writing style of a text to better address the cultural differences of the people who speak the second language (this is sometimes called *transcreation*).

Making Words Appropriate

When I'm given English materials that are inappropriate for other cultures, I inform the English writer or content provider about this fact and then adapt my translation accordingly. For example, if you ask youth on an international site if they wear Levi jeans or if their mothers drive them to a store, you're using references and concepts that are too North American and emphasizing North American products and habits. It's not that people in other countries don't wear Levi jeans or drive cars. The issue is that, if a publication claims to be "global" and targeting a global audience, it should keep the questions and statements more open-ended and less culturally loaded towards one particular culture. Localization means being very sensitive to cultural differences.

Kristen Choi, Web Translator

Handling Ambiguity

Language is, in itself, ambiguous. In English, we have numerous words with multiple meanings. For example, you can *draw a picture*, *draw attention*, and *draw water*. Technical communications specialist William Horton (1998) notes that it takes the *Oxford English Dictionary* 250,000 words just to define the word *set*.

If such words are used in the original language, the writer/editor must supply context that will reduce ambiguity. For example, no translator would have a problem understanding the difference between *draw a picture* and *draw water* because these phrases help to define *draw*. However, as communications specialist Kukulska-Hulme (1999:32) notes: "...context does not always show which role a word is playing: sufficient context is needed." She demonstrates this point by putting the word *last* into the phrase *the last option* and asking if this phrase means:

- The most recent option?
- The only remaining option?
- The final option in a list?

As Kukulska-Hulme demonstrates, *the last option* does not supply enough context to provide accurate meaning. However, she suggests that if *last* is put in a phrase, *the option selected when you last used the Edit menu,* the meaning is now clear because the context is sufficient.

When translators come across phrases such as *the last option,* they may be able to figure out the meaning from the larger context, but it's more likely that they won't be able to provide an accurate translation and will have to go back to the original writer/editor for clarification. This kind of situation creates bottlenecks in the translation process and increases costs through additional time and use of resources. It is extremely important, therefore, that original content be written clearly—a policy that needs to be set early in the content management process.

Translation Tips

Translating is a learned skill.

The ability to create quality translation/adaptation is an acquired skill. Many people think that a native speaker of a language can be a translator/adaptor. This isn't the case. In fact, native speakers may not even be good writers in their own language. It's also important to understand that translation takes time, no matter how short the text. Even a phrase may take a significant amount of time if the meaning isn't clear, the concept involved is unusual, the words are new or rarely used, or it requires adaptation. Our research into localization and our experiences in numerous bilingual projects (we work primarily in Canada where many documents must be published in both French and English) are summed up in Table 9.12.

Table 9.12   Tips for Translating Text

TRANSLATION ISSUES	YOU SHOULD...
Style and Meaning	■ Simplify the writing style in the original language.
	■ Have writers/editors eliminate jargon.
	■ Use editors, copyeditors, and proofreaders to ensure the original text is clear in meaning.
	■ Be aware that, although many countries may use the same language—for example, Spanish throughout Latin and South Americas, the words can have different meanings within the different cultures.

Table 9.12 (Continued)

TRANSLATION ISSUES	YOU SHOULD...
Teamwork and Process	■ Have your translator or translation team work with the English writer(s)/editor(s) before the English text is posted to the site. This collaboration will result in culturally neutral words and references and reduce the amount of adaptation required.
	■ Use a bilingual copyeditor to do a concordance, that is, ensure that nothing has been lost in the process of translation. The goal is equivalency in content, style, tone, level of language, and format.
Functionality	■ If the original language is English, text in the targeted language may be longer (as much as 25 to 30 percent) than the original. Ensure that the longer text suits your Web design.
	■ Have your translator(s) test the usability of translated content by seeing how it appears on different browsers and ensuring functionality from a user's perspective. (For more information on these issues, see Chapter 8, "Content + Technology: A Surprising Alliance.")

To Sum It Up

Content and logical management means that your organization must undertake the appropriate planning and decision making at each stage of Web site development. This chapter has provided you with some heads-up issues that we've come across in our experiences and through our research for this book. Although we recognize that your work in content management will be affected by any number of in-house events—for example, changes in organizational goals, staffing, technologies, and resources—we hope that this chapter can help you traverse this increasingly complex process that's an essential part of Web site production.

Resources for This Chapter

Books

International Technical Communication: How to Export Information about High Technology by Nancy Hoft. Information on management strategies, user analyses, writing for translation, and designing online documents. (John Wiley & Sons: 1995)

Guide to Macintosh Software Localization by Apple Computer Inc. This book remains a useful reference tool for international requirements and considerations. (Addison-Wesley: 1992)

Gestures: The Do's and Taboos of Body Language Around the World by Roger E. Axtell. An easy-to-read book that raises awareness about cultural differences. (John Wiley & Sons: 1991)

Global Interface Design: A Guide to Designing International User Interfaces by Tony Fernandes. A practical information tool on localization with many supporting visuals. (Academic Press, Inc.: 1995)

Language and Communication: Essential Concepts for User Interface and Documentation Design by Agnes Kukulska-Hulme. Information about language and communication concepts for people working in other fields. (Oxford University Press: 1999)

Digital Property: Currency in the 21st Century by Lesley Ann Harris. Discusses issues involved with intellectual property on the Web. (McGraw-Hill Ryerson: 1998)

Digital Copyright: Protecting Intellectual Property on the Internet by Jessica Litman. Provides a current perspective on U.S. copyright law and technology. (Prometheus Books: 2001)

Web Sites

From Plain English to Global English (www.webpagecontent .com/ra_article/49/3/). Although this site is primarily designed to offer useful advice and tips on how to write for people who use English as a foreign language, it also provides good information on how to write clearly for all English-speaking users.

ESL Idiom Page (www.eslcafe.com/idioms). An alphabetical listing of English idioms and their meanings.

The World Factbook (www.odci.gov/cia/publications/factbook/ index.html). Provides detailed statistical information about the demographics, politics, and economy of individual countries.

DOSFAN Electronic Research Collection (dosfan.lib.uic.edu/ ERC/index.html). Provides free online research through various U.S. Department of State databases.

The Association for Machine Translation in the Americas (www.isi.edu/natural-language/organizations/AMTA.html). An organization for people interested in studying, evaluating, and understanding the science of machine translation.

Foreignword.com (www.isi.edu/natural-language/organizations/ AMTA.html). A site devoted to translation information. Also includes a question-and-answer forum.

"Empowering users through user-centred web design" (www .its.monash.edu.au/web/slideshows/ucd/spusc.html). A conference paper by Dey Alexander that focuses on the principles of good design.

Web of Culture (www.webofculture.com/worldsmart/design_ icons.html). A commercial site that provides an overview of icons, color, and language requirements for global use.

Digital Preservation (dp.aiim.wegov2.com/go/wego.group.group ?groupId=1708). Information regarding the management of digital assets and large portal style sites.

CHAPTER 10

The Business of Web Writing/Editing

What's Inside:

- How to find work opportunities
- Pros and cons of a freelance career
- Tips to estimating work and setting fees
- Billing and business practices
- Invoices and payments
- Building good business relationships

The only reason for being a professional writer/editor is that you can't help it.

ADAPTED FROM A QUOTE BY LEO ROSTEN

From our experience, research for this book, and interviews with other writers/editors, we've found that the business of the Web—from contracts to copyright—is in as much a state of flux and uncertainty as any other aspect of the Web. This means that everyone—from those making a transition from the print world to those with Web experience—are asking questions such as:

- How can I find work?
- How do I estimate how long a job will take?
- What should I charge for my services?
- What should I put into a written proposal?
- What are the elements of a good contract?

We've also found that Web opportunities and business practices vary enormously both among countries and within a country. For example, if you live near the seat of a government, you're likely to get work on government sites. If you live in a city with high-tech

Work opportunities are generally *local.*

companies, you'll find work in online documentation. Your professional experiences will tend to be *local*, that is, types of work, organizational hiring practices, fee structures, and so on will depend on where you live and work. And even though the Web allows writers/editors to work from a distance, you're far more likely to find work close to home. One reason is that people still like to meet face-to-face, but another is that, by living in the same town or city as your client, you share similar experiences and knowledge—the kind of sharing that enables good business relationships.

Although this chapter is geared primarily for freelance writers/editors, people seeking full-time work will also find useful career information and tips. In today's highly competitive global market, employees are expected to be entrepreneurial within their own organizations and demonstrate the same kind of energy and initiative characteristic of self-employed people who have to hustle to find and maintain clients. Also, given the uncertainties of the Web world, many writers/editors may find themselves frequently changing employers, alternating between full-time jobs and contract work, or even moving out of the writing/editing field for an interim period of time until they can resume their preferred career path.

First Steps

Start with your interests, skills, and knowledge.

Two of the most common questions we get in our Web writing/editing workshops are "Where do I start?" and "How can I break in?" Our answer is: "It depends on you—your interests, your skills, and your knowledge." For example, do you have an education or training in a specific field? Then you'll have a knowledge base that will appeal to specific types of clients. One of the writers/editors we interviewed, Helen Byrt, has a Ph.D. in zoology and was always interested in science and medical writing. She's parlayed this specialty and her interest into a Web business, ScriptMedical, to help pharmaceutical companies provide information about drug products.

Or, perhaps you have a skill set that can help you make an easy transition from print to the Web. Paula Parks, a writer and adjunct professor of new media at the Columbia University School of International and Public Affairs, describes her work this way: "I write columns, features, and reports for business-to-business Web sites. My work has changed little, really, from the work I used to do at newspapers. Although, I don't do investigative reporting, I do write biting, hard-hitting reports and analyses. And it's all posted on the Web for my clients' clients to see."

"Where Do I Start?"

Your individual talent base and background will decide how you approach a new work area, what opportunities you'll find, and the direction you'll take. However, a good place to start a career writing/editing for informational Web sites is to explore different types of content and decide what interests you or falls within your area of expertise. For example:

- If you're a creative writer or enjoy editing narratives, you may be suited for work on children's sites or adult sites that are highly interactive.

- If you have a technical background, you're likely to find work in technical documentation or product information sites.

- If you prefer writing/editing light and humorous text, you may enjoy work on children's sites or in developing marketing/promotional content on an e-commerce site.

- If your area of expertise is writing/editing publications such as reports, brochures, booklets, and pamphlets, you'll find opportunities on government and large corporate sites that post information for the public.

We also suggest trying your hand at genres you've never written in before. For example, volunteer on a Web site whose project is outside your normal realm of experience and see if the writing/editing suits you. Because the Web is currently a medium of experiment rather than experience, you may discover some surprising insights about your interests and strengths. It's also important to remember that Web writing/editing isn't for people who have some special knowledge that others don't. In fact, such people don't exist. Rather, the Web is a new and untried medium with many unanswered questions. If you're willing to experiment, you may be the one to find some of the answers.

> Experiment in new genres.

In Chapter 1, we illustrated the Web site production process (see Figure 1.1). As a newcomer to Web production, you won't have expertise in this particular process, but if you've had any experience in publishing and/or broadcasting, you'll understand processes in general. This knowledge is an important asset when you seek Web content work. It means you'll have skills that clients are looking for, including:

- Experience in scheduling—benchmarks, milestones, and timeframes.

- Providing deliverables as requested.

- Working on teams with people in different areas of expertise.

- Using different technologies such as audio and/or video to deliver content.

- Mixing text with graphics such as illustrations, photographs, tables, and graphs to enhance meaning.

"How Can I Break In?"

> Consider a variety of strategies.

Writers/editors use many techniques to find out about work opportunities. We don't recommend cold-calling, that is, phoning a client that you don't know to try and sell your services.

Online Work-Posting Sites

You'll find a variety of sites online that provide information about full-time and contract Web content work or allow you to bid on projects. Some of these services are free, while others require subscription fees. Information about these sites is anecdotal, and we've found it impossible to judge whether these sites provide satisfactory results on a regular basis. Therefore, although we can't recommend the following sites, you may be interested in exploring what's "out there."

- **E-lance (www.elance.com/c/home/main/index.pl?):** Employers list projects for bids by freelancers.

- **Freelance Online (www.FreelanceOnline.com/index2.html):** A work-posting site that charges a small fee to subscribe.

- **Writing Employment Center (www.poewar.com/jobs):** Posts jobs in print, broadcasting, and the Web.

We'd like to hear from you if you've had experience with one or more of these sites, or if you know of others worth mentioning in a revised edition of this book. You can contact us through our Web site at www.wiley.com/compbooks/hammerich.

Most cold calls are likely to result in rejections even if you have experience. Rather, we suggest that networking, volunteering, and building your own Web site are your best strategies for getting work.

Other online sources for work opportunities are organizations that post job openings on their Web sites and general job boards. For the latter, we suggest narrowing your search using keywords such as "Technical Editor" or "Documentation Writer"; we've found that "Writer" and "Editor" rarely get good results.

Networking

One of the best ways to find out about work opportunities is to join a professional association whose members are involved in Web development and go to your local chapter's meetings. Although these meetings usually have an educational/training purpose, they provide excellent opportunities for networking—getting to know people in this new field, furthering your knowledge about the local scene, and making contacts that could lead to work.

> Connect with your colleagues.

Professional groups also regularly need guest speakers. If you feel comfortable with public speaking or want to give it a try, offer to provide a lecture or workshop. You may find that people are interested in your knowledge and that public speaking is something you're good at. We regularly speak at conferences, networking events, and educational seminars, partly to share our knowledge but also to network.

Volunteering

One of the biggest problems in getting work in a new field is not having experience. How can you get experience if managers won't hire you because you don't have it? An excellent way to break this vicious cycle is to volunteer and get some samples for your portfolio. Many different kinds of people and organizations want to develop Web sites but have little funding and are looking for free help. For example, volunteer to write Web content for:

- A community group
- Your friends' and family's Web sites
- A small start-up business
- A professional association

- Your local schools
- Your religious institution
- A local youth sports team
- A local nonprofit housing group

Build Your Own Site

Showcase for your talents.

Many Web writers/editors build Web sites to promote their skills, knowledge, and expertise to potential clients. A personal Web site is an excellent opportunity to tell the world about yourself, demonstrate your skills by providing samples of your work or links to sites you've worked on, and show that you know something about the technical side of Web production.

Tips to Breaking In

Table 10.1 on page 320 provides all the tips we've gathered from our own work search experiences and those of the various writers/editors we've interviewed.

Becoming Part of a Community

I join networking groups such as venture capital groups and DigitalEve and belong to about 30 different electronic lists. What I like about going to local chapter meetings is that I become part of a community. My strategy is to volunteer to do a job such as handing out name tags. First of all, it gives me something useful to do so I'm not just standing there looking lost. Secondly, I find that people gravitate back to me because I'm a familiar face and they've already spoken to me. I chat with as many people as I can and exchange cards. If I find someone who might be a good lead for work, I follow up with an e-mail asking if I can meet with them further and show them my portfolio.

Heather Finley, Marketing Communication Strategist
IlluminArts Communications
www.illuminarts.com

It Doesn't Have to Be Fancy

It's a very good idea to create your own basic Web site. Nothing fancy, just a place to describe your services, background, client list, and show samples of your work. You may even present your own online content project or publication there. It's extremely helpful when pursuing online work to be able to give your potential client/employer your URL and say: "Here's where you can find out more about what I offer." It's also amazing how much you learn by creating a basic Web site. HTML and other aspects of Web development are definitely *not* rocket science. You can easily teach yourself the basics from a good how-to book. Also, understanding what goes into building a Web site teaches you a great deal about the true opportunities and limitations of online media. Most importantly, creating your own Web site proves that you can work in online media. It also helps you establish your own identity, which increases your profile and gives you leverage. And it's an easy way for people to find you.

Amy Gahran, Online Media Content Consultant
www.gahran.com

Freelance Pros and Cons

For many writers/editors, the business of the Web means self-employment and contract work. Although you'll find in-house writing/editing positions, many opportunities exist for people who want to work independently. Deciding whether to work as a freelancer or as an employee is a matter of personal needs and lifestyle. Table 10.2 on page 321 provides some of the pros and cons of both types of employment.

> Web work is often by contract.

If you're considering self-employment, we recommend that you find a course or workshop that covers the basics of running a small business. Such courses cover a variety of topics that may be applicable to you such as:

- Budgeting and financing.
- Your country's tax and tax payment systems.
- Your country's requirements for business registration.
- Legal ramifications of different kinds of business structures such as sole proprietorship or incorporation.

Table 10.1 Tips to Gaining Experience and Breaking into the Web Business

ACTIVITIES	TIPS
Networking	■ Network at online discussion groups and at conferences, meetings, and other local events. ■ Remember that networking is a two-way street—you have to give as well as receive.
Volunteering	■ Let everyone know that you're available to provide help and expertise on their Web sites. ■ If you're employed, ask to work on your employer's Web site. ■ Create your own opportunities by offering advice and making useful suggestions to Web site owners. Many owners are aware that their sites have problems, but don't know how to fix them. If you gain work from this, it may turn into a paid opportunity. ■ Make yourself visible by critiquing Web sites for an awards site and/or writing about Web sites for an e-zine.
Personal Knowledge Development	■ Take a Web design course—the assignments can go in your portfolio. ■ Surf other writers'/editors' Web sites for ideas about building your own site. (Many of the writers/editors we interviewed for this book have their own sites. The Web addresses are below their names.)
Marketing	■ Focus on a niche market if you have specialized knowledge and expertise. Explore organizations and Web sites in this market. ■ Consider describing yourself in a new way if you find that the title "Writer" and/or "Editor" isn't working for you. Have a title such as "Web Content Strategist" or "Web Content Developer" if you're a writer or a "Web Content Quality Controller" if you're an editor. ■ Consider submitting your own site for a site award.

Being Business-Wise

If you've determined that you want to be a freelance writer/editor, then you need a set of business skills specific to this career path—skills involved with estimating the scope of a project, setting your fees, making project proposals, and negotiating contracts.

Table 10.2 Pros and Cons of Freelancing versus Being on Staff

	PROS	**CONS**
Freelancing	■ Flexible work schedule.	■ No job security.
	■ No dress code.	■ No vacation or sick pay.
	■ Can work at home, on site, or from another location.	■ No work-supported medical, dental, and/or insurance plans.
	■ May have more tax deductions (country-dependent).	■ Unpredictable income, and client payment schedules may cause problems.
	■ Continual mental stimulation because of a variety of jobs and clients.	■ Must pay for equipment and supplies.
	■ May be able to earn more than a full-time employee in equivalent position.	■ May have overlapping deadlines and no access to support writers.
	■ May be able to choose clients and types of projects.	■ May not have access to training unless self-funded.
		■ May feel isolated with little or no contact with a production team.
		■ Must handle paperwork and record-keeping for business.
On Staff	■ Steady income.	■ May work on projects that restrict personal writing style.
	■ Fixed working hours.	■ May not be able to follow personal interests or work on a variety of different kinds of Web sites.
	■ Vacation and sick pay.	
	■ Work-supported medical, dental and/or insurance plans.	■ Generally higher costs for business clothes.
	■ Provided with equipment and supplies.	■ Have to deal with office politics and supervisory issues.
	■ Training support.	■ Time and money spent commuting to work.
	■ Being part of a production team.	
	■ Possibility of advancing within an organization.	

First Meeting Qs & As

You've been asked to meet with a client and/or the production team. Perhaps, the client wants to look you over and find out if you're the right person for his or her project. Or, you may be the one chosen and this is your first opportunity to sit down and discuss the project in depth. Whichever is the case, you need to obtain as much information about the client as you can before this first meeting. If the organization already has a Web site and wants to recreate it, check the site for content and map its navigation patterns. If the client is building a Web site from scratch, request and look over any print materials such as annual reports and promotional brochures to better understand the organization. Figure 10.1 provides you with a checklist of Qs & As for a first meeting with a client.

> Ask clients
> the right
> questions.

Setting Your Fees

> Fees can
> vary
> significantly.

One of the hardest questions all freelancers face is how much to charge for work. We can't provide you with a definite answer, because your fee structure will depend on a number of interrelated factors:

- **Your market:** If you work locally, the supply and demand for Web writers/editors in your area will determine the bottom and top ends of your fee scale.

- **Your expertise:** The more experience you have, the more you'll be able to charge. However, it's important to remember that experienced writers/editors are expected to work faster and produce more polished results earlier.

- **The tasks you'll be doing:** Many clients expect to pay different rates for different tasks such as content organizing, writing, editing, copyediting, and proofreading.

- **If you'll have to hire subcontractors:** Some experienced writers/editors provide additional services such as copyediting, translating, and proofreading. If you're asked to supply a team, then you can charge a fee (usually between 10 and 15 percent) for managing your subcontractors in addition to your own work.

Given all these factors, Web writers/editors can currently charge between $35.00 (low level of expertise) and $150.00 U.S. per hour (high level of expertise).

Billing Considerations

Whatever you charge, your fee must exceed your expenses or you'll find it impossible to keep your business going. Although this seems obvious, some writers/editors *low-ball* an estimate to

Questions	Answers
Goals/Objectives What are the goals/objectives of the site?	☐ Market products/services ☐ Inform users about an issue ☐ Build membership in an organization ☐ Provide information about programs/services ☐ Promote users' productivity ☐ Educate users about the organization
Audience Has the target audience(s) been identified?	☐ Local ☐ Global ☐ Multilingual ☐ Shoppers ☐ Users of programs/services ☐ Potential members ☐ Employees

Web Site Content Areas
What are the logical content areas for the new or rebuilt site?
	☐ Organization policies and programs
	☐ Product/service information
	☐ Contact directories
	☐ Membership information
	☐ Online store/surveys
	☐ Privacy/legal statements
	   (For a more detailed list, see Table 3.1
	   Models of Informational Web Sites.)

Media Mix What media will be required/allowed on the site?	☐ Text ☐ Graphics ☐ Animation ☐ Audio ☐ Video ☐ Webcasts or video-conferencing
Content Specialists/Subject Matter Experts Who will be contributing content for the site?	☐ Subject matter specialists ☐ Marketing specialists ☐ Technical specialists ☐ Public affairs or corporate communications specialists ☐ Other
Content Availability Does content exist and what format is it in?	☐ Print ☐ Electronic ☐ Databases ☐ Already on a Web site
Scheduling Have dates been set for different stages of content development? (For an overview of the Web development process, see Figure 1.1.)	☐ Research and content gathering ☐ Delivery from content specialists ☐ First draft ☐ Final draft approval ☐ Prototype delivery

Figure 10.1   A sample Q & A checklist for the first meeting with a client.

get work and then find they can't survive easily on what they're charging. Taking on a job that doesn't pay adequately will affect your ability to achieve high-quality documents. Your tendency will be to get the project done quickly—a situation where mistakes occur and work becomes sloppy, thereby damaging your reputation and hence your chances of finding future work.

When you're starting out, it's a good idea to have a home office to keep your overhead low and to learn how to control your expenses. As you establish a client base, begin to have overlapping projects, and charge appropriately, you'll be able to run a profitable business. Table 10.3 can help you better understand how to determine costs and charges.

Table 10.3 Overhead and Billing Considerations

OVERHEAD	BILLING CONSIDERATIONS
Office Expenses ■ Rent ■ Insurance ■ Utilities ■ Phone/Fax ■ Internet account	■ Calculate office space costs based on space allocation within home or actual commercial space rent. ■ Keep track of actual bills for phone, fax, and Internet account.
Administration ■ Courier ■ Postage ■ Banking fees ■ Photocopying ■ Office/Computer supplies ■ Cabs/Parking ■ Project travel requirements	■ Keep track of actual amounts allocated per client/project. ■ Build in the administration costs into your fee or negotiate separate payment for different items. ■ Save all receipts for which you may collect reimbursement.
Computer Hardware/ Software Purchases ■ Warranties ■ Maintenance plans	■ Amortize your costs based on the estimated life of hardware/software (country-dependent).
Marketing ■ Business cards ■ Letterhead ■ Brochures ■ Personal Web site	■ Amortize your costs for marketing supplies and promotional materials. ■ Include the actual monthly costs of your Web site.

Table 10.3 (Continued)

OVERHEAD	BILLING CONSIDERATIONS
Labor Costs ■ Actual time spent writing/editing per project ■ Time for finding, proposing, and estimating work ■ Time for meetings, conferences, and workshops requested by the client	■ Bill for estimated or actual time required to complete the project. ■ Build into your fee the time you took to estimate a project or develop a proposal. ■ Ensure that your billing includes time spent on client-requested meetings, conferences, and workshops.
Profit ■ The amount of money over and above all expenses ■ May be fixed or variable	■ Should range from 10 to 30 percent above the actual costs.

Estimating and Keeping Track

Estimating how long a project will take can be difficult, even for experienced writers/editors. When trying to estimate your time, ask yourself:

> Estimating is a learned skill.

■ **How fast can I produce top-quality content?** As a freelancer, your reputation depends on what you show clients. You can't provide them with your first draft unless your level of expertise is so high that your first drafts are superlative—a very rare situation for most of us.

■ **Do I have previous experience with this topic?** You may have already worked with the subject matter or on related topics. If so, your background knowledge means that your learning curve will be much lower than someone who is new to the client's field. The more you know, the faster you'll be able to produce content at the appropriate level.

■ **Do I truly understand the scope of the project and what it entails?** Not all clients are good at communicating exactly what they want. If you use the Qs & As checklist for a first meeting (see Figure 10.1), you'll have a good perspective on the project. However, you'll always be dealing with unknowns. For example, if content specialists will be contributing text for you to edit, you'll have no guarantee as to the quality of the material, no matter what the client says. In our experience, you must anticipate the worst—the *glitch* factor—and build that expectation into your estimate.

- **Can I break the project into work units?** When dealing with a large project, you should try to find a way to break it into small units whose workloads you can estimate. In the print world, writers/editors often know the number of pages or words in a publication and can estimate based on those figures. However, a Web page can be as short as one line or equivalent to many print pages. Therefore, we find that breaking a project down by enumerating Web pages is not useful. You might instead try to estimate the amount of content per Web site section and how long each would take to write/edit. An "FAQ," for example, is likely to be short, while "Membership Information" will be longer.

- **Have I dealt with this client before?** A reality of freelancing is that some clients are easier to deal with than others. If you've worked for the client before, you'll know his or her personality, expectations, quirks, and work habits. If the client is new to you, your intuition will be the only guide you have to figuring out how well you'll communicate and work together. If you have any sense that the client will be excessively picky or insecure about making judgments, build in time for additional drafts and more phone calls and meetings than usual.

One of the best ways to build expertise in estimating is to keep close track of the amount of time you actually work on projects. Table 10.4 is a sample of the kind of chart we use to track writing/editing projects. In this sample, we accounted for time in quarters of days because we generally bill per diem.

Table 10.4 also demonstrates some typical characteristics of a successful freelance Web writer's/editor's work life:

- No project is full time during a week.

- On some days, the writer/editor works more than an average eight-hour workday.

- The schedule for this week had no day off.

Teach Your Clients

You're likely to find that some clients are more knowledgeable about the time a project will take than others. Others will not realize that, in addition to the initial writing/editing, a project can also require time for:

- Research (gathering information and reading)
- Concept development
- Revisions to final draft
- Client contact (phone calls and/or meetings)
- Travel to meetings or other venues

How do you educate clients? By breaking down an estimated project into logical, clearly defined steps and indicating how much time each step will take. You can also indicate a range of time for a task such as 12 to 15 days if you're unsure. If you do so, let the client know that you keep careful track of your time and will bill them according to "time spent." We've found that experienced clients often choose the upper end of the range rather than have to renegotiate the contract.

Freelancers usually juggle more than one project at a time—a necessity because they often have projects of different scope. Some will be small and quickly done, while others are large and spread out over time. In the latter case, the writer/editor will often have *down time* when a client is reviewing content, producing additional material, or seeking approvals. Freelancers can't

Table 10.4   A Sample Work-Tracking Chart

PROJECT	DAYS OF THE WEEK BY DATE							WEEK'S TOTAL WORK DAYS PER CLIENT
	3/11	3/12	3/13	3/14	3/15	3/16	3/17	
CSG Intranet	.50	1	.50		.25	1		3.25 days
Builders Ass'n Web site		.25		1			.25	1.5 days
MNF "Help" section	.75		1		.50			2.25 days
Personal Work Days	1.25	1.25	1.50	1	.75	1	.25	

bill for *down time*; as a result, they try to have other projects on the go so that they're working continuously. However, success also requires delivering top-notch content. Experienced freelancers have learned how many projects they can juggle at any one time without sacrificing the quality of their work.

Types of Billing and Rates

> Billing usually depends on project size.

In some cases, an organization already has a policy in place regarding how contractors must quote and bill for work. In other cases, you'll be asked how you charge for your expertise. The three traditional methods for billing are per hour, per diem, or by the project.

- **Per Hour:** Most clients want to know what you charge by the hour because this is the most common form of payment in the workplace. Charging by the hour can be best for small projects that may require less than a day's or week's work. It provides flexibility because you can bill odd amounts such as 11.25 hours. A small project charged by the hour usually only requires one bill submitted at the end of the project. As we noted earlier, Web writers/editors charge between $35.00 and $150.00 U.S. per hour.

- **Per Diem:** A per diem rate is your hourly rate multiplied by eight hours—for the eight-hour business day. Per diems work well for larger projects that require many days. Writers/editors who charge this way may bill in quarters of days such as 9.75 days. When working on a per diem, you'll generally bill the client at set times such as when you've provided certain deliverables or used up a certain amount of days. If a client and writer/editor have a strong and trusting relationship based on previous experience, a per diem project can be divided into monthly amounts and billed accordingly. This is an optimal situation because it provides you with a regular income for a period of time and payment isn't dependent on deliverables that can be delayed because of project problems. Per diem rates range from $280.00 (low level of expertise) to $1,200.00 U.S. (high level of expertise).

- **By Project Rate:** A project rate is a fixed billable amount for the entire length of the project—the number of estimated days multiplied by the per diem rate. The downside to this billing method is that, if you take longer than estimated to complete the work, you can't bill for the extra time. The upside is that if you take less time, you can still bill the same amount, thereby increasing your per diem fee. Generally, a project rate will remain the same unless the scope of the project has changed substantially. In this case, you should be able to increase your fee. It's a good idea to have a clause covering this situation in your contract.

The three different types of billings all have their pros and cons and depend on the project, the client, and your preferences. Table 10.5 provides you with some general tips with regard to billing.

Invoices and Payments

Part of your business accounting system is an invoicing process. Your invoice is a formal statement of work that you've accomplished the work, and the client has approved it. As we noted above, you may be invoicing at the end of a project, at time of deliverables, or according to a set schedule. Your invoice should be on your letterhead or generated from an accounting software program. As Figure 10.2 on page 332 demonstrates, it should include:

> Send professional invoices.

- **Date of invoice**—the day you create the invoice, not the day you delivered the work.

- **Client's name, company name (if applicable), and address**—the designated manager for the project.

- **Invoice number**—many organizations keep track of suppliers through their invoice numbers. If you don't have a system for numbering in place, consider one that will help you keep track of all the invoices you send during your fiscal year. For example, Invoice No. 03-02 would indicate your third invoice for the year 2002.

- **Contract/project number (if applicable)**—medium-sized and large organizations usually require this number in order to provide payment.

- **Description of work**—provide a straightforward, simple description of work completed such as "edited Web content." The client usually doesn't need a detailed list of all your services unless he or she requests a task log.

Table 10.5 Tips to Billing Practices

BILLINGS PRACTICES TIPS	
General Principles	■ Honesty is always your best policy. No one can dispute the number of hours you say you've worked, but if a client suspects that you're over-charging, your reputation will suffer.
	■ Provide good value for the client's money. Chances are, you won't have billing difficulties if you produce high-quality work on schedule.
Fee Structure	Be upfront with the client about costs built into your fee. If they ask, let them know that your fee includes:
	■ Costs of estimating
	■ Labor costs
	■ Administration
	■ Office items such as long-distance phone calls and couriers (if the latter aren't being billed separately)
Contractual Arrangements	■ Tell clients that projects are taking longer if the problems are coming from their end. Good clients will acknowledge this and add time to the project even if you haven't negotiated a change-of-scope clause in your contract.
	■ Bite the bullet when you have to. If a job is taking longer and/or requiring more couriers and long-distance phone calls than you estimated, chalk the loss up to experience and learn from your mistakes.
Payments	■ Know that most organizations pay within a certain amount of time from receipt of the invoice, *not* the date that the work was completed. Although this period can be 30 days, it can also vary from immediate payment to 120 days.
	■ You may ask the client if you can submit an interim invoice(s) during the project. Many clients accept this practice.
	■ Your cash flow problems are not your client's concern, and it's unprofessional to try and change billing schedules. However, you can ask your client how long they typically take to pay invoices to help you adjust your cash flow.
	■ If you are on a payment schedule, consider adding a statement showing the payment history to your invoices. This will keep the client informed regarding paid and unpaid bills.
	■ Ask if the client has a policy regarding late payments. For example, some clients will pay interest charges.

- **Time involved**—the time you spend depends on the project and how you bill. You may indicate hours or days spent, or a period of time such as "February to March, 2002."

- **Fee**—you can provide the overall fee or show the calculation of your fee such as "10 hours x $60 per hour = $600.00." Be careful not to miscalculate your fees or you're likely to get the invoice back for correction. The result is more waiting until you get paid!

- **Taxes and expenses (if applicable)**—these items aren't part of your fee and should be itemized separately.

- **Payment expectations ("Net 30 days," for example)**—although some clients may not honor your payment schedule, a formal statement of your expectations demonstrates that you expect to be treated in a professional manner.

- **A thank you**—we usually include a handwritten "Thank You" at the end of an invoice as a courtesy.

One problem of freelancing is that payments can be erratic. Some clients will pay promptly, while others will delay even if you have a 30-day payment clause in your contract and on your invoice. Late payers, however, are not always holding back money because of a poor cash flow. Many governments and large corporations are so bureaucratic that checks must go through various departments before being sent off. Not only can this take time, but if a key person goes on vacation or gets sick, your check may be sitting on a desk waiting for a signature.

In general, we've found that if billing is done appropriately, payments will follow with no hassle. However, if you haven't received payment within four to six weeks after the invoice date, we suggest that you phone the client and mention politely that you haven't been paid. If another two to three weeks pass without payment, call again. If a third phone call is necessary, you may consider it time to mention that you'll be putting the matter in the hands of your lawyer. And if that doesn't do the trick and the sum is large enough to warrant the expense, you may decide to bring in a lawyer. In our experience, this rarely happens as the first or second phone call usually produces payment.

Proposals and Contracts

One method of obtaining work is to submit proposals. Depending on the organization and/or the size of the project, you may

Writer/Editor Company Name

Address
Telephone
Fax
E-mail

Date: _____

Client Name
Client Company
Address

Re: **Invoice #02-048**
Contract #F897-329-6

For: Content development for MNF Group Web site
(Work from September 1 to November 15)

Fee:

- Concept development/meetings	5 days x $600/day	$3,000.00
- Writing to final draft	15.5 days x $550/day	8,525.00
- Copyedit services	4 days x $200/day	800.00
	Sub-total:	$12,325.00

Expenses: (see attached receipts)

- Out-of-town travel costs: $259.75
- Long-distance phone calls: $76.49

	Total Expenses:	$336.24
	Total:	**$12,661.24**

Many thanks, Writer/Editor Name

Payment due. Net 30 days.

Figure 10.2   A sample invoice.

receive a formal Request for Proposals (RFP) or a more informal solicitation—a client asking two or three companies or freelancers to bid on a job. When the project is large, requiring the expertise of many people, companies and freelancers often band together to provide services. In this situation, you may be part of a group submitting a proposal in a consortium approach or be in the position of a subcontractor with a lead company making the formal bid.

Table 10.6 illustrates some of the major areas that need to be included in a proposal. It's important to remember that, if a client asks for specific information, you must supply it in your proposal. In our experience, many proposals fail a first review because they don't meet even the minimum requirements for submission set out by a client. Your thoroughness and attention to detail is crucial to ensuring a positive result. And, if you win the contract, you'll have to live with the contents of your proposal so it's extremely important that you haven't underestimated timelines or budgets.

> Effective proposals require precision.

Many companies and freelancers who submit proposals are also providing ideas regarding the content of a project and

Table 10.6   Typical Proposal Items and Requirements

ITEM	REQUIREMENT
Covering Letter	Address the letter to the Project Manager and provide a brief synopsis of the submission and other key submission information such as project title and number, deadline date, and the format of the proposal.
Title Page	Provide the title of the project, your name/company title, and the date of submission.
Statement of Work/ Understanding	State the job requirements in your own words, rather than those of the client, to show your understanding of the project.
Proposed Methodology	Demonstrate your approach to the project such as how you plan to undertake content research, user interviews, writing/editing drafts, and so on.
Timelines/Deliverables	Describe what you expect to deliver and when. Include when you expect client approvals and how you'll handle time delays.
Billing/Payment Schedules	Indicate your billing structure—hourly, per diem, project rate, applicable taxes, and your expected payments in terms of benchmarks/deliverables.
Company and Team/ Subcontractor Profiles	Present yourself and others on your team, if applicable, through resumes, references, samples of work completed, and legal corporate information if requested such as a Tax Number, Corporation Number, and/or Legal Trading Name.

Protecting Your Ideas

As a former lawyer and now a business person who derives a considerable portion of his income leveraging his intellectual property, I have to say that NDAs are like locks on doors. They're really only designed to keep honest people out. Locks rarely deter determined thieves. Similarly, if someone is going to steal your ideas, or breach your confidentiality by passing them onto others, an NDA isn't going to stop them. It only provides a framework upon which to seek legal redress, generally in the shape of damages. But that doesn't mean you should completely ditch NDAs. They are a useful part of your intellectual property armory, but they shouldn't be used in a vacuum. You need to use all other skills that you possess—especially your intuition, common sense, and trust in a client.

Some people, fearing the loss or misuse of their ideas, resort to discussing them only in a vague or abstract manner. In my early days as a consultant, I wrote a number of proposals for clients outlining ideas I had for dramatically improving their business, but they weren't interested. So I sent colleagues copies of a proposal and asked for feedback. Most of them said: "We have no idea what it is you're trying to say." In holding back what I thought was the "genius" in my ideas, I'd pretty well gutted my proposals. Clients didn't know what to make of them, so they would simply pass. Now I go to great lengths to outline my proposal and then, explicitly, the benefits to the client. I'm not too worried that they'll just take the ideas and run because, as a rule, the client lacks the skills to execute the ideas, and if they take the proposal to a cheaper outfit—well, odds-on, they don't have the skills either.

Mark Neely, Author and Consultant
Infolution Pty Ltd.
www.infolution.com.au

how a project can be accomplished. You can label every page of your proposal "Confidential" and/or you may decide to incorporate a nondisclosure agreement (NDA) that asserts your ownership of an idea. The NDA is designed to protect the information and its release to your competitors. As well, you may find yourself signing an NDA if you gain work on a confidential project that involves client information such as patents, methods, technologies, processes, and so on. In general, NDAs typically state:

- The information that is to be protected.

- The parties involved.

- The time during which the information is protected—for example, the timing of a new product launch, a new law being announced, or a proprietary training product.

- The laws under which they are governed.

For more information on NDAs from a layperson's perspective, you can check out "A Practical Guide to Non-Disclosure Agreements" (www.technz .co.nz/business/nondisclosure/nondisc.htm).

A project proposal that gains you work will be the basis for a contract. The client will use your statement of work and methodology as well as your outline of benchmarks, timelines, and deliverables to draw up the agreement of work. As well, contracts usually include topics such as content ownership, termination of contract, nondelivery clauses, full handling of financial requirements, and so on. If you find yourself working with classified information or proprietary information, you may have to obtain a security clearance. These clearances usually come in several levels, each requiring different amounts of information. Your client should help you obtain the clearance, and you must release the required information when requested. Security clearances are often used for contracts with the military, police, government, and financial institutions and are useful if you wish to find work in these areas.

In our experience, most contracts are fairly written and protect both you and your client. However, you may come across one that is slanted only for the client. If you're uncomfortable with a

Copyright, or Who Owns What?

If you come from the print world as an author, journalist, screenwriter, and so on, then you're accustomed to owning the copyright to your work. However, as a freelancer writing content for informational Web sites, you'll generally find a clause in your contract indicating that you've sold your copyright—a common situation in work-for-hire contracts. Nevertheless, you need to be aware of your rights. You don't have to sell your copyright completely. Rather, you could sell limited use to your clients or retain ownership of those rights. If you determine that the copyright of your material is important to you, this subject should be included in your contract negotiations.

contract, it's a good idea to seek out professional help from a lawyer or ask someone who is experienced with contracts to review it with you.

Make-It or Break-It Relationships

Successful freelancing in Web content development depends on your ability to build excellent relationships with clients and production teams. You may be dealing with an experienced client/team with a lot of savvy and confidence, a harried client/team pressured by a boss to deliver content yesterday, or a client/team new to Web development and unsure about this new area of responsibility. No matter what the situation, we've found that building good working relationships means that you must:

> "People" skills are key to success.

- **Deliver high-quality content on time**—this creates trust in your abilities and reliability.

- **Understand that, to clients, their Web sites are the most important project in the world, no matter how small or large**—your ability to respect and empathize with this feeling means that clients will see you as a valuable ally in achieving their goals.

- **Never discuss your other ongoing projects**—consider the information involved with each project as confidential. Clients will respect your discretion.

- **Respect the skills and abilities of team members**—content may be "king," but the emperor wouldn't have any clothes without the hard work of information architects, designers, and programmers.

- **Realize your own limitations**—don't be afraid to ask for help or information. However, you must do this politely and be aware that other people are busy. Your team members will appreciate your respect for their time considerations.

- **Take responsibility for your mistakes**—if you've made an error, apologize to the appropriate team members but don't dwell on it. No one expects you to be perfect, but they will respect your honesty, sincerity, and ability to move on.

- **Stay out of office politics**—you may find that people want to confide in you. Listen and be sympathetic, but remain neutral and don't get involved by passing on gossip.

"Be nice..."

...really, that's the best way. When you work with someone, help them do their job—usually, this is accomplished simply by doing your own job in a competent manner. Don't adopt a superior attitude to anyone—you'd be surprised how quickly today's peon becomes tomorrow's boss, and how long their memories are. Thank people when they're helpful. Be useful. Don't talk about them behind their backs. Don't stab them in the back. If you think someone is good at his or her job and you're in a position to help them advance, do it. People do remember those who have done well by them, both professionally and personally. This doesn't mean you have to let people take advantage of you. Most people are normal folks just trying to do their job. If you help them do it, and do so in a pleasant, professional, and engaging way, it'll pay dividends in more work and building your professional reputation.

John Scalzi, Web Writer and Editor
www.scalzi.com

We've also found that specific areas in the process of Web site development often give rise to areas of "people" difficulties; for these, you'll need specific strategies to maintain good relationships (see Table 10.7).

To Sum It Up

Successful freelance writing/editing careers rarely happen overnight. They're a combination of top-notch professional skills, business savvy, and the ability to get along with a variety of people in different kinds of situations. Many writers/editors find that it takes several years to gain the experience and build a sufficient clientele so that they no longer have to search for work—rather, the work comes to them. Even so, social, economic, and/or political circumstances can alter; clients can go out of business or retire; and work sources can dry up. Because

Work change will be constant.

Table 10.7   Strategies for Maintaining Good Working Relationships

AREAS OF POTENTIAL DIFFICULTIES	YOUR STRATEGIES
Participants' Roles	Sometimes a client doesn't clearly set out roles or they begin to blur during the project. Your choice is to refuse additional responsibilities or take them on and charge more. In either case: ■ Be able to articulate the limits of your role as you understand them. ■ Sit down with the client and discuss the issue. ■ Be firm about your choice in a polite way. Explain that much as you enjoy the project, you can't take on the additional work because it's outside your expertise, or that you'd be delighted to participate more intensely in the project, but that this will require increased payment.
Communications and Instructions	Unfortunately, not everyone has good communication skills. If communications get snarled, you must: ■ Be patient. ■ Ensure that you speak and write clearly. Find different ways to say the same thing. ■ Be a good listener and try to *walk* in another's shoes. ■ If you don't understand something, don't blame the other person but say: "I need more guidance. Can you help me?"
Deadlines	Although the client may have set procedures and timelines out in a careful way, glitches often occur and pressures build. As the contractor, you'll be expected to work night and day on the project. When this happens, your best strategy is to be prepared for the time crunch and: ■ Put in the time necessary. ■ Do the best you can. ■ Don't complain. ■ Don't do *busy work* if you can hire someone to do it for you. On the other hand, don't give in to unreasonable demands that will affect your health and well-being. Be polite, but firm in stating your inability to meet the deadline.

change is guaranteed to be a constant in your work life, resilience will be one of your most important strengths. You'll need to be:

- Prepared for the unexpected—it's bound to come your way no matter how settled you feel.

- Flexible so you can adapt quickly and easily to changing situations.

- Open to new types of work because they may prove to be a major source of income.

- Aware of trends in your field so that you can see which way the wind is blowing.

Most importantly, you must have the capacity and willingness to be on a continuous learning curve because you are, or will be, a pioneer in this new and developing field, facing challenges that writers/editors have never faced before, and finding solutions to problems that have never existed before. We wish you the best of luck!

Resources for This Chapter

Books/Magazines

Web and New Media Pricing by J.P. Frenza and Michelle Szabo. Discusses business proposals and pricing models. Includes case studies about different kinds of projects. (Hayden Books: 1996)

Digital Property: Currency in the 21st Century by Lesley Ann Harris. Discusses issues involved with intellectual property on the Web. (McGraw-Hill Ryerson: 1997)

"Under Lock and Key" by Patricia Casey. An article on copyright and trademark issues for the digital world. (*AV Multimedia Producer*, March 2001, 23, no. 3, pp. 79-81)

Career Opportunities in Cyberspace by Harry Henderson. Includes employment prospects, occupational descriptions, and education/skill requirements. (Checkmark Books: 1999)

Web Sites/Discussion Groups

Online-Writing (talk.poynter.org/cgi-bin/lyris.pl?). An active ListServ for professionals who write, edit, and produce for the Web. To reach the ListServ, click on the second blue box to reach a page of discussion lists for online writers.

National Writers Union (www.nwu.org). A professional organization for freelancers working in U.S. markets.

DigitalEve (www.digitaleve.org). A professional organization for women in technology with chapters in the United States, Canada, the United Kingdom, and Japan.

The Society for Technical Communication (www.stc.org). Although aimed at those who develop technical documentation, this professional association has information useful for all Web writers/editors.

Editors' Professional Associations. There are numerous organizations on the web that provide information on professional development, conferences, and resources. Type "Editors Associations" in your search engine.

GigaLaw.com (www.gigalaw.com/index.html). A site with information on contracts, non-disclosure agreements, and other legal matters.

www.Writers.ca: What to Pay a Writer (www.writers.ca/whattopay .htm). The Periodical Writers of Canada's rate guideline for different types of writing assignments.

Seattle WriterGrrls (www.seattlewritergrrls.org/resource.htm# career). This site provides a good list of resources about contracting, writing proposals, and freelancing.

WritersMarket.com: How Much Should I Charge (www .writersmarket.com/content/charge.asp). A series of articles by freelancer Lynn Wasnak about estimating, billing, and rate guidelines.

Web Workshop.org (www.webworkshop.org). Articles about building Web sites and promoting a business.

HTML Goodies (www.htmlgoodies.com). Provides tutorials on building Web pages.

CyberAtlas (cyberatlas.internet.com). Reports on results from Web-related research and surveys worldwide.

ContentBiz (www.contentbiz.com). News, interviews, and case studies about e-commerce.

Tomalak's Realm (www.tomalak.org). Articles and links regarding usability, intellectual property, technology, and so on.

CHAPTER 11

After Words and For Words

The Web is a new medium whose potential and impact is, as yet, unknown. The reason is that it takes time for people to adjust, examine, explore, and experiment with a new way of communicating. Just as the producers of the first Gutenberg Bible reproduced the work of the medieval monk without altering the text or format to reflect the new possibilities of the printed book, site owners in the early days of the Web reproduced print materials by just dumping them online without altering text to reflect the possibilities of digital media. As futurist Steve Holtzman (1998:185) points out: "It puzzles me that there are people who expect that, in almost no time at all, we'd find great works by those who have mastered the subtleties of such completely new digital worlds. We are seeing the first experiments with a new medium. It took a long time to master the medium of film. Or the book, for that matter. It will also take time to master new digital worlds."

In Chapter 4, we noted that rhetoric in the Information Age required a new definition—one supplied by Richard Lanham as the "economics of human attention-structures." Management and organizational change researchers Thomas Davenport and John Beck (2001:3) concur, stating: "Understanding and managing attention is now the single most important determinant of business success." This message is only just getting through to most clients as the Web approaches its 10th birthday. Site owners are coming to the painful realization that their sites are inadequate. They're beginning to redefine their business plans and trying to understand what their clients really want in online content. The impact of these events will be ultimately beneficial to professional writers/editors who want careers in Web content development. Although the economic downturn is making organizations more cautious about investing in Web sites, we believe that the new focus on content will mean many more opportunities for work and career advancement.

However, it's also important to remember that advances in technology will continue relentlessly despite slow-downs. This means that you must be aware of trends in Web development and the possible ways they may affect content delivery. Therefore, we wish to briefly highlight new technologies that may have an impact on your career.

The Wireless Web

Although researchers are exploring new technologies to deliver the Web using standard power cables and connections in homes and businesses, a growing trend in Web content delivery is through devices such as wireless hand-held pagers and personal digital assistants (PDAs). One wireless technology under development is the "super phone" which will have extraordinary functionality beyond that of ordinary telephone capacity. Users will have color screens, video capabilities, interactive keyboards, mice for data entry, and touch screens.

These devices, which don't require standard phone or cable lines, use new programming languages and deliver the information via satellite technologies over private networks. Because the screens on these devices are much smaller than desktop monitors, the look-and-feel of the interface is minimal and content needs to be extremely concise. With these devices, content providers can enter data remotely and the information, tabulated on servers around the world, will be available in real time. The development of hand-held printers, another trend, will provide users with great flexibility and service levels in accessing information.

Convergence

Convergence begs the question: Will the TV and Web get married and live happily ever after? Although futurists still predict this outcome, early attempts at WebTV—which linked viewers to the Internet using standard TVs and specialized TV set top units—weren't particularly successful. However, producers are currently working on new ideas and new technologies to develop WebTV products such as interactive game shows that combine real people, animated characters, and computer programs working together to deliver new forms of entertainment. Given the constant growth in bandwidth and data storage combined with the enormous commercial possibilities of television, it's very likely that these attempts will continue until success is achieved. WebTV will open up many new opportunities for writers/editors with a creative bent and an interest in broadcasting.

Virtual Reality

Virtual reality (VR) has been around for a number of years. Originally, the technology required cumbersome headsets and huge platforms. Today, you'll find VR sequences on the Web on such sites as those owned by real estate companies that want to display interiors of homes to users. VR has also included *avatars*—computerized versions of yourself—that users could control by a mouse or joy stick in chat rooms and Internet gaming. More recently, VR is being used to deliver content for medical care for humans and animals, simulation training for space and scientific studies, and tele-immersion—a combination of VR and video-conferencing in which users feel as if they occupy the same space although they're actually in separate locations. Use of VR technologies is likely to open opportunities for writers/editors who have an ability to develop voice-over content, designed for the ear rather than the eye.

Personalization

Personalization refers to technologies that allow users to customize their Web tools in personal ways from the visual to the textual. Personalization also refers to technologies that allow content producers to identify users' lifestyle needs through their surfing and shopping habits and deliver personalized content based on those findings. Such personalized content is already beginning with online banking and will extend to online communities where users can be participants in investment clubs, entertainment centers, shopping networks, virtual travel centers, and so on. This type of personalization will require writers/editors who can deliver content targeted to specific audiences in a manner that is informal and yet accurate and concise.

The Semantic Web

Tim Berners-Lee, founder of the World Wide Web, and researchers James Hendler and Ora Lassila (2001:36-37) are exploring an enhancement to the current Web which they call the *Semantic Web*. Using technologies that provide machines with information as well as rules about sorting information, our computers will "become much better able to process and 'understand' data that they merely display at present." For example, concepts and ideas will be given Web addresses, their content interlinked through a hypertext-like function, and their material analyzed and personalized for users by software agents. The result will be machines that can provide us not just with data, but with data that has meaning, that is, a semantic value. Although this notion is in its infancy, the possibilities that it would create for writers/editors would be interesting given that conceptual content is difficult to develop with clarity and precision.

Internet 2

One purpose of the original Internet was to connect super-computers together for research purposes. This purpose went astray as the Web developed into a global medium for home and business use. Educational and research institutions are now working on developing Internet 2, a separate cyberspace, where they can link together to test new applications, run simultaneous tests, and develop new technologies without having to deal with the concerns of the Web where speed is hindered by mass usage and low speeds. Internet 2 is likely to open doors for writers/editors who have specialized knowledge in scientific and technological areas.

To Sum It Up

The difference between the right word and the almost right word is the difference between lightning and a lightning bug.

MARK TWAIN

No matter how digital media change, we strongly believe that the qualities of good textual content—clarity, credibility, conciseness, and coherence—will remain just as important in the future as they've been since most of humanity moved beyond oral cultures. As a professional writer/editor of content, you'll play an important role in the future of the Web by creating/editing good content, helping target content for specific audiences, and providing advice to clients on how to deliver content that best suits customers' needs and demands.

HTML Codes for Special Text Characters

HTML, which stands for Hypertext Mark-up Language, contains the codes that programmers use to create design elements for headers, bolds, italics, and so on. Below are the codes for special text characters such as *em* dashes, slashes, and fractions.

NAME CODE	NUMBER CODE	GLYPH	DESCRIPTION
	&#00 - &#08		unused
	&#09;		tab
	&#10;		line feed
	&#11 - &#31		unused
	&#32;		space
	&#33;	!	exclamation mark
&quot;	&#34;	"	double quotation mark
	&#35;	#	number sign (pound sign)
	&#36;	$	dollar sign
	&#37;	%	percent sign
&amp;	&#38;	&	ampersand
	&#39;	'	apostrophe
	&#40;	(	left parenthesis
	&#41;	)	right parenthesis
	&#42;	*	asterisk
	&#43;	+	plus sign
	&#44;	,	comma
	&#45;	-	hyphen
	&#46;	.	period
&frasl;	&#47;	/	forward slash
	&#48 - &#57	0-9	numbers 0-9
	&#58;	:	colon

NAME CODE	NUMBER CODE	GLYPH	DESCRIPTION
	`&#59;`	;	semi colon
`&lt;`	`&#60;`	<	less-than sign
	`&#61;`	=	equals sign
`&gt;`	`&#62;`	>	greater-than sign
	`&#63;`	?	question mark
	`&#64;`	@	at sign (commercial at)
	`&#65; - &#90`	A-Z	letters A-Z uppercase
	`&#91;`	[	left square bracket
	`&#92;`	\	backslash
	`&#93;`	]	right square bracket
	`&#94;`	^	caret
	`&#95;`	_	horizontal bar (underscore)
	`&#96;`	`	grave accent
	`&#97; - &#122`	a-z	letters a-z lowercase
	`&#123;`	{	left curly brace
	`&#124;`	|	vertical bar
	`&#125;`	}	right curly brace
	`&#126;`	~	tilde
	`&#127; - &#129`		unused
`&sbquo;`	`&#130;`	‚	single low-9 quote
	`&#131;`	ƒ	function sign
`&bdquo;`	`&#132;`	„	double low-9 quote
	`&#133;`	…	ellipses
`&dagger;`	`&#134;`	†	dagger
`&Dagger;`	`&#135;`	‡	double dagger
	`&#136;`	ˆ	caret
`&permil;`	`&#137;`	‰	per mill sign
	`&#138;`	Š	uppercase S with hacek
`&lsaquo;`	`&#139;`	‹	less than sign
	`&#140;`	Œ	uppercase OE ligature
	`&#141; - &#144`		unused
`&lsquo;`	`&#145;`	'	left single quote
`&rsquo;`	`&#146;`	'	right single quote
`&ldquo;`	`&#147;`	"	left double quote
`&rdquo;`	`&#148;`	"	right double quote
	`&#149;`	•	middle dot
`&ndash;`	`&#150;`	–	en dash

NAME CODE	NUMBER CODE	GLYPH	DESCRIPTION
&mdash;	&#151;	—	em dash
	&#152;	~	tilde
&trade;	&#153;	™	trademark sign
	&#154;	š	lowercase S with hacek
&rsaquo;	&#155;	›	greater than sign
	&#156;	œ	lowercase oe ligature
	 - &#158		unused
	&#159;	Ÿ	uppercase Y with umlaut
			non-breaking space
&iexcl;	&#161;	¡	inverted exclamation
&cent;	&#162;	¢	cent sign
&pound;	&#163;	£	pound sterling
&curren;	&#164;	¤	general currency sign
&yen;	&#165;	¥	yen sign
¦ or &brkbar;	&#166;	¦	broken vertical bar
&sect;	&#167;	§	section sign
¨ or ¨	&#168;	¨	umlaut
&copy;	&#169;	©	copyright
&ordf;	&#170;	ª	feminine ordinal
&laquo;	&#171;	«	left angle quote
&not;	&#172;	¬	not sign
&shy;	&#173;		soft hyphen
&reg;	&#174;	®	registered trademark
¯ or &hibar;	&#175;	¯	macron accent
&deg;	&#176;	°	degree sign
&plusmn;	&#177;	±	plus or minus
&sup2;	&#178;	²	superscript two
&sup3;	&#179;	³	superscript three
&acute;	&#180;	´	acute accent
&micro;	&#181;	µ	micro sign
&para;	&#182;	¶	paragraph sign
&middot;	&#183;	·	middle dot
&cedil;	&#184;	¸	cedilla
&sup1;	&#185;	¹	superscript one
&ordm;	&#186;	º	masculine ordinal
&raquo;	&#187;	»	right angle quote
&frac14;	&#188;	¼	one-fourth fraction

NAME CODE	NUMBER CODE	GLYPH	DESCRIPTION
½	½	½	one-half fraction
¾	¾	¾	three-fourths fraction
¿	¿	¿	inverted question mark
À	À	À	uppercase A, grave accent
Á	Á	Á	uppercase A, acute accent
Â	Â	Â	uppercase A, circumflex accent
Ã	Ã	Ã	uppercase A, tilde
Ä	Ä	Ä	uppercase A, umlaut
Å	Å	Å	uppercase A, ring
Æ	Æ	Æ	uppercase AE ligature
Ç	Ç	Ç	uppercase C, cedilla
È	È	È	uppercase E, grave accent
É	É	É	uppercase E, acute accent
Ê	Ê	Ê	uppercase E, circumflex accent
Ë	Ë	Ë	uppercase E, umlaut
Ì	Ì	Ì	uppercase I, grave accent
Í	Í	Í	uppercase I, acute accent
Î	Î	Î	uppercase I, circumflex accent
Ï	Ï	Ï	uppercase I, umlaut
Ð	Ð	Ð	uppercase ETH, Icelandic
Ñ	Ñ	Ñ	uppercase N, tilde
Ò	Ò	Ò	uppercase O, grave accent
Ó	Ó	Ó	uppercase O, acute accent
Ô	Ô	Ô	uppercase O, circumflex accent
Õ	Õ	Õ	uppercase O, tilde
Ö	Ö	Ö	uppercase O, umlaut
×	×	×	multiplication sign
Ø	Ø	Ø	uppercase O, slash
Ù	Ù	Ù	uppercase U, grave accent
Ú	Ú	Ú	uppercase U, acute accent
Û	Û	Û	uppercase U, circumflex accent
Ü	Ü	Ü	uppercase U, umlaut
Ý	Ý	Ý	uppercase Y, acute accent
Þ	Þ	Þ	uppercase THORN, Icelandic
ß	ß	ß	lowercase sharps, German
à	à	à	lowercase a, grave accent
á	á	á	lowercase a, acute accent

NAME CODE	NUMBER CODE	GLYPH	DESCRIPTION
â	â	â	lowercase a, circumflex accent
ã	ã	ã	lowercase a, tilde
ä	ä	ä	lowercase a, umlaut
å	å	å	lowercase a, ring
æ	æ	æ	lowercase ae ligature
ç	ç	ç	lowercase c, cedilla
è	è	è	lowercase e, grave accent
é	é	é	lowercase e, acute accent
ê	ê	ê	lowercase e, circumflex accent
ë	ë	ë	lowercase e, umlaut
ì	ì	ì	lowercase i, grave accent
í	í	í	lowercase i, acute accent
î	î	î	lowercase i, circumflex accent
ï	ï	ï	lowercase i, umlaut
ð	ð	ð	lowercase eth, Icelandic
ñ	ñ	ñ	lowercase n, tilde
ò	ò	ò	lowercase o, grave accent
ó	ó	ó	lowercase o, acute accent
ô	ô	ô	lowercase o, circumflex accent
õ	õ	õ	lowercase o, tilde
ö	ö	ö	lowercase o, umlaut
÷	÷	÷	division sign
ø	ø	ø	lowercase o, slash
ù	ù	ù	lowercase u, grave accent
ú	ú	ú	lowercase u, acute accent
û	û	û	lowercase u, circumflex accent
ü	ü	ü	lowercase u, umlaut
ý	ý	ý	lowercase y, acute accent
þ	þ	þ	lowercase thorn, Icelandic
ÿ	ÿ	ÿ	lowercase y, umlaut

The terms covered in this glossary are an alphabetical listing of those listed in the *Let's Speak the Same Language* section as well as others used elsewhere throughout the book.

Accessibility: The degree to which people with various disabilities can access Web content.

Affiliate program: A site link that leads users to another site where they can buy a product or service. If they do so, the owner of the original site receives a commission.

Application Service Provider (ASP): (1) A company that provides businesses with software services such as Web Hosting or HR Management, freeing the business from purchase and maintenance of complex software packages; (2) also the acronym used to designate Active Server Pages that allow interactivity and functionality on a Web site.

Archival page: An online storage location for historical information or data that can be generally retrieved by topic, date, or author.

Associative link: A link that is used for purposes of gaining information as opposed to simply traveling.

Audio/video components: Elements of the site, created in a studio or on location, that are inserted as sound or movie clips in the Web site.

Browser: A software application—a collection of software modules or components integrated into a single visual application—that allows the user to surf the Internet.

Business-to-business (B2B) sites: Sites created by businesses to inform and transact with other businesses.

Business-to-consumer (B2C) sites: Sites created by businesses to market products/services to individual consumers.

Client: (1) The person(s) who has contracted for the creation/ maintenance of the Web site. May be internal or external, and may possess varied backgrounds and degrees of Internet knowledge; (2) a software application that contacts and receives files from a server. Browser software is an example of a client.

Consuming: A user behavior that is akin to the print behavior of *extensive reading*, that is, reading long texts usually for pleasure and global understanding.

Content: Written material on a Web site. When written text is enhanced by graphics and video and audio materials, these elements become part of content.

Content management: The management of online documents and databases over time.

Content management system: A software tool to help site owners manage and deliver content.

Content specialist/Subject matter expert: Person(s) who "own" the content through their specific knowledge of the topic.

Convergence: The merging of media such as television and telephone with the Internet, thereby creating a single digital medium.

Converging links: Links that bring users from different locations to the same point.

Database: A collection of organized, searchable information.

Destination page: A page designed primarily to inform, although it may also contain some links. Can be *primary*, containing the main content of the site, or *secondary*, containing information not directly connected to the main purpose of the site.

Drill-down link: See "Embedded link."

Editorial style guide: A tool created by a writer/editor to ensure consistency in editorial decisions on a Web site.

E-mail broadcast: A delivery tool that organizations can use to issue content such as special announcements and membership newsletters.

Embedded link: An internal link placed within the body of the text as opposed to being on a navigation bar or submenu. Includes *drill-down links* that move users vertically through the site and *lateral links* that move users horizontally through the site.

External link: A link that allows users to travel off a Web site.

Extranet: A network that allows customers and/or suppliers access to a business's nonpublic information through a password-restricted login. Online banking is an example of an extranet.

File format: The structure of the data contained in the file, as indicated by an extension such as .doc, .txt, .html, and .bmp. Many software packages allow files to be saved in various formats that enable their use in other applications.

Foraging: A user behavior that is akin to the print behavior of intensive reading, that is, reading short texts to extract specific, detailed information.

Functionality: The technology underlying those features of a site, other than links, that allow users to undertake an activity.

Gestalt principles: Principles that emphasize the overall structure or pattern as the primary way we perceive form.

Graphical user interface (GUI): The design of a Web page that represents both the architecture and navigation of the site.

"Home" page: A site's first real content page that also displays navigation and design.

Hypertext: (1) A set of documents; (2) a system of links that allows users to access other documents on the Web, thereby allowing the user nonlinear access to information.

Icon: An image that is recognizable because it bears a similarity or resemblance to what we already know or conceive about an object.

Information architecture (IA): Organizing information into logically related groupings so users can navigate effectively through the content and find the information they seek.

Information quality: Information that is fit for use by information consumers.

Interactivity: The process by which users interact with content.

Internal link: A link that allows users to travel within a Web site.

Internally linked, scrollable page: A Web page in which the links in the first screen act like a table of contents that allows users to navigate without having to use the scroll bar.

Internet: The international network connecting networks and individual users, allowing them to communicate and exchange information through TCP/IP protocol.

Intranet: An in-house Web site that can't be accessed by outsiders and is designed to provide employees with nonpublic organizational information.

Knowledge base: Storage of organizational information, usually in a database form.

Lateral link: See "Embedded link."

Localization: The adaptation of a product to a specific location, incorporating local laws, customs, and language.

Meta description: A phrase or sentence programmed into the Web page that describes that page's content specifically for search engines.

Metasearch engine: An engine that uses keywords to search other search engines.

Metatag: A keyword or a group of keywords programmed into the Web page in order to generate search engine traffic.

Microcontent: A term used by usability researchers to describe small bits of text such as titles, headers, and labels.

Mind-mapping: A technique that encourages people to build a graphical display of information through creative and innovative thinking.

Naturalized language: Language based on beliefs in a workplace that have become so engrained and familiar to employees that they appear to be common sense.

Navigation: The routes that users take through a Web site to move from Web page to Web page.

Navigation design: The connection between the information architecture (IA) and the design of the graphical user interface (GUI).

Navigation link: A link that provides a path for users as they seek ways to travel on the Web. May be a connection to an area on the same Web page, within the same site, or to an external site.

Navigation page: A page designed primarily for navigation. May also contain some content.

Objective text: A term used by usability researchers to describe content that has been stripped of promotional phrases.

Parasocial interaction: Social interaction that is not direct, but mediated through a persona or an entity such as a Web site.

Pixel: A picture element—a dot that displays color in varying depths on a monitor.

Plug-ins/players: Software used to provide additional functionality to a browser such as audio, video, animations, cross-platform document delivery, and interactivity.

Primary destination page: A page that contains the main content of the site.

Proprietary: A piece of software code owned by a legal entity such as a database software manufacturer.

Psychology of art: A theory of human perception, based on the work of Rudolf Arnheim, that separates the concept of *seeing* from *perceiving*.

Real-time event: An online event that is delivered live to users' desktops.

Redundant link: A link that is duplicated on one Web page—for example, both on a navigation bar and in the text.

Rhetoric: The use of language for the purposes of persuading others.

Scannable text: A term used by usability experts to describe text that is short and has bulleted lists.

Scanning: A term used by usability researchers that actually comprises two print reading strategies: *skimming*, that is, quickly running the eye over text to get the gist of it, and *scanning*, that is, seeking particular pieces of information.

Screen candy: Graphic images or photographs displayed to attract or entertain the user.

Screen real estate: The space available on a Web screen for text, visuals, and navigation information.

Secondary destination pages: A page that contains information not directly connected to the main purpose of the site.

Server: A computer or software application that serves the requested files over a network. See also "Browser" and "Client (2)."

Shortcut link: A link that allows users to access information without drilling down through the site—for example, <u>What's New</u>.

Site map: A visualization of the information architecture of a Web site.

Site structure: Information organized in a hierarchy that fits the form of a *tree* model, *linear* model, or a *mixture* model.

Skin: A look-and-feel for players and browsers that users have designed by incorporating changes in color and texture, moving buttons to different locations, and adding or altering graphic images.

Spider: A computer program that roams the Web searching for sites to add to a search engine's database.

"Splash" page: The front end of a Web site that usually provides site identity through a title, graphics, and/or animation.

Stickiness: A site's ability to maintain users' interest and keep them as visitors.

Streaming audio: Real-time content conveying sound in a steady flow.

Streaming video: Real-time content conveying images in a steady flow.

Visual semiotics: A theoretical framework that explains how images make meaning in social and cultural contexts.

Visuals: All forms of design and graphics such as color, backgrounds, navigation icons as well as the media mix of illustrations, photographs, and animation.

Webcast: A real-time method of providing an audio and/or video event.

Web directory: A searchable index of handpicked sites organized into specific categories such as travel, health, business, education, and so on.

Web page: A rhetorical unit of content that may be visible on one Web screen or may require scrolling.

Web screen: A flexible unit of space that holds whatever Web page content appears on an individual user's monitor at a given time.

Web search engine: An automated software program known as a *spider* (also known as a *crawler* or *bot*) that builds a database of Internet sites which can then be searched through keywords input by a user. See also "Web site search engine."

Web site: A collection of Web pages arranged into hierarchical levels of grouped information, connected by navigation design, and presented through graphical user interface (GUI).

Web site search engine: A search function localized to one Web site. See also "Web Search Engine."

Web site section: A grouping of pages of related content on a Web site. Sometimes referred to as a *key content area*, a *channel*, or a *theme/stream*.

World Wide Web (WWW): A portion of the Internet that allows users to access information through browsers.

Writing/Editing: Writing/editing text on a Web site.

Adobe Acrobat. 2001. "The Best Way to Share Documents Online." (unpaginated). [Viewed May 30, 2001.] www.adobe.com/products/acrobat.

Albers, Michael J. 2000. "Information Design: An Introduction to This Special Section." *TechnicalCOMMUNICATION: Journal of the Society for Technical Communication*, 47, no. 2: pp. 163–166.

Albu, R. 1998. *An A–Z Introduction to the Study of Varieties of Present-Day English*. Iasi: Ars Longa.

Alexander, J.E. and Tate, M.A. 1999. *Web Wisdom: How to Evaluate and Create Information Quality on the Web*. London: Lawrence Erlbaum Associates, Publishers.

Arnheim, R. 1969. *Visual Thinking*. Berkeley, CA: University of California Press.

Barnes, H. 2001. "Create Customer-Focused Web Content." *e-Business Advisor*, February, 2001.

Barrett, E. 1989. "Introduction: Thought and Language in a Virtual Environment." In E. Barrett (Ed.), *The Society of Text: Hyptertext, Hypermedia, and The Social Construction of Information*. pp. xi–xix. Cambridge, MA: The MIT Press.

Barry, A.M.S. 2001. "Starving in the Midst of Plenty: The Relationship between Advertising Images and Eating Disorders." *Exposure: Journal of the Society for Photographic Education*, 33: pp. 12–18.

_____ 1997. *Visual Intelligence: Perception, Image, and Manipulation in Visual Communication*. New York: State University of New York Press.

Bartlett, A. 2000. *Mind-Mapping for Writers*. (unpaginated). Inkspot. [Viewed July 4, 2001.] www.inkspot.com/feature/bartlett.html.

Bazerman, C. and Paradis, J. 1991. "Introduction." In C. Bazerman and J. Paradis (Eds.), *Textual Dynamics of the Professions*. pp. 3–11. Madison, WI: University of Wisconsin Press.

Berners-Lee, T. 2001. "Web Accessibility Initiative." (unpaginated). W3C: World Wide Web Consortium. [Viewed July 4, 2001.] www.w3.org.

_____ 2000. *Weaving the Web: The Original Design and Ultimate Destiny of the World Wide Web by Its Inventor*. New York: HarperCollins.

Berners-Lee, T., Hendler, J., and Lassila, O. 2001. "The Semantic Web." *Scientific American*, May, 2001, 284, no. 5, pp. 35–43.

Bolter, J. 1991. *The Computer, Hyptertext, and the History of Writing*. Hillsdale, NJ: Lawrence Erlbaum Associates, Publishers.

Borges, J.A., Morales, I., and Rodriguez, N.J. 1998. "Page Design Guidelines Developed through Usability Testing." In C. Forsythe, E. Grose, and J. Ratner (Eds.), *Human Factors and Web Development*. pp. 137–152. Mahwah, NJ: Lawrence Erlbaum Associates.

Brandt, D. 1990. *Literacy as Involvement: The Acts of Writers, Readers, and Texts*. Carbondale, IL: Southern Illinois University Press.

Buzan, T. 1999. *Definition of Mind Maps*. (unpaginated). Buzan Centres. [Viewed July 4, 2001.] www.mind-map.com/MM/mindmap/DEFINITION.HTM.

Chicago Manual of Style. 1969/1982. Chicago: The University of Chicago Press.

Coney, M.B. and Steehouder, M. 2000. "Guidelines for Designing and Evaluating Personas Online." *TechnicalCOMMUNICATION: Journal of the Society for Technical Communication*, 47, no. 3: pp. 327–340.

Davenport, T.H. and Beck, J.C. 2001. *The Attention Economy: Understanding the New Currency of Business*. Boston, MA: Harvard Business School Press.

Davenport, T.H. and Prusak, L. 1998. *Working Knowledge: How Organizations Manage What They Know*. Boston, MA: Harvard University Press.

de Certeau, M. 1984. *The Practice of Everyday Life*. (S. Rendell, Trans.). Berkley, CA: University of California Press.

Dias, P., Freedman, A., Medway, P., and Paré, A. 1999. *Worlds Apart: Acting and Writing in Academic and Workplace Contexts*. NJ: Lawrence Erlbaum Associates.

Dillon, R.F. 2001a. "UI Design: Principles and Guidelines." Slide Presentation, Department of Psychology, Computer User Research and Evaluation Program, Carleton University, Ottawa, Canada.

_____ 2001b. "Integrating User-Interface Design into the Software Development Process." Slide Presentation, Department of Psychology, Computer User Research and Evaluation Program, Carleton University, Ottawa, Canada.

Discover. October, 2000. p. 94.

Dow Jones Reuters Business Interactive Limited. 2000. "The Reuters Guide to Good Information Strategy." (unpaginated). Reuters. [Viewed July 4, 2001.] about.reuters.com/rbb/research/gis.htm.

Dragona, A. and Handa, C. 2000. "*Xenes Glosses*: Literacy and Cultural Implications of the Web for Greece." In GE. Hawisher and C.L. Selfe (Eds.), *Global Literacies and the World-Wide Web*. pp. 52–73. London: Routledge.

European Association for Machine Translation. 2000. "Introduction: EAMT Machine Translation Workshop." (unpaginated). [Viewed July 11, 2001]. www.lim.nl/eamt/archive/ljubljana/introduction.html.

Fairclough, N. 1995a. *Critical Discourse Analysis: The Critical Study of Language*. London: Longman Group Limited.

_____ 1995b. *Media Discourse*. London: Edward Arnold.

_____ 1992. *Discourse and Social Change*. Cambridge: Polity Press.

_____ 1989. *Language and Power*. New York: Longman.

Farkas, D. and Farkas, J. 2000. "Guidelines for Designing Web Navigation." *TechnicalCOMMUNICATION: Journal of the Society for Technical Communication*, 47, no.3: pp 341–358.

Faulkner, C. 1998. *The Essence of Human-Computer Interaction*. New York: Prentice Hall.

Fleming, J. 1998. *Web Navigation: Designing the User Experience*. Sebastopol, CA: O'Reilly & Associates Inc.

Foltz, P. R. 1996. "Comprehension, Coherence and Strategies in Hypertext and Linear Text." (unpaginated). New Mexico State University Department of Psychology. [Viewed February 22, 2001.] www-psych.nmsu.edu/~pfoltz/reprints/Ht-Cognition.html. (Also in J–F. Rouet, J.J Levenen, A.P. Dillon, and R.J. Spiro (Eds.), *Hypertext and Cognition*. pp. 109–146. Hillsdale, NJ: Lawrence Erlbaum Associates.)

Freedman, A. and Medway, P. 1994. "Introduction." In A. Freedman and P. Medway (Eds.), *Genre and the New Rhetoric*. pp. 1–22. London: Taylor & Francis Ltd.

Gee, J.P. 1999. *An Introduction to Discourse Analysis: Theory and Method*. London: Routledge.

Gillette, D. 1999. "New Design for International Audiences." pp. 15–17. *Intercom*, December 1999. Society for Technical Communication.

Grellet, F. 1981. *Developing Reading Skills: A Practical Guide to Reading Comprehension Exercises*. Cambridge: Cambridge University Press.

Grice, R.A. 1989. "Online Information: What do People Want? What do People Need?" In E. Barrett (Ed.), *The Society of Text: Hyptertext, Hypermedia, and The Social Construction of Information*. pp. 22–44. Cambridge, MA: The MIT Press.

Gross, J. 2001. "Rescuing Troubled Web Sites." (unpaginated). *VarBusiness*, July 16, 2001. [Viewed July 30, 2001.] www.varbusiness.com/ components/search/Article.asp?ArticleID=28269.

Hall, E.T. 1966. *The Hidden Dimension*. Garden City, NY: Doubleday.

Halliday, M.A.K. 1994. *An Introduction to Functional Grammar: Second Edition*. London: Arnold.

Hansen, Y.M. 1999. "Visualization for Thinking, Planning, and Problem Solving." In R. Jacobson (Ed.), *Information Design*. pp. 193–220. Cambridge, MA: The MIT Press.

Harrison, C. 2001. "Mastering Rhetorical Knowledgeability: The World of the Writing Consultant." Paper presented at the Congress of the Social Sciences and Humanities, Canadian Association for the Teachers of Technical Writing, May 26, 2001.

Hart, G.J.S. 2000. "The Style Guide is Dead: Long Live the Dynamic Style Guide." *Intercom*, 47, no. 3: pp. 12–17.

Head, A. J. 1999. "Keeping Content King." (unpaginated). *Planet IT*. April 23, 1999. [Viewed March 23, 2001.] www.PlanetIT.com/ docs/PIT19990423S0025.

Hodge, R. and Kress, G. 1988. *Social Semiotics*. Cornell, NY: Cornell University Press.

Hoerner, J. 1999. "Scaling the Web: A Parasocial Interaction Scale for World Wide Web Sites." In D.W. Schumann and E. Thorson (Eds.), *Advertising and the World Wide Web*. pp. 135–147. Mahwah, NJ: Lawrence Erlbaum Associates.

Hoffman, D. D. 1998. *Visual Intelligence: How We Create What We See.* New York: W.W. Norton & Co.

Hoft, N. L. 1995. *International Technical Communications.* NY: John Wiley & Sons.

Holtzman, S. 1998. *Digital Mosaic: The Aesthetics of Cyberspace.* NY: Touchstone Press.

Horn, R.E. 1999. "Information Design: Emergence of a New Profession." In R. Jacobson (Ed.), *Information Design.* pp. 15–33. Cambridge, MA: The MIT Press.

Horton, W. 1997. *Secrets of User-Seductive Documents: Wooing and Winning the Reluctant Reader.* Arlington, VA: Society for Technical Communication.

Huang, K., Yang W., and Wang, R. 1999. *Quality Information and Knowledge.* Upper Saddle River, NJ: Prentice Hall PTR.

Isakson, C.S. and Spyridiakis, J. 1999. "The Influence of Semantics and Syntax on What Readers Remember." *TechnicalCOMMUNICATION: Journal of the Society for Technical Communication,* 46, no. 3: pp. 366–381.

Jaynes, J.T. 1989. "Limited Freedom: Linear Reflections on Nonlinear Texts." In E. Barrett (Ed.), *The Society of Text: Hypertext, Hypermedia, and the Social Construction of Information.* pp. 148–161. Cambridge, MA: The MIT Press.

Johnson, C. 1998. "The Ten Golden Rules for Providing Video Over the Web or 0% of 2.4M (at 270k/sec, 340 sec remaining)." In C. Forsythe, E. Grose, and J. Ratner (Eds.), *Human Factors and Web Development.* pp. 207–221. Mahwah, NJ: Lawrence Erlbaum Associates.

Johnson, B. and Schneiderman, B. 1999. "Tree-Maps: A Space-Filling Approach to the Visualization of Hierarchical Information Structures." In S. Card, J. MacKinlay, and B. Shneiderman. (Eds.), *Information Visualization: Using Vision to Think.* pp. 152–159. San Francisco, CA: Morgan Kaufman Publishers Inc.

Johnson-Eilola, J. 1997. *Nostalgic Angels: Rearticulating Hypertext Writing.* Norwood, NJ: Ablex Publishing Corporation.

Johnson-Sheehan, R. and Baehr, C. 2001. "Visual-Spatial Thinking in Hypertexts." *TechnicalCOMMUNICATION: Journal of the Society for Technical Communication,* 48, no. 1: pp. 22–30.

Kahn, P. and Lenk, K. 2001. *Mapping Web Sites.* Hove, East Sussex: RotoVision SA.

Kirsch, G. 1990. "Experienced Writers' Sense of Audience and Authority: Three Case Studies." In G. Kirsch and D.H. Roen (Eds.), *A Sense of Audience in Written Communication.* pp. 216–229. Newbury Park: Sage Publications.

Kolb, D. 1997. "Scholarly Hypertext: Self-Represented Complexity." *Hypertext 97: The Eighth ACM Conference on Hypertext.* pp. 29–36. New York: The Association for Computer Machinery, Inc.

Kress, G. 1998. "Visual and Verbal Modes of Representation in Electronically Mediated Communication: The Potentials of New Forms of Text." In I. Snyder (Ed.), *Page to Screen: Taking Literacy into the Electronic Era.* pp. 53–79. London: Routledge.

Kress, G. and van Leeuwen, T. 1996. *Reading Images: The Grammar of Visual Design.* London: Routledge.

Krug, S. 2000. *Don't Make Me Think: A Common Sense Approach to Web Usability.* Indianapolis, IN: MacMillan USA.

Kukulska-Hulme, A. 1999. *Language and Communication: Essential Concepts for User Interface and Document Design.* Oxford: Oxford University Press.

Lagon, O. 2000. "Culturally Correct Site Design." (unpaginated). *Webtechniques.* [Viewed July 3, 2001.] www.webtechniques.com/archives/2000/09/lagon.

Lakoff, G. and Johnson, M. 1980. *Metaphors We Live By.* Chicago, IL: University of Chicago Press.

Landow, G.P. 1991. "The Rhetoric of Hypermedia: Some Rules for Authors." In P. Delany and G.P. Landow (Eds.), *Hypermedia and Literary Studies.* Cambridge, MA: The MIT Press.

Lanham, R. 1993. *The Electronic Word: Democracy, Technology, and the Arts.* Chicago, IL: The University of Chicago Press.

_____ 1976. *Motives of Eloquence: Literary Rhetoric in the Renaissance.* New Haven: Yale University Press.

Latour, B. 1987. *Science in Action: How to Follow Scientists and Engineers through Society.* Cambridge, MA: Harvard University Press.

Laughnet. 1997. "Murphy's Laws for Programmers." (unpaginated). [Viewed July 4, 2001.] www.laughnet.net/archive/compute/murphy.htm.

Lemke, J. 1990. *Talking Science, Language, Learning and Values.* Norwood, NJ: Ablex Publishing Corporation.

Lynch, P.J. 2000. "VisualLogic: 10 Fundamentals of Web design." (unpaginated). [Viewed February 15, 2000.] patricklynch.net/viz/viz021500.html.

Macromedia. 2001. "Web Site Production Management Techniques." (unpaginated). [Viewed June 22, 2001.] www.macromedia.com/resources/techniques.

Marcus, A., Armitage, J., Volker, F., and Guttman, E. 1999. "Globalization of User-Interface Design for the Web." (unpaginated). 5th Conference on Human Factors & the Web. [Viewed June 30, 2001.] zing.ncsl.nist.gov/hfweb/proceedings/marcus.

Marks, W. and Dulaney, C.L. 1998. "Visual Information Processing on the World Wide Web." In C. Forsythe, E. Grose, and J. Ratner (Eds.), *Human Factors and Web Development.* pp. 25–43. Mahwah, NJ: Lawrence Erlbaum Associates, Publishers.

Mazur, B. 2000. "Revisiting Plain Language." *TechnicalCOMMUNICATION: Journal of the Society for Technical Communication,* 47, no. 2: pp. 205–211.

McAdams, M. and Berger, S. 2001. "Hypertext." (unpaginated). *The Journal of Electronic Publishing,* 6, no. 2. [Viewed July 4, 2001.] www.press.umich.edu/jep/06–03/McAdams/pages.

McCloud, S. 1993. *Understanding Comics: The Invisible Art.* New York, NY: HarperCollins.

McCoy, K. 1999. "The Second Computer Revolution." In S. A. Redmond. *Taking the Leap into New Media.* pp. 8–11. Cincinnati, OH: North Light Books.

Miller, G.A. 1956. "The Magical Number Seven, Plus or Minus Two: Some Limits on Our Capacity for Processing Information." (unpaginated). The WELL. [Viewed July 4, 2001.] www.well.com/user/smalin/miller.html. (Also in *The Psychological Review,* 63, pp. 81–97.)

Miller, M. 1999. *The Complete Idiot's Guide to Online Search Secrets.* Indianapolis, IN: Que.

Moore, P. and Fitz, C. 1993. "Gestalt Theory and Instructional Design." *Journal of Technical Writing and Communication,* 23, no. 2, pp. 137–157.

Morkes, J. and Neilsen, J. 1997. *Concise, Scannable, and Objective: How to Write for the Web.* (unpaginated). [Viewed April 3, 2001.] www.useit.com/papers/webwriting/writing.html.

Morris, M.D. 2001. "The Power of Quiddity." *Intercom,* 48, no. 3, pp. 19–21.

Mullet, K. and Sano, D. 1995. *Designing Visual Interfaces: Communication Oriented Techniques.* Mountain View, CA: Sun Microsystems, Inc.

Neilsen, J. 2000. *Designing Web Usability: The Practice of Simplicity.* Indianapolis, IN: New Riders Publishing.

_____ 1998. *Microcontent: How to Write Headlines, Page Titles, and Subject Lines.* (unpaginated). September 6, 1998. [Viewed February 13, 2001.] www.useit.com/alertbox/980906.html

Neilsen, J. and Coyne, K. P. 2001. *Corporate Websites Get a 'D' in PR.* (unpaginated). [Viewed June 19, 2001.] www.useit.com/alertbox/20010401.html.

Nelson, T. 1999. *Ted Nelson's Computer Paradigm, Expressed as One-Liners.* (unpaginated). Keio University. [Viewed April 16, 2001.] www.sfc.keio.ac.jp/~ted/TN/WRITINGS/TCOMPARADIGM/tedCompOneLiners.html.

_____ 1996. "Orality and Hypertext: An Interview with Ted Nelson." (unpaginated). In J. Whitehead (Interviewer), *Cyberspace Report.* [Viewed March 4, 2001.] www.ics.uci.edu/~ejw/csr/nelson_pg.html.

Norman, D.A. 1998. "Want Human-Centered Development? Reorganize the Company." (unpaginated). Nielsen Norman Group. [Viewed June 5, 2001.] www.nngroup.com/reports/want_hcd_reorg.html.

Odell, L. and Goswami, D. 1985. *Writing in Nonacademic Settings.* New York: Guilford Press.

Onesoft Corporation. 1998. "The Extranet Solution." In P. Lloyd and P. Boyle (Eds.), *Web-Weaving: Intranets, Extranets and Strategic Alliances.* pp. 55–65. Oxford: Butterworth-Heinemann.

Pang, A.S. 1998. "Hypertext, the Next Generation: A Review and Research Agenda." (unpaginated). *First Monday,* 6, no. 11. [Viewed March 3, 2001.] www.firstmonday.dk/issues/issue3_11/pang/index.html.

Pastore, M. 2001. "U.S. Share of Internet Users Continues to Shrink, 'Hypergrowth' Over." (unpaginated). CyberAtlas. [Viewed May 21, 2001.] cyberatlas.internet.com/big_picture/geographics/article/1,1323,5911_769451,00.html.

Peterson, J.H. 2000. "Online Editing: Minimizing Your Turnaround Time." *Intercom,* 47, no. 3, pp. 9–11.

Powell, T. 2000. *Web Design: The Complete Reference.* Berkeley, CA: Osborne/McGraw Hill.

Prencipe, L.W. 2001. "Trademarks and Metatags Don't Mix." (unpaginated). *InfoWorld*, April 20, 2001. [Viewed July 30, 2001.] iwsun4.infoworld.com/articles/ca/xml/01/04/23/010423calist.xml.

Raskin, Jef. 2000. *The Humane Interface: New Directions for Designing Interactive Systems*. Reading, MA: Addison-Wesley.

Redish, J.C. 2000. "What is Information Design?" *TechnicalCOMMUNICATION: Journal of the Society for Technical Communication*, 47, no. 2: pp. 163–166.

Robinson, B. and Versluis, E.B. 1985. "Electronic Text: A Choice Medium for Reading?" In D. Chandler and S. Marcus (Eds.), *Computers and Literacy*. pp. 26–40. Philadelphia, PA: Open University Press.

Rouet, J–F. Levenon, J.J., Dillon, A., and Spiro, R.J. 1996. "An Introduction to Hypertext and Cognition." In J–F. Rouet, J.J. Levenon, A. Dillon, and R.J. Spiro (Eds.), *Hypertext and Cognition*. Mahwah, NJ: Lawrence Erlbaum Associates, Publishers.

Saunders, F. 2000. "Web Wonders." *Discover*. June, 2000.

Shaw, D. 2001. "Playing the Links: Interactivity and Stickiness in .Com and "Not.Com" Web Sites." (unpaginated). *First Monday*, 6, no. 3. [Viewed July 4, 2001.] firstmonday.org/issues/issue6_3/shaw.

Shedroff, N. 1999. "Information Interaction Design: A Unified Field Theory of Design." In R. Jacobson (Ed.), *Information Design*. pp. 267–292. Cambridge, MA: The MIT Press.

Shields, R. 2000. "Hypertext Links." In A. Herman and T. Swiss (Eds.), *The World Wide Web and Contemporary Cultural Theory*. pp. 145–160. London: Routledge.

Shriver, K. 1997. *Dynamics in Document Design: Creating Texts for Readers*. New York: John Wiley & Sons.

Slevin, J. 2000. *The Internet and Society*. Malden, MA: Polity Press.

Smith, A. 2001. "Why Is Usability So Hard?" (unpaginated). Human-Computer Interaction Resource Network. [Viewed May 19, 2001.] www.hcirn.com/reflect/whyhard.html.

Spilka, R. 1993. *Writing in the Workplace: New Research Perspectives*. Illinois: Southern Illinois University Press.

Spyridakis, J.R. 2000. "Guidelines for Authoring Comprehensible Web Pages and Evaluating their Success." *TechnicalCOMMUNICATION: Journal of the Society for Technical Communication*, 47, no. 3: pp. 359–382.

St. Amant, K.R. 2000. "Resources and Strategies for Successful International Communication." pp. 12–14. *Intercom*, September/October 2000.

The Stanford-Poynter Eyetrack Study 2000. (unpaginated). The Poynter Institute. [Viewed May 19, 2001.] www.poynter.org/eyetrack2000.

Strunk, W. and White, E.B. 1959/1979. *The Elements of Style.* New York: MacMillan Publishing Co.

The American Heritage Dictionary of the English Language: Fourth Edition. 2000. (unpaginated). [Viewed March 12, 2001.] www.bartleby.com/61/80/R0218000.html.

Toub, S. 2000. "Evaluating Information Architecture: A Practical Guide to Assessing Web Site Organization." Argus Center for Information Architecture. [Viewed April 28, 2001.] argus-acia.com/white_papers/evaluating_ia.html.

Tufte, E.R. 1997. *Visual Explanations: Images and Quantities, Evidence and Narrative.* Cheshire, CONN: Graphics Press.

Tuman, M. 1992. *Word Perfect: Literacy in the Computer Age.* London: Falmer Press.

Turner, M. 1999. "Fundamental Web Design Principles?" (unpaginated). The Fifth Australian World Wide Web Conference. [Viewed July 4, 2001.] ausweb.scu.edu.au/aw99/papers/turner/paper.html.

Tyner, K. 1998. *Literacy in a Digital World: Teaching and Learning in the Age of Information.* Mahway, NJ: Lawrence Erlbaum Associates, Publishers.

Usborne, N. 2001. "Write Like A Good Listener." (unpaginated). ClickZ Today. February 19, 2001. [Viewed May 22, 2001.] www.clickz.com/article/cz.3400.html.

User Interface Engineering. 2000. Annotated Table of Contents for *Web Site Usability: A Designer's Guide.* (unpaginated). [Viewed April 23, 2001.] world.std.com/~uieweb/booktoc.htm.

_____1998. *As the Page Scrolls.* (unpaginated). [Viewed April 23, 2001.] world.std.com/~uieweb/scrollin.htm.

Vygotsky, L.S. 1934/1986. *Thought and Language.* (A. Kazoulin, Trans.). Cambridge, MA: MIT Press.

Weeks, R. 1999. "The Medium is the Message but What Language are We Speaking?" In S. A. Redmond, *Taking the Leap into New Media.* pp. 14–17. Cincinnati, OH: North Light Books.

Whitehouse, R. 1999. "The Uniqueness of Individual Perception." In R. Jacobson (Ed.), *Information Design*. pp. 103–129. Cambridge, MA: The MIT Press.

Wick, C. 2000 "Knowledge Management and Leadership Opportunities for Technical Communicators." *TechnicalCOMMUNICATION: Journal of the Society for Technical Communication*, 47, no. 4: pp. 515–529.

W3C: World Wide Web Consortium. 1999. "Web Content Accessibility Guidelines 1.0." (unpaginated). [Viewed July 3, 2001.] www.w3.org/TR/WCAG.

Wurman, R.S. 2001. *InformationAnxiety2*. Indianapolis, IN: Que.

_____ 1989. *Information Anxiety*. New York, NY: Bantam Books.